Pregnancy Stories

Real Women Share the Joys, Fears, Thrills, and Anxieties of Pregnancy from Conception to Birth

cellaro

Publisher's Note

This publication is designed to provide accurate and authoritative information in regard to the subject matter covered. It is sold with the understanding that the publisher is not engaged in rendering psychological, financial, legal, or other professional services. If expert assistance or counseling is needed, the services of a competent professional should be sought.

Distributed in the U.S.A. by Publishers Group West.

Copyright © 2001 by Cecelia A. Cancellaro
New Harbinger Publications, Inc.
5674 Shattuck Avenue
Oakland, CA 94609

Cover design by Amy Elizabeth Shoup
Cover photograph by ©Annie Griffiths Belt/CORBIS
Edited by Jueli Gastwirth
Text design by Michele Waters

ISBN 1-57224-236-1 Paperback

All Rights Reserved

Printed in the United States of America

New Harbinger Publications' Web site address: www.newharbinger.com

02   01

10   9   8   7   6   5   4   3   2   1

First printing

For my mother, Elizabeth, and my daughter,
Ruby Elizabeth

Table of Contents

Acknowledgments

When I came up with the idea for this book, I was in the second tri-mester of pregnancy and had just started to feel the reassuring kicks and pokes of my daughter, Ruby Elizabeth. When I began writing, Ruby was four months old and spent most of her waking hours nes-tled into one of my arms, nursing and nursing and nursing, while I often used the other to poke away at the keyboard. Now, as I add the final touches, Ruby is a very mobile fourteen-month-old who visits me often as I work in my little corner of our dining room, sometimes for a cuddle, but usually just to try and press the illuminated on/off button on the computer's hard drive. Her presence has been my source of motivation, inspiration, and illumination.

My agent, Anne Edelstein, has been wonderful from the begin-ning, providing enthusiasm and good advice.

Kristin Beck, Jueli Gastwirth, and the staff at New Harbinger Publications exemplify the best qualities one could hope for in a pub-lisher. For their savvy, creative, committed, and spirited approach, I am grateful.

The extraordinary care of Domenica Dominguez (and the sweet and sharing personality of her son, Enzo) made it possible for me to leave Ruby for a few hours every week, knowing that my little girl was being loved, stimulated, and completely entertained while I was get-ting some much-needed uninterrupted work time.

Without my Park Slope new moms group, adjusting to life as a mom would have been much more difficult and much less fun. The advice, the laughs, and the shared cheese toast and Veggie Booty are much appreciated.

My father, Anthony Cancellaro, has always been a big sup-porter. This year, as I grappled with new motherhood and a book deadline, his constant encouragement and belief in my abilities made both challenges seem more manageable.

I owe a major debt to the fathering, partnering, and editing skills of my husband, Eric Zinner, without which, this book would still be just an idea. He has provided an enormous amount of love, support, and guidance throughout.

Finally, my deepest thanks go to the women who so generously shared their stories with me. Their honesty, insight, and spirit have enriched my life and the pages that follow.

Introduction

I became a pregnant woman at the age of thirty-six, confident that I was well prepared for the task at hand. I'd wanted a child for as long as I could remember. In fact, I should have had a couple already according to the life plan I'd sketched for myself when I reached the age at which one begins contemplating such things. Although my husband and I had only been married for a year, the "baby project" had been discussed for much longer than that and we'd carefully constructed a plan of action that suited our desires and our lifestyle.

So there we were, the first step of our plan not only implemented, but implemented in record time, poised to begin our journey to parenthood. But from the time my daughter was small enough to be mistaken for a pinto bean until she very slowly made her way through the birth canal eight months later, I found myself obsessively searching for information that would allow me to understand and feel comfortable with the many mystifying aspects of pregnancy. I became overwhelmed with the multitude and magnitude of changes—both physical and emotional—I was experiencing and with the powerful effects each one of them had on me. At a time when I expected to be feeling nothing but happiness, excitement, and fulfillment, I was alarmed when more negative emotions—fear, anxiety, confusion—took hold.

My husband was wonderfully supportive, but how could he possibly understand how disconcerting the constant queasiness and exhaustion of a first trimester could be, or the sudden fear the slightest unusual cramp could trigger? The midwives I saw were experienced, knowledgeable, and patient, but I only got to see them once every four weeks, leaving me hungry for reassurance during the intervening twenty-eight days. And the shelves and shelves of pregnancy books (and believe me, I read more than my share), as intelligently and sensitively written as many of them were, spoke in generalities and statistics that I found lacking. I was tired of books that told me what pregnancy *should* be like. I wanted a book that would tell me about the variety of ways that actual women experienced pregnancy.

It wasn't enough, for example, to read about what an amniocentesis is, how it is performed, and why it is recommended to some women. I wanted to know why particular women made the decision to undergo this diagnostic test, whether they experienced any strong emotional reactions in the process, and what the actual procedure was like for each of them. Did it hurt? Were they nervous? How did they feel during the long waiting period for results?

Similarly, I was eager to know if other women experienced the fear of miscarriage as acutely as I did, or if they, like me, had unexplained bleeding during their pregnancies. Did anyone else spend hours poking their stomach, worrying why they weren't feeling their baby move more regularly as soon as they reached their second trimester? I wanted to hear how they were coping with the many irritating and sometimes debilitating symptoms that often accompany pregnancy, to learn how they felt about their growing bellies, their swelling breasts, and their changing appetites. What kind of effect was pregnancy having on their sexual desire and on the ways in which their partners were relating to them? Were they exercising? And what about weight gain? What kinds of feelings accompanied those frequent, and no longer private, weight checks?

In a word, I wanted experience. I longed to hear about what other women were going through and how they were dealing with it. It was this kind of information that I found most useful, most comforting, and most honest.

All pregnant women rely on their friends for advice and support, and so did I. My friends generously shared their maternity clothes, their baby gear, and, most importantly, their enlightening stories about pregnancy from which I learned a tremendous amount. But there were a limited number of them and I found myself wanting more. I then turned to the Internet, where I found hundreds upon hundreds of other pregnant women, who all seemed to be in search of the same kind of information and encouragement that I was. These mothers-to-be generously shared their stories with their counterparts around the world, describing their joys, their fears, and their vulnerabilities. Whether they were discussing their deeply held beliefs about the pros and cons of prenatal diagnostic testing or inquiring whether anyone else finds themselves leaking urine every time they cough, these women were gaining knowledge and power through each others' words.

It was other women's stories, more than anything, that sustained and guided me through the long nine months of my pregnancy, and it was clear to me that I was not the only woman who felt this way.

From morning sickness to constipation, Braxton-Hicks contractions to preterm labor, preeclampsia to gestational diabetes, hospital births to home births, it's a fact that pregnant women rely on each other as they navigate their way through the ups and downs of that marathon-like forty week endurance test.

Unfortunately our culture does not make it easy for pregnant women to find the care and wisdom that other women can provide. Women often live far away from their families and lead extremely busy lives. The primary, and often only, sustained relationship that a pregnant woman has with someone other than her partner is with her health care practitioner and, as wonderful as this relationship might be, it is not enough. One need only listen to the conversations that take place between pregnant women in doctors' offices, in childbirth classes, and in baby stores, to see how eagerly and openly women share their experiences with one another as well as how much satisfaction these exchanges bring.

The desire to provide a structured forum for pregnant women to communicate with one another motivated me to begin collecting the stories that comprise this book. Throughout my pregnancy and my early months of new motherhood, I talked to and corresponded with hundreds of women about pregnancy. I was moved and inspired by their willingness to be so open and their hope that their stories would, in some way, offer guidance, support, and even a laugh or two to other women.

In the pages that follow you'll find the stories of a very diverse group of women who have one thing in common—pregnancy. Their ages vary as do their lifestyles and their geographic locations. Care has been taken to present as wide a range of experiences as possible. The stories included are not meant to provide specific guidelines. Instead, they are meant to express the many and unique ways that real women experience pregnancy.

The chapters of the book represent the major stages and themes of pregnancy. Many women have written stories for more than one chapter so if you find that you identify with a particular contributor, you can often follow her through various stages of her pregnancy. The age listed after each woman's name indicates the age she was during the pregnancy she has written about. The list of contributors at the end of the book provides a brief biographical sketch of each woman as well as a list of the chapters in which her stories can be found. There is also a glossary of pregnancy terms and a list of pregnancy resources to provide further information on a variety of the issues and ideas mentioned throughout these pages.

What follows is not meant as a substitute for the advice of experts and health care providers. However, it is my hope that the varied stories in this book will bring the experts' words to life by letting women speak for themselves. Not every story will speak to every reader directly, but the knowledge, support, and sense of companionship they offer will help us to better understand our own unique experience of pregnancy and more fully appreciate the amazing strength we come to possess during this awe-inspiring transformation.

Chapter One

Ready, Set, Go: Conception and First Trimester Experiences

The decision to have a baby is one of the most significant we'll ever make. For many of us, though, it actually turns out to be the easiest part of the conception process. Rarely in our lives are we confronted so directly with something as wondrous and as unpredictable as our body's ability to create life. We quickly learn that there are things we can do to make the conditions ideal for conception, and some of us approach it with the precision and drive of a physicist on the trail of a Nobel prize. At times, successful conception requires outside help, and fortunately, there are a host of options available to those struggling with infertility. Whatever the situation, it's impossible to know if it will take one month, eight months, or two years to conceive, or whether we will conceive at all. Because we've spent most of our lives trying *not* to get pregnant, the disappointment that now accompanies our menstrual periods each month really takes some getting used to. We soon realize that little has prepared us for the anxiety, fear, and panic that our pregnancy mission can trigger. When we are finally successful, we'll be more than happy to put the often bumpy road to conception behind us.

Of course, many pregnancies begin in a very different way. Perhaps completely unexpected and attributed to failed birth control or a careless encounter, or maybe not entirely unexpected but still met with ambivalence and caution, these pregnancies bring a different set of issues to the table. Regardless of whether we've approached the little window on the home pregnancy test with giddy anticipation or serious dread, once we've decided to forge ahead, the indisputable, and at times unwieldy, realities of the first trimester are there to greet us.

The first trimester is generally considered to be the first fourteen weeks of pregnancy, beginning with the first day of our last menstrual period. For most of us, a missed period and a home pregnancy test will be the first two confirmations. However, there are women who say they knew they'd conceived the moment it happened. There are many symptoms—physical and emotional—associated with this stage of pregnancy, some more common than others. Nausea, vomiting, fatigue, increased urination, increased appetite, mood swings, and breast tenderness are some of the most talked about. Others include light-headedness, excessive salivation, irritability and anxiety, menstrual-like cramps, constipation, and food aversions.

Suffering through these tedious afflictions is no fun at all, but the hardship is definitely eased by the sheer magic of the situation. No matter what else we're feeling, we're sure to be struck by the realization that we're in the midst of something incredible. As our pregnancies progress there will be many opportunities to revel in just how strong and capable our pregnant bodies can be.

Lauren, 32 Years Old

Lauren was in her early thirties when she and her husband started trying to conceive. They'd been together for a very long time, both of their careers were on track—hers in publishing, his in academe—and they felt quite prepared to start a family. Even though it didn't last very long at all, Lauren's journey to conception illustrates just how anxiety-ridden this process can be.

The first month we tried, I was completely convinced that I was pregnant. I had all the symptoms—exhaustion, tender breasts, emotional ups and downs, hunger—you name it. I thought about it constantly, spent hours staring in the mirror, trying to get used to what I was sure was a pregnant body. Imagine my surprise when, on day thirty-one, my period came along just as usual! I was horribly depressed—of course this meant I was doomed to a lifetime of infertility.

Toward the end of the second month of trying, my husband and I went away for a weekend in the country with some friends. By the time we arrived at the house, I had cramps and tender breasts and was tearfully resigning myself to the fact that I was about to get my period. When morning came—and with it sheets of rain, closing off all of our options for romps in the countryside—I surrendered myself to my childless fate. When our friends started mixing pitchers of margaritas, I held out my glass, and I plunged into the hot tub with the rest of them (after all, what are alcohol and hot tubs to women who certainly aren't pregnant?).

A few days later, it dawned upon me that my period had never come. Surely I wasn't pregnant. Surely the cramps and tender breasts, those misleading symptoms from last month, weren't really signs of pregnancy this time. Surely I had not had four margaritas in one day during my first trimester. Surely, I, always the responsible one, had not already inflicted some horrible deformation on my poor baby? It never occurred to me, of course, that these melodramatic reactions were the only surefire sign of pregnancy I'd had so far—hormones!

Of course I was pregnant, and, of course, my son was born strong and healthy, with no signs that margaritas or hot tubs or anything else had done him any harm. Maybe next time I won't have all those margaritas while I'm trying, but maybe next time, I won't freak out if I do.

Anne, 31

Anne and John had always planned to have children. John is the youngest in a family of seven and his siblings had been procreating for years. When they decided to make their first contribution to the next generation they were both in their late twenties, they'd recently bought a house, and things were going just as expected, until, of course, the unpredictability of the conception process took over.

After ten months of trying to conceive our first child (and I mean trying—taking my temperature every morning to track ovulation, having sex every other day during the "fertile time," staying in bed and elevating my hips after sex, etc.) my husband and I had some basic tests done to check our fertility. My husband's sperm test results were abnormal and my doctor told me that it was highly unlikely that we would get pregnant the old-fashioned way. On the one hand, it was a relief to have a concrete reason why we weren't getting pregnant; on the other, it was shattering news to receive. It was just before Christmas and I consoled myself by thoroughly enjoying the freely flowing wine that accompanies the holidays.

The next month my period was more than two weeks late so I decided to take a pregnancy test. The results showed I was, in fact, pregnant. I was overjoyed, of course, but also very fearful that because my husband's sperm weren't "normal," something would be wrong with the baby or I would have a miscarriage. I am a strong believer in the power of positive thinking so I concentrated on all the positives—that I was pregnant, that I felt good, and that everything was progressing normally. I don't think ten minutes went by that I didn't think about being pregnant, and there were definitely times I wished I could "escape" myself and just forget about it for a while. When the twelfth week finally passed, I was hugely relieved and felt as if I could finally begin enjoying being pregnant.

Even after our daughter was born, I was always a little nervous about whether we'd be able to get pregnant again. Since we weren't planning on trying for a while, I put these fears aside, although we did put my husband on a recommended vitamin regimen that we read might help things along when the time came. Much to my surprise, a mere nine months after my daughter's birth, this vitamin regimen and one careless evening resulted in my second pregnancy. Even as I write this, however, just having delivered my second daughter, I can still feel acutely the fear of not being able to have a baby, and I continue to be amazed at the mere existence of my children.

Shannon, 25

Deciding on the best time to have a baby is complicated and sometimes even the most carefully wrought plans change in light of something bigger. A frightening car accident made Shannon and her husband, Rob, realize that they didn't want to wait any longer.

When I think about how my son, Andrew, began and how he came into the world, everything in between seems dull by comparison. My husband and I didn't plan on trying to have a child for at least a year after we were married; he was still finishing his undergraduate degree, neither one of us was working full-time, and we had no medical insurance. It was on our three-month anniversary that our decision changed: It was mid-October, and we left one morning to take a short drive through the mountains, hoping to find the local artisans who sell jewelry so that we could buy some early Christmas gifts. As soon as we reached the spot where they typically sold their wares, however, we not only realized that they weren't there but also that the weather on top of the mountain was quite different from the valley. Snow was beginning to fall for the first time in the season.

We began our descent, watching the flakes accumulate on the road and growing more nervous. As we came around a curve, my husband was driving too fast for conditions and we started to skid into the other lane of traffic toward the edge of the road—and a 500-foot drop with no guardrail. Somehow, something pushed us back in the right direction and we found ourselves in a deep ditch on the right side, with our car perpendicular to the road and sticking out into traffic. We considered ourselves very lucky as we got out to inspect our situation, until a pickup truck came along, had the same sliding problem, and rammed into our car, which in turn swung around and hit my husband who was standing nearby. Time seemed to stand still as I considered life as a widow at twenty-two.

Fortunately, at the end of the experience, my husband sustained no major injuries and was released from the emergency room with a few stitches and a torn knee ligament. But we began to seriously rethink our decision to wait to have children: If one of us had died that day, what would the other have had to show for it, other than a photo album and fond memories? After much prayer and discussion, we decided that we would "take the goalie off the ice," so to speak, if we could get medical insurance that covered maternity. One month after our insurance policies were approved, we were pregnant.

In spite of the fact that we had gone off the pill, we were still shocked to find out that we were pregnant. I had always heard that it can take a while to become pregnant after discontinuing the pill, but obviously that wasn't the case for me. It was actually difficult for us to accept at first. Although we did have health insurance, my husband was only working part-time while he finished school, and I was being paid on an hourly basis to teach English as a Second Language at a university, neither of which would be lucrative enough to provide for a third person in the family. There were more than a few nights in the beginning weeks that I cried and wished the baby wouldn't have come so soon; not that I ever wished any harm to come to my baby, but we were struggling to figure out how we would take care of him once he was born.

Because we were so stressed about the news, I wound up doing away with any of the fanfare with which I hoped to make our announcement and told my parents (who live 1,500 miles away) over the phone. I needed their support more than I wanted to surprise them with a cute announcement, and they were very helpful in allaying my fears and encouraging me to be excited about the baby.

Physically my first trimester was fairly uncomplicated. I did have "all-day" sickness—nausea, for the most part—but only

vomited once. Outwardly, my body changed very little; however, by
8 P.M. each evening, I was more than ready for bed. I was really surprised to see just how tired I was at the end of the day, given that I
was barely pregnant, but I felt reassured when someone told me that
a pregnant woman at rest uses as much energy as a mountain
climber at work. (Whether that's true, I don't know, but it made me
feel better anyway.)

All of my appointments with my certified nurse-midwife went
smoothly, and I looked forward to having her as part of our labor
experience. We knew we were expecting a boy from our second
ultrasound; Andrew was not shy about being seen, and the person
performing the ultrasound assured us that if the baby was *not* a boy,
she needed to find a new job!

I became pregnant a second time when Andrew was just fifteen
months old, but sadly that pregnancy ended in a miscarriage when I
was thirteen weeks along (see Shannon's story in chapter seven). As
I write this, six months later, I am twenty-one weeks pregnant with
another baby. Other than the fears I've experienced because of my
recent loss, the early months of my current pregnancy have thankfully been uncomplicated.

Martha, 38

*Unlike Lauren, Anne, and Shannon, Martha knew it was going to be
difficult for her to conceive. When she met the man who later became
her husband, together they decided to embark on the journey to conception knowing that it would be long and arduous. Even so, it is
impossible to completely prepare yourself for the fear, uncertainty,
and grief that accompany the struggle with infertility. As writer Judith
Schwartz (1997), in her essay "Waiting for Brendan," put it, "A large
belly came to represent all that was lacking in me and in my life, the
embodiment of all my failings." In Martha's case the challenges did
not disappear once she was, finally, pregnant.*

I always knew I was going to have trouble getting pregnant. In my
early twenties I was diagnosed with polycystic ovaries, a hormonal
disorder that causes enlarged ovaries that contain numerous cysts
and is often responsible for infertility and irregular menstruation.
Since then, I just pretended I didn't want to have children. Of course
all that changed after I met the man who would become my husband. I remember telling him early on in our relationship, like on
our fifth date, that I didn't think I could have children. I thought he
should know and was shocked when he didn't break up with me on
the spot.

As we were going through infertility treatment, I was totally unpredictable. Every negative pregnancy test or menstrual twinge was cause for withdrawal. I wanted to suffer alone. It was my body and, therefore, my fault. Even though I was taking all the drugs and undergoing all the procedures, I think my husband suffered more since he had even less control.

I had many friends who were having trouble getting pregnant. I talked to them a lot. I learned the language of infertility. Before ever starting treatment I knew about cycles, estradiol levels, lining measurements, follicle growth. I wasn't prepared for the roller coaster ride until my husband and I began the treatment ourselves. In the beginning we were so naive; we actually thought we would get pregnant on our first try. A round of Clomid and then insemination. I remember that weekend well. I got inseminated on a Saturday morning and we went away for the night with another couple. We were told to have intercourse that night—I think that was the last time we actually had a good time having sex. We smiled on the beach. We thought we had made a baby. Two weeks later I got my period. Not much time for grieving: We jumped right back in, and that was how we lived our life for the next two years.

We graduated to in vitro fertilization (IVF). All of my friends who had not been able to conceive had gotten pregnant on their first IVF. I gave myself shots. Jerry gave me shots. I made a lot of eggs, a lot of lousy eggs. Three IVFs and twenty pounds later—still no baby. We changed doctors twice. The third one was our last hope. I inquired about his statistical success rate for women of my age and condition. He stated it's 100 percent or 0 percent, either you get pregnant or you don't. He was right. Infertility is a condition like no other: It is all or nothing. It's not like wanting a Lexus and getting a Chevy. You just get a car or you don't. So, I appreciated the honesty behind his statement.

After the fourth IVF we were hopeful. (I learned a lot about hope and the human mind. Amazingly, after each attempt I thought I would get pregnant.) The schedule called for blood testing for pregnancy two weeks from the day of retrieval. It was a Saturday morning. I woke up at five, bleeding. I went into the bathroom and cried. I climbed back into bed and tried to sleep. My husband and I spent the morning in bed, planning our life as a childless couple. The bleeding stopped and I took a pregnancy test—threw it in the garbage after a minute—retrieved it an hour later and thought there were two lines. We couldn't be pregnant, could we? The next morning I woke up at 5 A.M.—took a pregnancy test and woke my husband telling him that there was a positive test result in our bathroom (which I still have). We went to the clinic and had my blood drawn. At 12:15 P.M. the next day, I got call-waited. It was the clinic—I was pregnant! My husband was taking a shower. Fully clothed, I opened the curtain and hugged him, crying, the water beating down on the two of us. Remember this moment, he said. I do. Two years, three clinics, four IVFs, and we thought getting pregnant was the hard part. We were wrong.

Those first few weeks were harrowing; my beta number did not double as expected, I spotted the entire first trimester, and on more than one occasion, my husband and I sat in bed playing cards mourning the child we thought we would never meet. I was not allowed to have sex, go on an airplane, or do anything considered mildly risky. My husband had to give me intramuscular shots of progesterone in my rear every night for nine weeks. By the fifth week it hurt to sit down. Despite mandatory testing for HIV (for which I carry no risk), I had never been tested for Tay-Sachs and, in my ninth week of pregnancy, learned that I was a carrier. The week we had to wait for my husband's results was filled with terror. It was the only time I made him call the doctor for results, which luckily came back negative.

The first time we heard the heartbeat I cried. But I never really believed I was pregnant, not until my son was born.

Sara, 36

When Sara and her partner, Terry, decided to have babies, they, like Martha, had to seek outside support. They had everything a couple needs to start a family—a loving relationship, a warm home, and an intense desire for children. However, they were lacking one necessary ingredient—sperm.

When we started trying to conceive our second child, we were a two mom, one daughter, three cat, one dog, one grandmother, lesbian-headed family. We live in a suburban town in a typical suburban house, a split-level ranch. My partner, Terry, carried our first child Hannah, who is now a bubbly, independent, kinetic three-year-old. I adopted Hannah as her second parent (Terry maintained her parental rights and responsibilities) when she was eleven weeks old. Terry's biggest complaint about my own pregnancy is that my delivery story topped her own in terms of drama, but I'm getting ahead of myself.

Our first child was conceived via donor insemination using a sperm bank. We had the option of using the same donor with our second attempt, the difference this time being that I would be the one trying to get pregnant and carrying the child. We decided to use the same donor—not because we thought it incredibly crucial to have a genetic link between the children, but more so because we had the option, and at some point, the children might feel it important to be genetically related (although they might not). If we could give them that link, why not? Our goal was to each try to carry a child, and to adopt any further children; three children was probably our limit (although we realize that such limits are often random at best).

Our donor is what is called a "yes" donor, meaning he has agreed to meet any progeny from his sperm bank donations when they turn eighteen, if the progeny request a meeting. As with the decision to use the same donor, we didn't know whether the children would want to meet their genetic father, but if we could give them that option, why not?

With Terry's pregnancy, all of our inseminations were done at one of two doctors' offices. For me, we decided, based on our previous experience, that the process was really rather simple (thaw out the donor vial, insert pretty much like the usual event—minus particular plumbing and plus a substitute needle-less syringe), and that we would try a certain number of cycle attempts at home. This added a comfort factor (home is more comfortable than a doctor's office), which we thought might help our chances of conceiving reasonably quickly. However, this did involve certain logistical issues. The vials of donor sperm must be kept frozen in liquid nitrogen, much colder than your average kitchen freezer. There are several ways of doing this, but we opted for purchasing a small liquid nitrogen "dewar" (i.e., a tank), storing it in the basement, and trekking it to a welding supply place to refill it with liquid nitrogen every couple of weeks. This gave us the convenience and total control of inseminating at the right moment. Other options included coordinating shipping from the sperm bank to coincide with ovulation.

With the plan and equipment in place, we then started obsessively tracking temperatures, testing for ovulation using an ovulation predictor kit, and inseminating twice per cycle. We succeeded on cycle eight, just shy of the length of a full-term pregnancy. I was pretty sure that I was pregnant before my period was due, because my normal cycle includes about four to five days of spotting before my period actually starts and that time, I had none. I did a pregnancy test two days before my period was expected, and a faint line showed up. We were finally pregnant. And stunned. I think part of us thought it might never happen. We were thrilled.

My first trimester was pretty uneventful. I had nausea from time to time, I completely lost my taste for coffee as well as ice cream, and I was extremely tired.

I did have some very odd food cravings. I ate large quantities of liverwurst for a few weeks at the beginning (and I'm sure it was no coincidence that the blood test I was given during this time was my first ever that did not come back with anemic results). The idea of olives seemed good, so we bought a few jars, although I never ate many of them. I also wanted foods like stuffed grape leaves and bagels with lox.

We told many friends and family about our pregnancy pretty early on—anyone who knew we were trying to conceive got the news of our success fairly quickly. I told work colleagues at around week nine or ten, mostly because I was behaving so oddly that I didn't feel I could keep up the charade much longer. They were pleased because my due date fell during our summer session. I teach in a graduate teacher-training program, and replacing a faculty member for part of the semester is difficult. I was annoyed at essentially "losing" my maternity leave since it was vacation time anyway, but that paled in comparison to my excitement about finally being pregnant.

I started reading an Internet bulletin board for women who were expecting the same month that I was, but in many ways I felt quite different from the majority of them, although a few other two-mom families did post. I was also in the odd position of having never gone through a pregnancy before, but having already parented an infant/toddler/preschooler. Despite feeling a bit out of sync in some ways, I did continue to read the board as time allowed.

Dakota, 45

Although it is now common for women in their forties to get pregnant and give birth to healthy babies, the available statistics about potential problems are always the source of much anxiety for women in this age group. Dakota had known for a long time that she wanted a child, and when she was in her early forties the circumstances in her life were finally right. When her first two pregnancies ended in miscarriage, however, she was sure that her opportunity had passed.

I was forty-five and had lost two babies since I was forty-two. Those were terrible years and I can scarcely remember anything specific about them except that feeling of low-grade, intense pain that I had from the moment I got up until I went to bed at night. I had given up on having children.

I had headaches and cried without provocation at work, in restaurants, at home, in the movies, in church, everywhere. My temper was out of control, worse than ever. I surmised that the extreme psychic discomfort and the physical malaise I felt were symptoms of incipient menopause combined with the sense that I was an infertile old woman straight out of the Old Testament without the prospect of redemption.

I made an appointment to see the gynecologist to verify that my childbearing years had come to an end. The doctor listened to my symptoms, nodded sympathetically, murmured comforting words in that soft South African accent of his, and ordered blood tests to see the levels of various hormones. They do this to figure out if a menopausal woman should start taking estrogen supplements.

Well, the tests showed I was two months pregnant. What I thought were symptoms indicating change of life were, in fact, symptoms of pregnancy. People don't necessarily associate headaches with pregnancy, but I had fierce ones during that time.

I can pinpoint very accurately my emotional and physical responses during the third month of the first trimester. I was happy because I thought I might in fact have a child at the end of it all. I was panicked because I was old and the chances of having a child with problems were very great. One day I felt nauseous and was elated because I had heard the worse you felt the healthier the baby would be. Perversely, I felt physically terrific. I wasn't sleepy, not tired, nor ravenous, nor really nauseous. I tell every expectant mother I know not to worry if they don't feel bad.

The real torture was that I couldn't tell anyone about it. The doctor had advised discretion. Since I had told everyone I was pregnant the first time after the first five minutes, I took the advice to heart. By the end of the third month, my coworkers were staring at me thinking I was quickly gaining a middle-age spread.

Miriam, 34

Not all women experience a burning desire to have babies. When writer Amy Herrick's husband decided he wanted one, she was "taken aback." However, "In the end I agreed to give it a try because I figured it might be one of those things I'd regret never having done, like eating sushi or riding the Cyclone at Coney Island. It wasn't exactly that I wanted to do it, but I was worried that if I didn't do it, I would always wonder what I'd missed" (1997).

In Miriam's case it wasn't until she became unexpectedly pregnant that she decided she wanted a child. A college professor and writer, she was living with her husband in one state and commuting to another to work. She'd decided that it was time to change this situation, but pregnancy was not part of her initial plan.

The first sign that I was pregnant but didn't know it was that I began to want to buy a house. One day I was driving through my favorite neighborhood and saw a "For Sale" sign in front of a house I loved. Suddenly, I just had to live in that 1920s bungalow with the boldly colored sunroom off to the side. I pulled over, and scrawled the agent's name and number on a scrap of paper.

That was before I "knew," before I realized that I couldn't remember my last period (had I brought tampons on that trip in mid-December? What about the week before when guests visited?). Weeks passed. I was busy so I didn't think much of it. I was living in one state four days a week and commuting to my job in another state for the other three. I was terribly tired, but I chalked this up to my compressed schedule. I was nauseous and stomach-sick. Must have been the small planes, wintry skies, and the irregular meals I was eating away from home.

Eventually my psyche took hold and one night my dreams were filled with images of a small baby growing inside my body. I woke that morning in an uncertain sweat. Still, I drove to the drugstore for a home pregnancy kit. I had no idea where they were located and was too shy to ask. What a surprise to find them over by the condoms, and to learn that there were so many choices. I bought a double-pack, just in case I needed extra opinions, and went home.

I hoped to wait until my husband, Rob, got home at the end of the day, but by midafternoon I could no longer hold off. With a private show of bravado (What is the proper emotion for a pregnancy test? Should one's girlfriends be present? One's lover?), I dutifully peed over the white wand and placed it on the edge of the sink to dry. I washed my hands and walked out of the room to pass the longest three-to-five minutes of my life. Sure enough, the second hole showed a pink line, which, on this test, meant that I was pregnant.

I hesitate to write my response, because it was complex, and I wonder about my daughter's reactions were she to read this years from now. Simply, I was shocked. It was rainy and dark that afternoon and for several hours I curled up on the couch to protect myself from a world that had just opened new fault lines in a major way. I had been planning to take the next years off from teaching and turn to more artistic writing. I felt cheated, as if I had been in charge of my destiny and now I realized that I wasn't. And then the most amazing thing happened. The shock and turmoil lifted. Just like that, and as quickly. The world was a bigger and different place than I ever had thought it would be. I was pregnant. I was going to have a baby.

The odd thing was calling the doctor to get a referral for an obstetrician. I told the nurse who answered that I'd taken a home test and was pregnant. She asked what I planned to do. Her response startled me, because even in the whirlwind of surprise I'd never imagined but one choice, to have the baby. Although I support abortions, it felt much nicer to call the obstetrician's office where the nurse congratulated me, told me how wonderful it was, and chatted happily while she scheduled my first appointment.

Aside from being tired, hungry, bloated, and a bit nauseous, I loved being pregnant without it showing to much of the world (though other pregnant women seemed to know). All my life I've made connections with others through similar interests, achievements, and intellectual passions. Rarely had I recognized things my body did as a source of connection with other women. All of a sudden I felt warmth for and from other women who were or had been pregnant. As we shared the news I received much kindness from men and women who were committed to building new families. When our friends Barry and Phyllis came over for a celebratory dinner, they bore a bouquet of purple irises, bottles of sparkling water, and a box or two of the small-size stone wheat crackers that were helping Phyllis through her own pregnancy.

This is my best memory from those first few weeks: On an airplane, the woman next to me pulled out a huge pile of pamphlets about pregnancy. "I'm fourteen weeks," she confided. "I just came from my doctor's office and they gave me all this stuff to read." At the time I was ten weeks, and had barely told anyone. We became immediate friends. We read her materials, passed pamphlets back and forth, pointing out interesting or disturbing facts ("Will our feet really get bigger, permanently?"). She shared her experience with clothes; she'd been wearing a combination of hers and her husband's, but next week "it's maternity clothes for me."

When I felt queasy, she told me to keep eating pretzels. "The salt's not great for us, but it's better than the cookies." The woman a seat ahead on the other side of the aisle chimed in with advice to drink ginger ale. When I thought my stomach wouldn't hold out, my new pregnant friend rounded up the vomit bags in the seat pockets in front of us. In the end I didn't vomit. She did, and I held the bag and together we made sure the experience was as dignified and discreet as could be, and the flight attendant helped too. We left the plane and hugged good-bye. She gave me an extra apple from her bag. I can't remember her name, but she taught me about the kindness of strangers and the intimacy of sharing pregnancy with other women.

Jennifer, 26

When writer Ariel Gore (1998) started experiencing early pregnancy symptoms she blamed it on food poisoning. The state of semi-denial she was in lasted for a few weeks. "As I sat there playing mind games with myself, the little mass of cells that would become my daughter was busy dividing, redividing, and implanting itself on my uterine wall, where it would remain for nine confusing, nauseating months."

Pregnancy was the furthest thing from Jennifer's mind when she, too, started showing early signs. Her life was full and fulfilling just as it was. She was married, very committed to her work as an events coordinator at a performing arts center, and a devoted and regular visitor to her local gym.

I was not expecting to become pregnant. I had been taking birth control pills for over a decade, and I considered the possibility of pregnancy to be "taken care of." When I started waking up a bit nauseated, I thought I had the flu. When my breasts became unbearably tender and full of fluid, I went to the doctor who prescribed a diuretic. When I finally skipped a period, I was more than two months along (though I didn't know that at the time), and I still didn't think I was pregnant. I thought I'd developed a horrible disease, or suffered radiation poisoning from the microwave, or had been exposed to some other environmental toxin.

Five days after my period was due, I broke down and bought a pregnancy test. I almost had a heart attack when the results were positive. When I informed my husband, he was as disbelieving as I was. I hadn't taken antibiotics, I didn't skip any pills, I just didn't understand how I could have conceived anything. I felt extremely guilty for being unhappy because I knew there were women who desperately wanted a baby and couldn't have one, and here I was, pregnant on a fluke and feeling like my life was over. I just didn't feel ready for the whole thing, and I was terrified of motherhood. I knew nothing about raising a child. I knew even less about being pregnant. I considered every option briefly but because of the unusual circumstances, I felt as though fate had given me this pregnancy and I decided to go ahead with it. My husband had always wanted children and even though he didn't expect to have one so soon, he was basically ecstatic. I, on the other hand, was never convinced that having children was for me so it took a little longer to digest the news.

My first trimester was half over before I even knew I was pregnant, and once I knew, I felt really stupid for not realizing it sooner. My breasts were so tender and full of fluid that I had to wear two bras to manage the daily bounce factor. I felt exhausted and was sleeping anywhere from twelve to eighteen hours a night. I had to pee every five minutes. I didn't develop morning sickness, for which I am grateful. I did, however, develop a voracious appetite, and I grew out of my skirts and pants almost overnight. No one told me that your waist was the first thing to go, or that pregnancy first widened your middle into a rectangle before a frontal maternity bulge alerted the world to the fact that you were, in fact, pregnant and not just putting on the pounds. (The same bulge that anyone and everyone seemed to want to touch without even asking if it was OK with me.) I was also having trouble keeping my wedding ring on. The ring still fit on my finger, but painful little blisters formed wherever it touched my skin. My doctor had no explanation for it, and the ring sat in my jewelry box until my daughter was four months old.

Because I became pregnant on the pill, I worried that the pills I took before I knew I conceived had harmed the baby. This made me very nervous about miscarriage, so I didn't tell the world I was pregnant until I was an estimated sixteen weeks along. I just gradually stopped tucking in my shirts and prayed no one would notice. It seems silly now, but I didn't want to tell everyone about my unexpected pregnancy only to go back and un-tell them should I lose the baby. Besides, sharing the baby with just my husband was kind of romantic.

I got in to see my selected obstetrician a month after I found out I was pregnant. My doctor was very educated and sincere, and I felt completely at ease with her. She answered my neurotic questions, estimated my due date, and invited me to listen to the baby's heartbeat. She said it was a bit early, but sometimes the heartbeat could be heard earlier on slender women. On the third swipe of my abdomen, she found it. I remember being shocked by how fast it was, and I couldn't believe there was something alive inside of me. At that moment, I decided to overcome my fears, take a deep breath, and face the future head on. Fate had offered me a gift I knew I couldn't turn away. That little heartbeat was depending on me, and I felt strong and capable and very happy.

Audra, 24

Audra was still nursing her one-year-old son when she discovered that she was pregnant again. The news came as a big surprise and she spent a good deal of her first trimester emotionally coming to terms with the pregnancy, while observing how differently her body was responding this time around.

I was shocked and upset to find myself pregnant again only one year after my son Clark was born. I was only three months away from graduating from university and on the verge of finally starting a career in dietetics. It seemed like we were just beginning to see the light at the end of the tunnel, financially, only to find that our plans had to be delayed for at least another year. We hadn't really talked about having more children, and we were really in a nice groove with Clark. I felt guilty for resenting the pregnancy and tried to deny and repress the feelings I was having.

My husband and I talked about it a lot, after deciding it was best to deal with our emotions before rather than after the baby arrived. We both felt so torn—happy to have another baby to love, but guilty for taking away Clark's status as only child and star of the family. Also, the pregnancy left my nipples sore and milk supply low so I put a rush on weaning. I had planned to nurse for longer, and felt robbed in that respect too. We didn't even tell anyone about the pregnancy until I was nine weeks along (which is a long time for me to keep a secret!). After our families and friends were aware and supportive of the coming attraction we felt much better equipped to handle it.

The first trimesters of my two pregnancies were very different. With my first, I felt great during most of the early months. I was queasy and weepy for a few weeks, but by my ninth week, I was flying high. I didn't throw up once, didn't feel too tired, and had an insatiable appetite. Unfortunately I put on ten pounds before the baby was the size of a sunflower seed, but I felt great. I did have one scare, though. I was six weeks pregnant and, momentarily forgetting it, sprinted for the bus. As I climbed on I felt something "pop" inside me. I looked down and saw that blood was pooling in my sandals from where it had run down my legs under my dress. I got off the bus and took a cab to the hospital where my husband met me. I was crying very hard, certain that I was losing the baby. A nurse gave me a urine test that confirmed I still had the pregnancy hormone hCG (human chorionic gonadotropin) in my system, but she said that I could be in the process of miscarrying and that there was nothing they could do. The bleeding had slowed to a trickle and the emergency room was so full that I didn't end up seeing a doctor. After five hours of waiting, I just went home. I saw my own doctor the next morning and had an ultrasound. How relieved I was to see the teeny heart beating. Nobody knows what caused the bleeding. My doctor suspected that I had a cyst on my ovary that ruptured. After that unusual and highly emotional episode, the rest of my first trimester went off without a hitch.

The first trimester of my second pregnancy was definitely an emotional ride, but it didn't contain the same kind of excitement and drama as the first. I was, however, downright nauseous for several weeks, and I even lost my breakfast once. I felt so tired and ill that I lost weight, and it didn't help that I was chasing around my very active toddler. Those early months with baby number two were much more somber and I felt quite introspective. Although neither baby was "planned," my first pregnancy was a celebration while my second one started out as a burden. I feel terrible writing this, thinking that my sons will one day read it, but as the baby blossomed inside me, so did my love for him. I just needed the first trimester to feel sad that things weren't working out the way I had anticipated. I've realized since that all the best things that have happened in my life were unplanned.

Ginette, 31

Ginette, like Audra, was shocked to discover that she was pregnant again when her first child was just a year old. Sadly, just as she was getting excited about the idea, she lost the pregnancy. She and her husband decided to try again about eighteen months later and were extremely happy when they succeeded, but Ginette was surprised at how rough the early months of the pregnancy were. And that was not the only surprise she would have.

One year after my son Joshua's birth, I found myself pregnant again, unexpectedly. I felt completely unprepared for another baby so soon. After the shock wore off my husband and I became excited and began making plans for our new family. Then, at fourteen weeks, I miscarried. I was terribly sad and also felt very guilty for my initial feelings about not being ready for a second baby, but life does go on, even though we still think of this unborn baby often.

When Joshua was approaching two and a half years old, we decided to start trying to have a second child. We were thrilled when I became pregnant within six months. It took eight months of trying for us to get pregnant with Joshua. At around seven weeks into the pregnancy, I started bleeding and cramping. We were very scared and I was sure I was going to miscarry again. While waiting in my general practitioner's office to be examined, I tried very hard not to cry, but I couldn't help myself. It really did feel like my heart was breaking. The doctor examined me, determined that my cervix was still closed tight and said that we would have to take it one day at a time. My husband insisted that I lay in bed for the rest of my pregnancy or at least until this episode subsided. I did this for a week during which time the bleeding slowed down to spotting. At that point, I called my doctor to tell him that I could not go on any longer with the doubts I was carrying around. I insisted on having an ultrasound, which he scheduled for that afternoon. We were both shocked and extremely relieved when the technician said, "There is the heartbeat. It looks great, nice and strong!" Within a week or two, the cramping finally slowed, then disappeared, as did the spotting.

One day during the time of my husband-imposed bed rest, my son Joshua discovered his mommy and daddy upset and crying. We explained to him that the baby in Mommy's belly was sick and we were not sure if it was going to get better but that we would hope and pray. He took this news as well as a three-year-old can, not really understanding, yet still realizing that something was going on. He left the room and went off to color. When he came back he had two little pieces of paper, one colored orange and one colored blue, which he put on my stomach saying it was medicine to make the baby better. We cried, but little did we know that this gesture was a premonition of things to come.

Around my ninth week my morning sickness got worse and my belly expanded. I felt very sick, nauseated, and had terrible headaches. I wasn't vomiting, but I could not bring myself to eat. I remember my husband and mother-in-law trying to force feed me apples and a vitamin supplement, yuck! I lost ten pounds and my doctor was concerned. I was given medication for my nausea (Diclectin), which helped, and I took it until my seventeenth week.

This experience was very different from my pregnancy with Joshua. My first trimester with Joshua was what I would call "typical." I felt nauseated most of the day and had lots of heartburn but nothing as extreme as what I was experiencing the second time around. With Joshua, at twelve weeks, the clouds finally broke and the morning sickness lifted. With this pregnancy the sickness lasted well into my second trimester. And it was during the second trimester, in my twentieth week of pregnancy, that a routine ultrasound gave us the shock of our lives—the baby that I was carrying was actually two babies! We were going to have twins.

Whitney, 33

Like Ginette, Whitney had already experienced one miscarriage when she started bleeding early in her first trimester. Although many women who bleed or spot during their pregnancies have healthy pregnancies and healthy babies (see Ginette, Audra, and Cynthia's stories in this chapter), this can definitely be a sign that something is going wrong, especially when accompanied by cramping.

When I became pregnant for the fourth time, I'd already experienced a partial molar pregnancy, a miscarriage, and a healthy pregnancy that resulted in the birth of my now two-year-old daughter. When my daughter was nine months old my husband and I began to talk about a second child. Because I had not resumed my period after I'd stopped breastfeeding three months earlier, I became concerned about my future procreation abilities and my doctor agreed to let me try Provera for one month to stimulate menstruation. It worked and my period arrived but I was frustrated when the following month, once again, I did not menstruate.

A self-exam in the shower shortly thereafter revealed a breast lump. My doctor assured me that everything was probably fine but that he would like to do a mammogram. "You aren't pregnant, are you?" he asked. It was more than three weeks since my period was due, with still no sign of it, so just to be sure I took three pregnancy tests prior to the mammogram. All three were negative. I couldn't be pregnant. Maybe my body was still off schedule. Still, I canceled the appointment and decided to reschedule as soon as my period arrived.

About a week later I started noticing that I was amazingly hungry throughout the day. Then one afternoon while cleaning up my daughter's toys, I fell asleep on the floor—this was unheard of, as I do not even nap in beds. I decided to take another home pregnancy test. Much to my surprise it was positive. How was this possible when the other three were negative? We were thrilled. I was already having extreme signs of nausea, tiredness, and hunger—wasn't it a bit early for all of this? Boy, this was going to be a long pregnancy!

Then one day I felt a very sharp pain in my side, had slight cramping, and began to spot lightly: I must be miscarrying, I thought. I'd been there before and was devastated. I went in for an ultrasound and because it was hard to tell exactly when I'd ovulated, it was unclear how large the fetus should be. However, the doctor was pretty certain that something was wrong and that I was indeed miscarrying. Blood work would confirm this, he was certain.

Soon after, a surprised call from my doctor revealed that even though my body was showing signs of miscarriage, my hormone levels were doubling, not dropping. He wanted me to go in for another ultrasound to see what was going on. I didn't allow myself to think I might still be pregnant so I was shocked and relieved when the ultrasound was fine—no heartbeat yet, but it looked like a normal pregnancy after all. But those cramps still haunted me.

Five days later I began to spot again, this time more heavily. Another ultrasound was scheduled. Another surprise. After some exploring the technician noticed that there were two sacs. The doctor confirmed this and I was told that I was miscarrying one of the fetuses, hence my symptoms. All was fine with the remaining pregnancy, and he even saw a heartbeat this time. I was informed that the other sac would more than likely be absorbed by the living fetus and that I would probably not pass it. Relieved, and yet a little sad, I went home again to tell my husband that all was fine. Surprisingly, he was more upset about the lost twin than I was. I was just so relieved to still be pregnant.

But the scares continued. I soon started bleeding heavily again and was sure I was miscarrying the healthy baby. Another ultrasound and, once again, I was told that things were fine and that I must be passing the sac they thought I'd absorb. I was beside myself but decided I had to quit worrying. Luckily, soon after that, all of the bleeding subsided, and, happily, the rest of my pregnancy was uneventful and resulted in the birth of a full-term healthy baby boy.

Emily, 35

Nausea and vomiting are often a part of the first trimester. Deceptively called "morning sickness," it can strike at any time of the day and for some women lasts all day long. When Emily became pregnant she never knew she could feel so awful. What at first seemed like a severe case of morning sickness was later diagnosed as hyperemesis gravidarum. Much more extreme and dangerous than morning sickness, women suffering from this condition experience excessive nausea and vomiting, dehydration, and weight loss. If not monitored carefully, the illness can have serious effects on the health of both mother and baby. Constantly vomiting, battling dehydration, and losing weight throughout her first trimester, there was nothing about her pregnancy or her life that Emily was able to enjoy during those early months.

The first trimester of pregnancy was not the happiest time of my life. There was no "glow of womanhood," no joy at having entered the long sought-after club of "maternity." Instead, I puked morning, noon, and night for four months. I got so dehydrated that I needed IV fluids. I was up most nights from midnight to 4 A.M. (which made work during the days hard). I lost seven pounds.

I poured over pregnancy books, looking for something that would offer me a way to understand morning sickness (I found particularly self-serving the explanation that the more "sick" you were the healthier the pregnancy). But nothing prepared me for finding my husband's breath nauseating. Or for sleeping on a mattress on the floor by myself for four months because every time my husband turned over in bed I thought I was on the sinking Titanic. The doctors kept telling me it didn't matter if I couldn't eat—just drink (how ironic, the baby will take what it needs from you no matter how sick you are). But drinking made me the most sick.

I resorted to eating watermelon and grapes off-season for their water content (the store clerk actually asked my husband if he really wanted those three pounds of grapes at $7 a pound). One time my husband cooked a pork chop whose aroma (or stench, in my case) permeated every corner of the house, leading me to lock myself in one room for hours while he opened all the doors and windows. (By the end of the first trimester, he was eating his meals in the car.) I was only able to work about four hours a day, canceled all trips, and basically dropped out of life for a while. But I got through it, with a healthy share of cynicism, fear, and crying. And I had an otherwise healthy pregnancy—I gained a total of forty pounds, had a relatively easy delivery (karmic payback), and a healthy baby girl.

In my Zen moments, I know the experience taught me something. It prepared me for the stark reality of parenting. Some people say that the reason pregnancy takes nine months is so that you can slowly prepare for the disruptions having a child brings. It just happened a lot earlier for me. From six weeks into my pregnancy I was forced to give in, slow down, and let go, which are the ultimate lessons of parenting.

Gina, 24

Gina had problems with preterm labor during her first two pregnancies and knew this might happen again during her third. But she never expected the severe nausea, vomiting, and fatigue that made her life with two small children and a full-time job as a paralegal so incredibly difficult to manage.

As soon as my husband and I decided to have a baby, I got pregnant. We were faced with a different situation than most couples, because I already had two children when we got married. I was scared of having another baby but my husband wanted one right away. Looking back, I am glad we didn't wait.

I was in my midtwenties when I became pregnant with my third child, and I was balancing an entire family and career. This made me feel more mature than most women my age who did not seem to have as much responsibility or as many worries. My first two pregnancies were wonderful in many ways, but they had also been quite difficult so I was definitely a bit worried about what my already full life would be like while I was carrying this child.

The very beginning of the first trimester of this pregnancy was actually great. I felt just like, well, myself! But, before I knew it, I started having all the symptoms of what people say is a "healthy" pregnancy. After that initial easy period, I was sick nonstop. I woke up nauseous, went to sleep nauseous, and vomited constantly. My days at work were terrible. I was completely exhausted by the time I got home. Just looking at food made me sick. I normally loved to eat junk food, but I couldn't even look at a cookie without wanting to throw up. The great part about this was that I only wanted to eat things that were actually good for me, like fruits and vegetables.

Emotionally I definitely felt a little depressed. I was in bed by 7:30 P.M. every night. My wonderful husband was in charge of everything, but my kids (then seven and five years old) needed me too. I felt like I was letting my entire family down, but I could do nothing about it. Sleep was the only way to relieve my symptoms. This was by far the worst first trimester I ever had. With my other two pregnancies I was nauseous for about two or three weeks, but the third time it lasted for months. I knew it was going to be a very difficult pregnancy. I kept thinking positively and asking God continually to give me strength so I could persevere until the end.

Cynthia, 36

Physically, the first trimester can certainly be debilitating, but for some of us it's the emotional and psychological symptoms that are paralyzing. Fear of losing the pregnancy and anxiety about the health of the fetus can be all consuming, as can the feeling that we're suddenly losing control of our lives and our bodies. Cynthia was totally unprepared for the places that her emotions led her during this time.

Even though I was convinced that it would take a while to get pregnant because of my age, we were successful on our first try. A very good start, yes, but, generally, my first trimester was not a happy time. I was thrilled to be pregnant but not at all prepared for the ups and downs of those first three months. I became obsessed with statistics about miscarriage and complications that could arise because I was over thirty-five. I read every piece of scary information I could get my hands on in books and on the Internet. Feelings of fear and anxiety consumed me and I wasn't completely comfortable sharing them since they often seemed irrational. A life was growing inside me and I couldn't see it, feel it, or do anything to ensure its well-being. I have never felt so out of control.

To make matters worse, I experienced some brown spotting on a couple of occasions, sending me into complete panic. On the second occasion, I was sent for an ultrasound, which allowed me to see the little "bean" that was growing inside me and its beating heart. This certainly helped to reassure me . . . but only for a short time. My midwife told me that if something were to go wrong in these early months, there really wasn't anything I could do to prevent it and that as difficult as it was, I had to "give myself over to nature." I tried to do this when I wasn't obsessively checking my vaginal discharge to be sure it wasn't brown or red.

When I hit the sixth or seventh week, I started to feel a lot more tired and a lot hungrier. If I didn't keep my stomach full at all times, I became queasy. My queasiness was at its worst on my subway ride to and from work every day. My forty-minute commute was extremely unpleasant and I wore sea bands (acupressure wristbands meant to decrease nausea), drank lots of water, and did an awful lot of deep breathing to keep myself from losing it on the train every day. I hardly made social plans, and after a full day of work and worrying, I couldn't find the energy to do much else besides go home and read or watch television.

When I hit my twelfth week and felt like I might be able to start relaxing, I woke up one morning to a significant amount of bright red bleeding. My husband and I rushed off to see our midwives. I was sure I was miscarrying and he too, although usually the positive one during these bumpy months, was quite shaken. After an examination showed a closed cervix and a uterus that had definitely grown since my last visit, the midwife tried to listen to the baby's heartbeat with the Doppler and couldn't find it. I was then sent off for an emergency ultrasound.

The technician covered the monitor that was facing me until she could have a look. This scared me even more. About two seconds after she put the wand on my belly, she said, "Your baby is fine." We then watched in amazement as we saw the baby with its beating heart squirming around on the screen. They never could determine why the bleeding happened and I was advised to stay off my feet for a week (which I did). The whole episode certainly prolonged the fear and anxiety of my first trimester and I was well into my second before I finally started to calm down.

Tass, 29

The emotional challenges of early pregnancy can be even more extreme if you've embarked on the road to single motherhood. In addition to the usual difficulties, single pregnant women often have to deal with the criticism and disapproval that society continues to direct toward them, even today. For many, though, the desire to have a child far outweighs this lack of support. Writer Anne Lamott (1993) describes it like this: "I could have had an abortion—the pressure to do so was extraordinary—and if need be, I would take to the streets, armed to defend the right of any woman for any reason to terminate a pregnancy, but I was totally unable to do so this time psychologically, psychically, emotionally."

Similarly, when Tass found out that she was pregnant, she felt strongly about keeping her baby, even though her ex-boyfriend (her baby's father) and her family thought she was making a big mistake.

I first suspected I was pregnant when I was on holiday with my family. I'd had a dream that I was pregnant and then at the airport as we were leaving I had a fainting spell. My period was late, but I have always been irregular. The first thing I did when I landed back home was to buy a home pregnancy test. It was hard to read so I did another—positive. I was very nervous and apprehensive. My boyfriend who I loved very much and wanted to spend the rest of my life with had broken up with me eight weeks earlier. If I was pregnant, then I had conceived on our last weekend together when we'd gone away to try and work things out.

The way he found out I was pregnant was not the way I planned it. We both happened to be at the same party one night and he came home with me. Unfortunately, I'd left the test sitting in the open and he saw it. He was angry and said that he needed to think and that we would go to the doctor to get it confirmed. When we did, the doctor confirmed what I already knew. I knew straight away that I wanted to keep this baby. Ten years earlier I had a pregnancy terminated and I didn't want to go through that again. I have always wanted children and it seemed as though fate was dealing me a second chance. For some reason I felt that if I decided not to have this baby, I would never be given the opportunity again.

I was very worried though. I had no permanent job or even a place to live. Just before my ex and I broke up we'd been planning to move out of the country. He had been away on business for three months and, when he returned, he said that he had doubts about our relationship. But I had already given up my job and my apartment and was staying with friends on the assumption that we would soon be leaving the country together. My life was already one big mess, and here was another complication, being pregnant.

My ex decided that he didn't want to have this baby with me. He didn't love me anymore and he felt trapped. I begged him not to make me do this alone. I cried all day, every day.

Deep in my heart I still knew that I wanted this baby, but I asked for guidance from many sources to help me make my decision. I even went to a psychic (who, by the way, didn't even pick up that I was pregnant!). When I called my mother I'd decided that whatever she said, I'd do. Her first words were, "Well, you'll have to have an abortion." I booked the appointment the next day. My ex said he would pay for it, drive me there, and look after me when it was all over. I continued to cry for days. I didn't want to do this but felt that I had no choice. With no job, no apartment, and no money, how could I possibly have this baby? Especially by myself.

The odds were certainly against me, but I couldn't help feeling that by having an abortion I was making the worst mistake of my life. I mentioned this to my ex's sister who is a counselor. She recommended that I see another counselor and she stressed how important it was for me to be sure that I was making the right decision.

When I went to see the counselor I was armed with a list of all the negatives and positives of *not* having the baby. There were quite a few more positives on this list, but the one negative that stood out was my fear of losing the will to live if I decided to terminate the pregnancy.

She listened to me for two hours and recommended that I postpone my decision until I was more certain. When I canceled my appointment at the clinic, I felt the biggest relief. For the first time in nearly three weeks, I felt calm. My ex was away working, but I called him and let him know. His only reaction was, "Well, you know how I feel."

My mother called two days after my scheduled appointment at the clinic. She hadn't called at all that week so had no idea that I'd been to see a counselor or that I'd canceled my appointment. She was very quiet when I told her that I still hadn't made up my mind.

The next day I had a call from both her and my step-dad (who has been like a father to me all my life). They told me that I was making a huge mistake and that I would be ruining my life. I couldn't believe what I was hearing. I told them that it was up to me to decide what to do and that I didn't want to talk about it anymore. They hung up on me.

I didn't hear from them again or from my ex. But as the weeks passed I became more and more certain that I wanted to keep my baby. My friends rallied around me and supported my decision. I knew I was doing the right thing.

Even with all of this emotional upheaval, I had no physical discomfort during those early months. I didn't get morning sickness or any other symptoms—I guess God didn't want to give me too much to handle all at once. How could I have possibly coped with anything more?

❈ ❈ ❈

As the first three months come to a close, we have had our official initiation into the world of pregnancy. Whether we were dealt a particularly difficult hand, or whether we were lucky enough to experience only minor discomforts, at the end of the first trimester we've reached a milestone of sorts. Having gotten this far, we start to believe that we actually can get through this, and it's likely that we've already learned a lot about the need to relinquish some control in the process.

As psychologist Harriet Lerner (1998) has written, ". . . there is no other normative experience in our lives, apart from our own birth and death, that puts us through such massive change and transformation in such a relatively brief time. The challenge is to embrace the full experience, and sometimes just get through it as best we can."

Chapter Two

Am I Glowing Yet? Second Trimester Experiences

We're usually pretty happy to part company with our first trimester. Once those early months have passed, the rate of miscarriage drops dramatically and many of the irksome symptoms disappear. The second trimester, generally considered to be the fifteenth through the twenty-seventh week, is when bellies begin to grow and civilian clothes are traded in for maternity gear. Lots of women report that great sex can be expected in months four, five, and six, and some even experience a sex drive stronger than ever before. These months also bring one of the most exciting parts of pregnancy—movements from the baby within.

For many of us, this is when the pregnancy starts to seem very real. Some women feel wonderful during this time, first trimester symptoms behind them and the discomforts of the third trimester months away. Unfortunately, many others don't. For some, nausea and vomiting have not subsided, heartburn and indigestion have begun, and mild swelling (often in ankles, feet, and hands) has set in. Other possible symptoms include leg cramps, occasional nosebleeds and nasal congestion, headaches, forgetfulness, and varicose veins. By now, we'll probably have shared the news of our pregnancy with family, friends, and coworkers, and if we haven't, our body is sure to give it away soon.

For those of us who decide to have diagnostic testing, the second trimester is when many of these procedures will take place. The alpha-fetoprotein (AFP) test, that can identify neural tube defects or an increased risk of chromosomal abnormalities, is usually administered around the seventeenth week, and amniocentesis, which detects genetic abnormalities as well as other problems, is conducted around the same time. Some women have ultrasounds throughout their pregnancy, but in many cases the only, and most extensive, ultrasound is performed somewhere around the twentieth week. Although this close examination and measurement taking can trigger anxiety for parents-to-be, by this time our babies are putting on such a show that one only looks on in wonder.

Choosing a childbirth method, pondering names, and beginning to get our homes ready for a new baby are some other things we might be doing during these middle months as we prepare ourselves both psychologically and practically for what lies ahead.

❉ ❉ ❉

Jennifer, 26 Years Old

Many of us feel stronger than ever as our bodies harbor and nurture our unborn babies, this strength erupting as we give birth and move on to motherhood. In the words of writer Louise Erdrich (1995), "Women are strong, strong, terribly strong. We don't know how strong we are until we're pushing out our babies. We are too often treated like babies having babies when we should be in training, like acolytes, novices to high priesthood, like serious applicants for the space program."

By the time she entered her second trimester, Jennifer had begun to embrace her unplanned pregnancy. She began to feel not only special but also quite powerful as her body ripened and her baby grew.

After the shock of becoming pregnant while taking birth control pills subsided, and I'd told everyone on the planet that I was indeed expecting a baby in the near future, I entered my second trimester with a smile on my face. During my fourth month (which the ultrasound would point out later was actually my fifth month), I began feeling that special glow reserved especially for pregnant women.

I felt the baby's first kick on Mother's Day. I couldn't believe the timing. I was lying on the couch and I felt something tap my stomach. It was not a fluttering movement like the books described; it was a punch. I looked down and actually *saw* something tapping me from the inside. At first I was freaked out, and I felt like one of those alien hosts portrayed in all the sci-fi movies. Then I became wildly excited and called everyone I knew. It was as if the baby knew it was Mother's Day and decided to give me a supportive pat.

Once the baby started kicking, I felt very important. A baby was growing inside of my body, growing because of me, and I was caught up in the cosmic fate of it all. It felt as if I were fulfilling some evolutionary purpose, a biological design older than the ages, and carrying this baby was my destiny. I felt extremely feminine and proud of it. Every time the baby kicked, I was drawn into a private conversation to which no man would ever be invited. It seemed to me that if I could grow a baby, I could do anything.

Emotionally, I felt my best in the second trimester. I accepted my role as "mother" and became less anxious. Of course, I had no idea what that meant or what to expect. I still thought my life would stay relatively the same, kind of like when you get a puppy. Sometimes they whine, potty on the floor, and chew on the table leg, but they're content sleeping in the sun and eating what you give them. I figured I had a huge list of willing babysitters, so I could still go to the mall now and then. The powerfulness of pregnancy masked my complete yet blissful ignorance of mothering an infant.

I also felt my best physically during this time. I had a little bulging ball under my maternity tops, and even though my behind was growing wider every day, I didn't feel especially fat. I felt great and could eat my weight in hamburgers. I still had energy to do what I liked (movies, restaurants), and for those few months, I could still get myself out of the bathtub unassisted. Additionally, my sex drive reached an all-time high, making my husband a fan of the second trimester as well.

When my first ultrasound took place, I learned that my baby was due an entire month earlier than we'd expected. As a result, I kicked into high preparation gear. I went to every prenatal class offered at the hospital where I planned to deliver. I placed my name on five day-care waiting lists. I interviewed and chose a pediatrician. I made yellow curtains for the nursery and bought a darling white chifforobe for the baby's clothes. I also stocked the baby's bookshelf with all my childhood favorites. I wanted everything in place when the baby arrived.

If I were only allowed one word to describe my second trimester, I would choose "calm." My doubts and fears lessened, my body felt strong, and my mind felt ready. In retrospect, I know that it was actually the calm before a big storm, but I will always be grateful for that brief glimpse of contentment. As my pregnancy took a turn for the worse (I developed preeclampsia—pregnancy-induced high blood pressure—at the start of my third trimester), I drew upon the positive energy of those middle months to sustain me through the turbulent waves of uncertainty. (See Jennifer's story in chapter five.)

Trudi, 32

Feeling the baby move for the first time was for Trudi, as it was for Jennifer, a moment that changed the course of her pregnancy. In fact, when asked what the best parts of pregnancy are, most women will mention the tapping, kicking, and rolling of their little ones as a highlight. In Trudi's case, her son's first detectable move was well-timed and it helped her find her way through that awkward stage when you don't quite look pregnant but you can't button your pants either.

If you're lucky, your second trimester is comparatively a lot easier than the first or last. And I was fairly typical—the morning sickness that had plagued me passed within the first couple of weeks, and soon, as predicted, I felt fine. Energy renewed, food aversions subsided, and appetite, well, tremendous. That little tiny bit of weight that I'd gained in the first trimester, only enough to make my jeans somewhat tight, soon expanded along with my waistline. By the end of the fourth month, I had gained nearly ten pounds and was officially in what I have fondly come to call "the chubby stage."

A pregnant woman's changing body was something I'd thought about even before I'd conceived. I never thought, however, that I would have any issues with my physique, so I was very surprised when I did (blame it on the hormones). The chubby stage is the horrible in-between place when your regular clothes don't really fit, but you're still not quite ready for maternity wear. In fact, until a friend of mine gave me crucial advice about how to expand my jeans (wrap a coated elastic band around the button, thread through the buttonhole, and loop back around the button), I was pretty uncomfortable.

Because I couldn't feel the baby move yet, it was very difficult to comprehend that my rapidly changing body shape had something to do with my offspring—of course my logical mind knew that, but emotionally, it was harder to make the leap. Clunky. Unattractive. Frustrated. I just wanted to get into maternity clothes, but alas, it wasn't until my sixth month that I was really in need of drawstrings and drop waists. I don't mean to sound shallow, but I think most women will agree that not being able to fit into your clothes is a drag. Ultimately, I found the remedy: I bought myself one or two pretty blousy items, and accessorized to the max. Oh yeah, and a pair of fabulous sexy shoes.

The chubby stage came to a merciful close—at least in my mind—the first time I felt my baby move. I had been reading up on what I could expect in terms of feeling the baby for the first time, and all the "experts" gave the same helpful characterization: It may feel like you have gas. I had been experiencing gas from the beginning of my pregnancy and it took on a variety of forms—sometimes a sharp, shooting twinge, other times just a little bubbly action in my stomach—so this description was not very useful in terms of preparing me for what I would actually feel. I couldn't imagine it, save the image from the movie *Alien* I had burned in my mind, although I did know that the pushing around the child would be doing that I could actually see and feel on the outside, as well as on the inside, wouldn't occur until much later.

Because my doctor asked me at my four-month check-up if I had felt any movement yet, I began to think about the baby moving more often than not. I was always dragging my husband's hand to my belly, hoping the little one would suddenly kick or something. After a while, I realized that the watched pot would probably only boil if I wasn't obsessing, so I laid off trying to feel the baby.

That fateful night, long into my fifth month—almost the sixth month, in fact—when it finally happened, I proved the watched pot theory was right on the money. I'd worked late and was tired and hungry and in a rush to get home. I hopped into a cab, and for the first time all day, relaxed. About halfway through my journey, lost in my thoughts and basically zoning out, I felt a little poke inside my stomach. Hmmm, I thought, I must be really hungry. Then the poke happened again, in almost the same spot. I broke into a huge grin, and said out loud (and the cabbie must've thought I was crazy), "Hey you, I guess you really are in there." At that instant, I knew for sure that my child had moved for the very first time. And it was thrilling. After that, I didn't experience the baby move again for a week or so. For the record, it didn't feel like gas—in fact, it didn't feel like anything else I had ever felt before.

Gina, 24

Pregnancy is definitely a lesson in learning to let go. Many say this serves as a needed initiation into the world of motherhood when we'll have to give up so much control that the art of hanging on by our fingertips becomes our gold medal event. This "letting go" can be a gradual process that unfolds slowly as our pregnancies change our bodies, our minds, and our emotional states, or it can come about abruptly, triggered by something urgent that cannot be ignored.

During the second trimester of Gina's third pregnancy, she felt awful and was living in fear of preterm labor, which had been a problem during both of her previous pregnancies. In spite of her past experience, Gina still found it incredibly difficult when the events of her pregnancy made her life feel somehow out of her control.

I kept telling my husband, friends, family, and myself that the exhaustion, nausea, and vomiting would soon end because the second trimester is much easier than the first. But this second trimester was much worse than it had been with my other pregnancies. I was still throwing up, but thankfully, just once a day after dinner.

When I hit my twentieth week a tremendous amount of fear came over me. I felt like I wasn't going to make it to the end. I was still working full-time, had two children and a husband to take care of, and I felt like I was at the end of my rope.

That same week I went into preterm labor. My husband was on his way to a softball game when I told him that I was having cramps. We called the doctor and off we went to the hospital. I was put on bed rest for a week. I was not to clean, do laundry, or work.

My mother gave birth to two premature children (I'm one of them) and I experienced premature labor during both of my other pregnancies. In fact, my first pregnancy ended with my daughter's birth at thirty-two weeks. Because of this history, my doctors were very concerned. (See Gina's story in chapter five.)

My relationship with my husband was very challenging during this time. He was so overprotective that I would become upset. I was tired of everyone doing things for me. I soon realized that I couldn't let my pride get in the way. Before too long, I would be myself again and, more importantly, I would have a healthy baby in my arms. I knew I had to do whatever I could to take care of myself for the sake of the baby.

Amanda, 31

When Amanda called her doctor, around her twenty-third week, to report lower back pressure as well as rhythmic pain in her abdomen, the entire course of her pregnancy shifted. She was hospitalized and treated for preterm labor and, when released, varying forms of bed rest were required for the duration of her pregnancy. She never completely shook the fear of losing her baby, but lots of support from family, friends, and coworkers made her life manageable.

Preterm labor kept me off my feet and out of the office for four months. While bed rest was nerve-racking, boring, and isolating, it was also somehow very liberating. Up until that point, my life consisted of surviving the workday. I stood almost two hours a day on the subway and my job as a publicist at a publishing house was hectic, making it hard to leave the office at a decent hour. By the time I finally did get home, I'd eat a bowl of cereal and fall dead asleep by 7:30 P.M. Everyone kept saying that by my second trimester the fatigue would go away. Because it never did for me, bed sounded like a nice place to be.

I was about twenty-three weeks along when preterm labor made me take to my bed. (See Amanda's story in chapter five.) My husband ordered cable TV, my mother bought me some lovely maternity pajamas, and I settled in for the long haul. My days took on a routine that mostly involved watching television and eating cereal. I sent fetal monitor readings to a nursing service twice a day via a phone line. The nurses there read them and called me back within a few minutes to tell me if any contractions were registering and to see how I was feeling. This monitoring kept me from panicking at the slightest contraction-like twinge. Before I got the monitor, my husband and I made several additional (and, as it turned out, unnecessary) trips to the emergency room because I was convinced I was going into premature labor again.

When I first heard I'd be home and on my back for a while, I thought I'd do a lot of challenging reading, maybe do some writing. But frankly, I was incredibly tired and rather brain dead. I felt a lot of guilt about what I saw as my own apathy and wish now that I'd just enjoyed the rest more. It was the last one I'd have for a long time. After about a month and a half, I did begin working from home on a couple of projects. We bought a laptop, which was great because I could work wherever I was most comfortable. I also began going online and found some good chat rooms and Web sites that dealt with bed rest.

My friends and family were incredibly wonderful during this time. My husband waited on me hand and foot and my sister brought me magazines, books, and endless optimism. My friends cooked for me or brought over take-out and made me feel like I was still part of the world. There are always people, however, who will make you feel bad about your situation. Once I started working, I came into contact with a few insensitive types who got me thinking that maybe I should just get up and see what happens. Who knows if this bed rest is really necessary? I opted to trust my instincts and stay put for the remainder of my second trimester (and the whole of my third).

Thankfully, my manager at work supported me and I was able to finish my projects on a good note. I realize now how fortunate I was to have been working for two women who gave me a lot of leeway during this time. My job might not have been perfect and I eventually left it to stay home with my baby, but, at the time, the support I received kept me afloat, both emotionally and financially.

Bed rest, I know, is torture for some women, but for me, the sedentary life wasn't that difficult an adjustment. I liked the rhythmic quality of my days, and I think it actually prepared me well for the somehow timeless, stay-at-home marathon to come. Even now, as I chase my two-year-old around, I think back on my bed rest as time that was purely mine. It was all about taking care of myself and my yet-to-be-born baby. I may not have read the classics or kept an insightful journal, but I did bring that baby to term, which is all that really matters.

Lynn, 42

During pregnancy, we often spend a great deal of time managing fear and vulnerability while trying to maintain some degree of emotional equilibrium. When her second trimester began, Lynn was eager to put the worries of her early months behind her. Like many of us, she embarked on these middle months with renewed energy and a sense of well-being. Unfortunately, the glowing ideal of the "Golden Trimester" is not realized for every expectant mother.

As an older mom, a bit sedentary by inclination, I felt obliged to do something to maintain a semblance of fitness during pregnancy. I had found only one option for prenatal exercise in the evening hours, so the choice was simple, and I joined a prenatal yoga class when I was just eight weeks pregnant. Starting a prenatal class so early yielded unanticipated consequences. When other students listed the aches and pains of pregnancy, our teacher was surprised when I called out "breast pain!" Apparently, most women start classes at a point when excruciating backache, leg cramps, and breathless wheezing have eclipsed the memory of mammary torture. So when our svelte, nulliparous yoga instructor spoke glowingly of the "milk factory," she didn't know the high price that some of us pay for industrial expansion.

Yoga class provided another boon in the earliest days of pregnancy. John and I held our secret very closely in the first trimester. In our early forties, we were well past the point when others expected us to breed a new generation. Our siblings and peers were busy with their kids; no one was watching or wondering as we quietly adjusted to the idea of parenthood for ourselves and waited for results from genetic testing. In yoga class, by contrast, I was moving in a sea of expectant moms. When I arrived each week in non-maternity clothes, my classmates simply nodded when I spoke of spellbinding fatigue and raging emotion. As worn and ragged as I felt embarking on this adventure, in gestational age I was the junior member of the class.

I welcomed the support that came from being among my own pregnant kind. It was in this class that I met Jane, who offered a world of calm and experience from her vantage point of late pregnancy. As she sailed toward her eighth month and I moved haltingly through my second, we spoke with closeness, and I treasured the matter-of-fact way in which she accepted my confidences. Whatever I volunteered, she'd encountered before, and confirmed my experiences in her soothing, gravelly voice. And our bumper stickers, medical choices, and cars all matched. When we left class together each week, I was happy to feel I was making my first contemporaneously pregnant friend. In a happy corner of my mind I envisioned our children as playmates, fantasizing that her first child and mine would someday enter kindergarten hand-in-hand.

As the secret of my pregnancy felt more pressing with family and friends, my connection to Jane grew more important. When I missed class during the week of my chorionic villus sampling (CVS), a diagnostic test that can detect various genetic abnormalities, she was the one person I told where I had been. In an utterly pragmatic voice, she assured me that risks were really very rare. It was so soothing to share the facts that had caused me such distress and be met with her confident assurances. Even before we got our results, Jane acknowledged the risks, but minimized the fear.

My second trimester began in a whirlwind of activity. The chromosomes were unambiguously whole, and knowing the gender made our future baby seem so real. When we could put it off no longer, we shared the news with incredulous family and friends. Even my boss showered me with loving good wishes and the promise of flexible work hours. I bought maternity clothes, and struggled to put the worries of the first three months behind me with positive affirmations, good thoughts, and good nutrition.

And then Jane's baby died.

With no risky behaviors, no troubling history, and no humanly possible way to predict its occurrence, Jane suffered a complete abruption of the placenta in her ninth month of pregnancy. Incalculable. Irreversible. Inconsolable. Between the terrifying trip to the hospital and the emergency cesarean, Jane's baby died before she was fully delivered.

Jane and I haven't seen each other since her baby died. We've had searching and open conversations on the phone. We've expressed mutual yearning for the new friendship. But when we make plans, she cancels, and I get the message. I doubt we will see each other face-to-face and belly-to-belly—not while I am expectant with predictable hopes and aches, and her vision of motherhood has been so brutally rearranged.

I wonder if I would have the strength even to dream, as Jane does, that she will have a healthy live baby someday in the future. How can a person spend another forty weeks full of the hopes and aches of pregnancy, while knowing—really knowing—that it's possible there will be no baby at the end of it all? How do individuals face the realities, weigh the possibilities, and leave trepidation behind as they approach the dangers of gestation, birth, and parenthood?

In my first trimester, I had dreamed of monsters, and guarded myself against bonding with the unknown fetus. Genetic testing resolved some fears, but others swooped in quickly to take their place: spina bifida; an empty skull; blindness; cerebral palsy. I was haunted and unreasonable. When an hour-long ultrasound showed standard development in all areas, I felt unmoored by the doctor's bland acknowledgments of "normalcy," so inadequate was his neutrality in the face of my exaggerated fears.

Jane's baby died in my second trimester, and a new and tragic outcome was added to my repertoire of nightmares. I resented that anyone—coworkers, family members—could react to the news of pregnancy with joy, as if one could anticipate unalloyed good news. In the tear-filled days after Jane's awful loss, I heard the sad truths behind others' good cheer. My sister's best friend endured death in childbirth, just as my sister skated "out of the woods" of her first-trimester worries. A friend and coworker quietly asked, "Did you know that my baby also died at term?" Heartbreaking stories spilled over with the slightest provocation, as if surface tension alone was keeping the tears and the memories contained.

As I slip into the home stretch of gestation, I still find emotional balance elusive. The baby's heartbeat is terrific, and she's active enough to pulverize my liver and execute back flips on my spine. My belly is expanding at a slow and steady rate, and the milk factory could feed the population of a midsized city. I passed my glucose test, which I take as license to eat all the ice cream the baby so obviously desires. I know statistically how rare it is to suffer the tragedy that befell Jane and her family. The challenge is to use those cold statistics to hold fears in abeyance, and yet honor the boiling reality of Jane's true experience.

I don't want to forget Jane's tragedy, or close the door to connection with my fellow travelers in this less-than-perfect world. At the same time, how can I relish the great good fortune that is gracing my precious corner of existence? In this, I take my cues from my littlest niece. At six years old, Daisy believes this pregnancy is a perfect present that John and I made just for her. Jubilant about a joyous future with our baby, Daisy bends down daily to kiss my belly hello, and again to kiss and gently hug the baby good-bye. The skin stretches over a lifetime of unfathomable mystery, but I accept her tender blessings, and try to learn from her fearless love.

Tass, 29

Finding a way to stay positive in the shadow of emotional chaos was also a major challenge for Tass during her second trimester. Physically, she was "glowing," but the unpopular decision she'd made to proceed with her pregnancy was taking its toll. In the midst of intense sadness, frustration, and loneliness, Tass managed to find strength in the life that was growing inside her.

They say that things get worse before they get better, and, in my case, this was never truer than in my second trimester. The fact that I had decided to go ahead with this pregnancy without the support of the baby's father or my family guaranteed that my life was going to be very challenging. Physically I felt great and my body was changing shape rapidly. I had been underweight previously and the extra weight made me look healthy. I took walks every day and I really started enjoying eating (earlier in the pregnancy, my appetite had not been the best). Emotionally, however, things were still very difficult. Money was a big worry even though I'd managed to save enough to move into an apartment of my own, with the help of my best friend and an older lady friend, Sybil, who'd become like a mother figure to me.

The only contact I had with my mother was an e-mail she sent telling me that I was selfish and on this long, hard road by myself. I didn't bother replying. On the other hand, the father of my baby and I had a turbulent time in the first month of this trimester. He exhibited his anger in numerous ways and accusations came flying from everywhere. According to him, his family, whom I had always respected and cared about, never wanted to hear from me again and he didn't want any part of this baby's or my life. I was incredibly hurt by this treatment.

Then I began therapy with the counselor I'd seen when I first learned that I was pregnant. Through my work with her, I slowly began to gain an understanding of the actions of others and a better insight into who I was. Most importantly, I severed all contact with my ex and began focusing on my baby and myself.

At eighteen weeks I had my first (and only) ultrasound. Sybil came with me. When she saw the baby on the screen, she cried. She said she had never seen anything so beautiful and how sad it was that my ex and his family were missing out. I too felt sad but also very happy. I learned that I was having a girl and this news made the pregnancy feel more real to me than it ever had. We went back to Sybil's apartment where she had blue and pink champagne waiting for us to celebrate. I had the ultrasound on videotape and I showed it to everyone—whether or not they expressed interest in seeing it! I was so proud of my little girl.

When I was twenty weeks along I found out through the grapevine that my ex was now back with his ex before me. I've never experienced such heartfelt sorrow and jealousy. But in a way, this news helped me put things in perspective. I decided that I could no longer cry myself to sleep every night and torture myself with thoughts of him. It wasn't good for me and it wasn't good for the baby. I had to look after my emotional, as well as my physical, well-being. This was hard, especially because my hormones were raging, but I found an inner strength that I never before knew I had. Around the same time, I found a support board on the Internet for women who were single and pregnant. It helped me to realize that I wasn't alone in what I was going through, and that was the single biggest step in my emotional recovery.

Toward the end of this trimester my ex made contact. He wanted to put all the animosity behind us. I wasn't sure at first. I was just beginning to feel strong again and was afraid that contact with him would bring up all the hurt and emotions of the past. We met twice that month and even though the second meeting did not go well at all, I managed to put it behind me. I even forgave him for all the hurt he had caused. I did this for the sake of my baby. I didn't ever want her to experience this kind of negativity in her life and I knew that if I wasn't able to come to terms with it, she would feel it through me. I still had quite a few moments of sadness, but I'd learned to recognize and deal with them appropriately. I also found an excellent yoga-style exercise book for pregnant women that helped me focus in my moments of stress.

Physically I was having the best pregnancy one could hope for. I wasn't putting on any excess weight (I was "all baby"), and my only problem seemed to be a skin rash that lasted only a little while. About this time I also heard from one of my mother's sisters. She started calling me every few days to make sure I was OK and to tell me how much she loved me. I began to feel that I had a family after all, and I started looking forward to the new direction my life was taking.

Ginette, 31

According to What to Expect When You're Expecting *(Eisenberg, Murkoff, and Hathaway 1991), between 50 and 80 percent of women who have had cesarean births are able to have a vaginal delivery subsequently. Ginette hoped she would be one of them. As she entered her second trimester, she had no idea that she was about to receive some news that would change everything about her pregnancy.*

My first appointment with my obstetrician took place when I was sixteen weeks pregnant. One of my main concerns was that he would be open to the idea of a VBAC, (vaginal birth after cesarean) and I was pleased to learn he was. My first son, Joshua, was a very big baby at birth (ten pounds, eleven ounces, twenty three and a half inches long), and after seventeen hours of back labor and irregular contractions, never getting further than four to five centimeters dilated, a cesarean was performed. I was also concerned at the initial appointment that I had not yet felt my baby kick and I mentioned this to the doctor. He said that was perfectly normal and, of course, I felt my first kick later that evening.

I went for my scheduled ultrasound at twenty weeks. The technician was great, really taking her time and measuring everything carefully. At one point she gestured to the screen and said, "There are the feet." It wasn't very clear, but we thought we saw three feet. A little later she told us the heartbeat was 142 beats per minute (bpm), then five minutes later she said the heartbeat was 145 bpm. I said, "Well, that's consistent." She responded, "No not consistent, two heartbeats, two babies." Well, I guess that explained the three feet! I almost fell off the table. The silliest, nervous, giddy laughter took over and we were beside ourselves.

The technician continued on with her examination referring to the babies as Baby A and Baby B. Now it all started to make sense to me—the fact that I was so big, that I'd been so sick, and the unexplained bleeding. Perhaps this was the reason this pregnancy was so different from my first. I also thought back to a time during my first trimester when my three-year-old son, after hearing that the baby might be sick, brought me *two* pieces of colored paper to place on my belly that he said would make the baby better. *Two* pieces. Did he know something we didn't?

Eight days after the ultrasound I went to my general practitioner because I had a sore throat. He was excited to receive the ultrasound report from my obstetrician and learn that we were having twins. He asked if I knew the sex of the babies and when I said no, he asked if I wanted to. I immediately said yes and he told me that he was 90 percent sure, based on the ultrasound image, that I was carrying two boys. From that point on, we started calling Baby A (left side), Jonah, and Baby B (right side), Jackson. We felt like we were getting to know them already.

Even though I was carrying twins, my birth experience turned out the way I'd hoped and I was able to deliver my sons vaginally. (See Ginette's birth story in chapter eight.)

Sara, 36

Sara's second trimester was proceeding in a fairly typical manner. She was no longer constantly tired, she was feeling her baby move, and she and her partner were discussing names. Nothing could have prepared her for how it was to end.

Moving into the second trimester felt like a breath of fresh air. Suddenly I no longer felt like sleeping all the time, I regained my energy, and food was somewhat more pleasurable (albeit still with a constrained sense of desire—bland soft comfort food ruled, like homemade macaroni and cheese). Unfortunately, my partner, Terry, continued to believe that an imposter had taken over my body, since I was an ultimate grump. This tendency toward grumpiness had started in the first trimester, but got even stronger in the second.

Midwife appointments continued at one-month intervals, and they were in large part unremarkable. My blood pressure was borderline high but not worrisome, certainly not close to putting me into the preeclampsia ballpark. We opted out of doing most diagnostic tests, because we knew we wouldn't abort unless the fetus was unviable, and that would show up on the level-two ultrasound at week twenty. We were willing to do less invasive tests like the triple screen blood test, but our midwife convinced us that we probably shouldn't put ourselves through it, if we weren't going to do anything in the event of bad results. We took her advice, all the more impressed with our prenatal providers. My weight continued to climb, but not alarmingly—I hit and passed the 200-pound mark at week twenty-four, having started my pregnancy journey at 184.

Terry and I continued to discuss names. The twenty-week ultrasound confirmed that we were expecting a boy. It was very exciting to see our son on screen—he was positioned quite differently than our daughter, Hannah, had been, and, in a way, we were more educated this time around and could really soak in the images. They measured fingers and arms and toes, and at the end we asked for the gender check. The technician skooched around to the right vantage point and said, "There it is." We had to ask what we were looking at. It certainly looked different than Hannah's labia picture.

I was feeling some kicking. All of it was very low, the baby was transverse (lying side to side instead of up and down) facing down, with his head on my left, and all the arm and leg kicks seemed to be right above my cervix. He was that way at the ultrasound, and he never changed position. The kicking was a very cool feeling—it wasn't all that frequent, but it was strong, and it made the baby's presence feel very, very real. One night, I was spooning behind Terry in bed, and some kicks woke her up out of a sound sleep. I, on the other hand, slept right through them.

All in all, the pregnancy felt fairly uneventful and was without fear or complications. I was a grouch, but presumably that was a phase that would be cured by delivery. Then exactly as I entered my twenty-sixth week, all hell broke loose. I experienced a sudden onset of eclampsia, without the warning of preeclampsia. In short, my body became allergic to being pregnant, and I needed to be unpregnant very quickly. Our son, Tobias Charles, was delivered that afternoon—fourteen weeks early.

Although my son and I both made it through this incredibly traumatic event, there were many frightening moments, days, and weeks before my family could see the light at the end of the tunnel. (See Sara's birth story in chapter eight.)

Caroline, 33

Deciding which, if any, diagnostic tests we'll have and what we'd do in the event of bad results, are very personal decisions that require a great deal of thought. When her obstetrician gave her the alpha-fetoprotein (AFP) blood test, which can detect neural tube defects and some chromosomal abnormalities, it was presented as a routine measure and Caroline's age and history did not put her into a high-risk category. When the results indicated that there could be a problem, Caroline's life was thrown into a state of turmoil. Because

*this test only measures risk and is not a diagnosis, and has a high
rate of false-positive results, further testing was advised.*

I was excited to enter my second trimester and enjoy the "honey-
moon" period. By the middle of my fourth month, however, I was
still feeling sick. I was light-headed in the morning, rather exhausted
most of the day, and still nauseous.

Then I received a call from my doctor saying that my AFP test
came back with a higher than normal risk for Down's syndrome. I
was at work, and my husband was unreachable at jury duty. I was
hysterical. Further testing was recommended. We spent the next two
weeks in a haze. It took one week before I could get an appointment
for an amniocentesis and a meeting with a genetic counselor. The
counselor was very informative and sensitive. I put a towel over my
head for the amnio and it was over very quickly. It was virtually
painless, though the general creepiness of it affected me all day.

The next day, my husband and I went on our scheduled vacation. It was a really tense trip because we kept thinking about the
test. I couldn't stand it anymore and we flew home early. I was
lucky that I only had to wait one week for the results. The genetic
counselor called me to say the baby was fine and healthy. Though all
along my odds had been good, it took at least another week for me
to get over the whole experience. Then I started feeling better both
mentally and physically.

Martha, 38

*Martha's difficulties did not end after her long struggle to conceive.
Because her pregnancy was considered high-risk from the beginning,
she had level two ultrasounds on a regular basis. In addition to measuring gestational age and fetal growth, these ultrasounds also examine the brain, heart, kidney, umbilical cord, amniotic fluid volume, and
placental position. It was during one of these diagnostic tests that
Martha learned some very frightening news.*

We learned about the hole in our baby's heart during my fifth
month. By that time, I had already vowed to write a book—the title
was going to be *The Best Bad Thing* since every time we got bad news
we were told, "It's the best bad thing to have." I was considered a
high-risk pregnancy so I was going to the doctor every two weeks
and having level two ultrasounds on a regular basis. In my fourth
month during a routine high-level ultrasound, while talking cava-
lierly with the doctor about football, he started telling us that everything looked good in spite of the problem. I stopped him in the

middle of his sentence since I had no idea to what problem he was referring. He asked us if anyone had told us that the umbilical cord only had one artery (versus a normal cord, which has two arteries). He then went on to explain that the single artery has a detrimental impact on blood flow. This meant that the baby might thrive better outside the womb, so there was a chance that an early delivery would be necessary. I would have to be even more closely monitored. In addition, cardiac and chromosomal problems were associated with one-artery umbilical cords. So despite normal amnio results I continued to worry about chromosomal abnormalities.

I wanted to have a real conversation with my doctor so I requested a consultation appointment. He basically dismissed our concerns as unnecessary; I was intimidated and never asked him about doing a fetal echocardiogram to check the baby's heart. A few weeks later, during a routine ultrasound the technician asked me if I was going to have a fetal echo because "she couldn't get a good look at the heart." I later learned that this was a euphemism for "there's a problem."

A fetal echocardiogram confirmed a hole in the ventricular wall of the heart. Of course, they could only guesstimate the size. Medication, surgery perhaps, but not to worry, it is the best bad thing to have—treatable and that rarity of medical conditions—curable. After a pediatric cardiologist delivered that news, my husband left for a four-day business trip. From that moment on I dreamed about handing over my child, who I had not yet held, to a surgeon to open up his chest and operate. I cried a lot.

Noah was born with a hole in his heart and during the first year of his life we gave him medication to treat it. Surgery was still discussed as a possibility, but there was also a chance that the condition would correct itself. When Noah was examined shortly after his first birthday, my husband and I received the very good news that the hole had closed on its own, much to our great relief.

Cynthia, 36

After the emotional difficulties of her first trimester, Cynthia proceeded to the middle months with extreme caution. With an amnio scheduled and persistent anxieties about the unexplained bleeding she'd experienced, she was fearful that her pregnancy would remain stressful. Early in her second trimester, however, things started to look up.

The heavy bleeding I experienced at the very end of my first trimester made the beginning of my second much less relaxed than I'd hoped. No one knew what caused the bleeding, and even though an ultrasound showed a healthy baby, I was still very anxious. When I visited my midwife during my fifteenth week I was looking for reassurance, and although my uterus had grown and my cervix was closed, she couldn't find the baby's heartbeat with the Doppler. She assured me that this was not at all unusual this early, but I was extremely disappointed and concerned.

It was around the same time that I started to feel much better physically. The nausea subsided and people kept telling me that I looked great. I found myself loving the look of my pregnant body and was actually excited when my "civilian" clothes no longer fit and I had to start buying and borrowing maternity wear.

During my seventeenth week, I had an amnio. I was very worried in the weeks leading up to our appointment, but the procedure itself was fast and almost painless. And there was an added bonus: We got to see our baby again since an ultrasound was done immediately before and during the procedure. We wanted to know the sex of the baby (I thought there would be enough surprises on the day she was born), and learning that I was carrying a girl really allowed me to start bonding with this little being who now seemed more real than ever.

The last time we'd seen her on screen she looked like a little space creature. Now she actually looked like a baby, an adorable baby, kicking her feet, spreading her fingers, even sucking her thumb. Watching her and watching my husband's face as he watched her, filled me with happiness, although I was definitely aware of an underlying feeling of vulnerability as well.

My husband and I waited two long weeks and one day for our amnio results, both feeling surprised that we didn't know what we would do if we received bad news. Before the procedure I think we both felt fairly certain that we would terminate the pregnancy if something was "terribly wrong" with the baby. While we waited, however, we realized that our definition of "terribly wrong" was unclear, and we became less sure of ourselves as the days passed. My husband called for the results (I was too nervous) and luckily, they were good.

With the amnio behind us, and the second trimester treating me so well, I found myself feeling great about being pregnant. When I started to feel my little girl moving around inside me (around my nineteenth week) I felt even better. At first it felt like a flutter or a fish flipping around and I always took it as some sort of meaningful private communication. I no longer had to wait for my midwives to put the Doppler on my belly to feel confident that she was fine, now she had her own way of telling me how she was doing.

My body felt rounder, sexier, and more full of life as each day passed. I had lots of energy, and even though I was starting to feel the effects of carrying around so much extra weight (I'd gained twenty seven pounds by my twenty-eighth week), for the most part, I felt like I was finally starting to get the hang of this pregnancy thing.

Angela, 28

With the renewed energy that often comes in months four, five, and six, we can accomplish an enormous amount. Pediatricians might be chosen, car seats purchased, perhaps we'll even have decided on a name. In spite of some hardship she'd recently experienced, Angela found herself ready and able to make the most out of trimester number two.

My second trimester was pretty uneventful in comparison to the first and the third. During the first, I missed so much work due to all-day morning sickness that my very unsympathetic employer decided to fire me. I was the major wage earner in our family and the loss of my salary was a tremendous blow. We lost the house we had bought ten months prior and just as the morning sickness subsided we moved from a 2,400 square foot house to a 760 square foot trailer. During my third trimester, I discovered that I had gestational diabetes and I also had to deal with periods of bed rest due to preterm labor. In comparison, the second trimester was a breeze.

During the midsection of pregnancy, I expected to start showing, gain weight, and feel the baby kicking, and I was surprised that these things didn't happen when I thought they would. I was excited to feel the baby move as early as fourteen weeks, which is very unusual, especially for first-time moms like me. It felt like mice tumbling in my belly and it was wonderful! At around twenty-one weeks she really started to kick. Although I could feel her move, the pregnancy still didn't feel real because I hadn't gained one ounce and I wasn't showing at all. No one believed me when I said I was pregnant. Finally, at twenty-three weeks, my belly just popped out overnight. It was amazing. I finally felt pregnant. This was a great, comfortable time during my pregnancy free of random emotions and awful morning sickness.

During these months, we started getting the nursery ready. I kept busy painting, wallpapering, and making lists of things we needed for the baby. In my resting time, I spent hours on the Internet researching many topics including immunization, circumcision, breastfeeding, and home schooling. As a first-time mom, I was overwhelmed with the controversy surrounding these issues and the heavyweight decisions that came with them. Being informed made me feel much more secure about my impending motherhood.

Miriam, 34

Once the idea of pregnancy, and all that it means, really sinks in, it's not uncommon to begin a careful examination of the details of our lives. Simultaneously, we try to imagine how things will change once a baby is added to the mix. Anyone who already has children will quickly point out to the uninitiated that they can't possibly conceive of what's in store, but, nonetheless, we try to plan as best we can for the monumental changes that will soon be upon us.

As Miriam's belly grew, so did desires about what she wanted her life to be like after the baby was born. As she made her way through this very happy time, she found herself plagued with frustration about the impossibility of "having it all."

I didn't show very much for the first four months of my pregnancy. In month five, however, I gained eight pounds, overnight, it seemed. My belly stuck out proudly and the secret was there for all to see. Each evening I would lay on the couch and caress my belly, for hours, especially after I could feel the baby kick and move. All I cared about was my pregnancy, and I talked about it to anyone who would lend an ear.

I loved my new rounder body, and adored the ease of wearing leggings and big comfy shirts. Alongside the bonus of looking adorable in black A-line tunics came the dread of facing radical changes to what my life had been. I had finished teaching for the semester and I was on leave for the next year. I had been commuting to a university job in another state, but I could not imagine continuing that while raising a young child. I wondered whether I would ever again find work in my field, and I feared that I was squandering the career I had worked so hard to build. I had earned a doctorate and a tenured professorship and a shoot-for-the-stars career that was supposed to continue, uninterrupted, forever.

I was also clear about my commitment to being a full-time, hands-on mother. It surprised me, but I knew intuitively, strongly, that I wanted to be home with the baby: me, who had never before held a baby, let alone dealt with diapers, comforting, feeding, nursing, and entertaining a small child for hours on end. My desire wasn't political or ideological. It didn't stem from a sense of what other women should do. I just knew that I couldn't put my daughter in full-time care while I worked, and since we depended on my husband's larger income, it was impossible for him to be the primary caretaker.

All of this seemed so contradictory. It left me feeling heavy as I pieced together sociology, history, feminism, and my own personal desires, trying to make sense of why this was happening to me now and why social structures hadn't changed enough to allow me to do everything I wanted to do. If I gave up my job, there was no guarantee that anything nearly as good would be available later on. If I gave up caring for the baby—well, that wasn't emotionally possible for me. What about that fantasy of doing it all? I was angry that the models for paid labor and parenting and careers and identity are still so rigid.

In the midst of all this angst my mother came to visit. She totally supported all the things I wanted to do in life and sympathized with the conflicts. We talked and talked and talked. Then she had enough. A new strategy was in order. "You'd be less depressed," she asserted, "if you didn't insist on wearing black maternity clothes all the time." Hipness was out. We popped into the car and drove to the mall. "It's air-conditioned," she reminded me. "When it gets too hot this summer you can go there and walk up and down for exercise in the cool air." Was this my mother? The one who runs her own six-figure consulting business and encouraged achievement over fashion? Was she really counseling me on the creative uses of a shopping mall?

We found the maternity shop. "Would you like a glass of spring water?" the saleswoman asked as we walked in. "I'll set it down in your dressing room." We went to town, so to speak, picking from the sale and full-price racks. I picked out a green bathing suit, and several lightweight cotton shirts in shades like pale pink that I never would have worn if I weren't pregnant, but what fun we were having. I broke all previous fashion barriers by pulling on a pair of soft-washed denim shorts with a drawstring and a pregnancy panel that were, no fooling, the most comfortable item I have ever worn.

Maybe this story stays in my mind because it's about how pragmatic I've grown through pregnancy and motherhood. New clothes didn't make the big issues disappear (how could they?). They did, however, make me more comfortable, in a small, private way. The big issues still weigh on me, but for better or worse, I've learned to live with the frustrations of how slow real change will be, and still attend to the small changes and interventions that make daily life a little happier now.

※   ※   ※

Learning to appreciate the "small changes and interventions" of the "now" is an important component of the life of a mother. Writers Myla and Jon Kabat-Zinn (1997) suggest that pregnancy itself often helps us to better appreciate those moments. According to them, "The increasingly dramatic changes that occur in our bodies and in our very perceptions, thoughts, and emotions invite new degrees of wakefulness, wonder, and appreciation."

As we head into the home stretch, it's likely that we've already discovered many new things about ourselves by the way we've experienced and responded to our pregnancy thus far. With six months of experience behind us, not only are we looking and acting more and more pregnant as each day passes, but for better or worse, the world is also responding to us in that way. Smiles from strangers, predictions from neighbors about whether we're carrying a girl or a boy, and lots of belly-patting (some with and some without permission) serve to remind us that this seemingly intimate, inner experience is actually making our lives suddenly very public.

Chapter Three

Are the Bellies Ripe? Third Trimester Experiences

During our third trimester, weeks twenty-eight to forty, we become more and more eager to meet our little boarders. We've carried them around for quite some time and now is when they really start to get heavy. Babies do most of their growing during this trimester, making many of their mothers quite uncomfortable. Trying to find restful sleeping positions will become a popular nighttime activity, and many of us will experience shortness of breath and backache due to the size and position of our now almost-fully-cooked babes. Itchy bellies, swelling ankles, feet, and hands, bleeding gums, and heartburn are some other common third trimester symptoms. As our bodies prepare to give birth, our uteruses might even warm up with a few practice contractions (which oddly carry the name of the English doctor who first described them, Braxton-Hicks).

By now, we have an image of our ideal birth experience. Childbirth method, pain medication options (to use or not to use), labor coaches, and, in some cases, even music to labor by have been chosen. All of this has certainly helped to prepare us, but while we wait around for the first contraction, our joy and anticipation will be interrupted from time to time by nervous thoughts about what *exactly* lies ahead.

The hugeness of our third trimester bellies combined with the enormity of impending birth and motherhood make it difficult to focus on little else. Describing one point toward the end of her pregnancy, artist Anne Mavor (2000) says, "My big tummy is making the decisions now. The bigger it gets, the more I live in it. Me and my tummy are the entire world and I don't care about anything else."

❀ ❀ ❀

Sara Michelle, 33 Years Old

As her very active son grew and grew, his presence gave Sara Michelle a focus unlike any she had known before. Finding herself pleasantly detached from everything else, she was able to revel in the mystery and wonder of the final weeks of pregnancy.

As my stomach grew rounder and my breasts swelled to yet another size, I felt a kind of satisfaction. There was no mistaking it now—I was clearly pregnant. I even started to feel beautiful, in a healthy, fecund way. During my sixth and seventh months I often wore a stretchy black miniskirt over tights with bright, man-tailored maternity shirts to work, and I felt really cute and proud of my new pregnant-professional look. A coworker, who had recently had a baby, said that among the women in our office who had tried to dress for success in maternity wear, I won the award for style. I feigned modesty: "Oh, you've got to be kidding!" I said, but was, of course, immensely pleased.

Looking at myself naked in the mirror was a whole different story. I never really got used to seeing my bulging body and stretched skin. Even though I knew that the way I looked was normal, I felt deformed, even ashamed. My exaggerated shape seemed excessively sexual, immodest.

The strong movements my baby started making helped keep me focused on what was happening inside my body. He was very active, and when he kicked, my stomach would jump out sideways. Sometimes this would happen in meetings, and I would laugh, wondering how anyone could have missed the internal judo kick I had just been dealt. Whenever I lay down, the baby would shift positions and I would feel as though my internal organs were on a roller coaster ride.

Aside from these physical sensations was the growing realization that I was approaching the biggest transformative event of my life. This awareness made me feel more and more detached from many things, especially what was going on at work. It enabled me to complete my responsibilities without caring as much about the personalities and politics involved. I had a deep secret, a stranger and best friend hiding within me, and that dwarfed everything else. It was a strangely liberating perspective, unlike any I had ever had before.

My new attitude took on more significance when, just two weeks before I went on maternity leave, my boss announced that he was resigning and that a major restructuring of our department was going to take place. The managers overseeing the reorganization were all very worried about me—although my suspicion was that they were not as concerned about my health or finances as they were about my possible proclivity toward filing lawsuits. They kept assuring me that my job would be safeguarded.

This was all rather amusing because I had been secretly hoping to take more than a three-month maternity leave, and maybe even quit the company altogether. I remember my anxious coworkers asking me what my plans were, whether I would return, and my shrugging and telling them that I would have to wait and see. I felt suspended above the fray, circling like a bird in the wind who can barely see the little people and busy activities below. Remaining aloof worked to my benefit—three months later my position was eliminated, and I was given the choice of another one or a severance package. I happily took the latter.

The only serious physical discomfort I experienced was a kind of carpal–tunnel–like syndrome in my hands and arms. My fingers had begun to tingle at the beginning of my last month, and the sensation became more and more intense. Typing, which I did for hours on end at work, became especially painful and distressing. I tried to drink a lot of fluids, keep active, and elevate my hands and feet on pillows at night. I even had a couple of massages, but nothing helped. After the birth, the condition faded slowly.

Even with this discomfort, I was not that impatient to deliver. I had given myself one week off from work before my due date, and then had a second week before my labor began. (See Sara Michelle's birth story in chapter eight.) I relished the extra time to prepare—I stocked up on supplies, and I worked on filling my mind with positive thoughts. I walked a lot during those days, trying to stir the baby into action. But I knew that he would take his own sweet time. My son, and his readiness, were mysteries. And my resignation to that, too, was liberating.

Cynthia, 36

As we get closer to giving birth, we'll probably start thinking about what kind of mother we'd like to be. Perhaps we have very strong ideas in this regard or maybe we've resolved to keep an open mind and take things as they come. After all, we haven't even met the other member of this complicated relationship. Whatever the case, it's pretty clear that our own mother will figure significantly in these thoughts. Perhaps we'd like to emulate her, or use her as an example of what-never-to-do. Maybe the harsh realities of pregnancy and soon-to-be new motherhood have made us appreciate her in a whole new way. Or we might just simply want to ask her how she made her way through these major life events.

During the final third of Cynthia's pregnancy her joy was tempered by the fact that her mother was not there to share it with her.

By the time my third trimester rolled around I was feeling pretty confident about my ability to be a pregnant woman. I certainly had the body for it, as well as the wardrobe, complete with the most unattractive underwear a girl could ever have as well as a kind of girdle/belt type contraption that was meant to help support the weight of my ever-inflating belly. Yes, there were times when I forgot about my current state and actually thought I could roll over in bed or stand up from a reclining position without several strategic maneuvers. And yes, I never went anywhere without a healthy supply of tropical fruit–flavored Tums. For the most part, however, I had finally mastered the pregnancy thing. As birthing classes began, baby paraphernalia was purchased, and my midwife appointments became more frequent, I actually began to believe that everything was going to be fine.

The closer I came to becoming a mother, however, the more I found myself thinking about my own mom who'd died nine years earlier. I knew that having a baby without her around would be difficult, but I'd no idea just how much sadness I would feel. It was as though the grieving process (which never really ends, just changes over time) had started all over again. I longed to share my pregnancy with her and to hear about hers. I wanted her to see me as my body and life transformed. Most of all, I wanted her to take care of me as I experienced all the fears and vulnerabilities that impending motherhood plentifully supplies. I felt envy that all three of my siblings had their children while our mother was alive and sorrow that my daughter would not benefit from her abundant and masterly grandmothering skills.

During this time, when most babies are settling nicely into an obedient head-down position, my daughter, who'd been head down for weeks and weeks, decided that it was time to stand up. I knew something was different because the movement I was feeling had changed; when my midwife confirmed my baby's breech positioning, I wasn't completely surprised. I did, however, wonder what this said about the personality of my soon-to-be-born little girl. Being the "good girl" that I am, who always does what's expected of her, my daughter's in utero decisions and my inability to do anything about them provided much fodder for thought.

Was my daughter already exhibiting signs of feisty behavior? Was this my first real, albeit subtle, taste of learning that a child's behavior is not really controllable? Or that my daughter might not be like me at all? You may think it odd that I attributed will and intent to her decision when, in all likelihood, she might just have been looking for a more comfortable position. Yet, as I fretted about what a breech presentation might do to my plans for an unmedicated birthing center delivery, I felt as though I was being taught some very important lessons about motherhood.

At the suggestion of my midwives and many other resources I consulted, I began to do daily exercises that have been known to coax babies out of the feet-first position. These included lying on an ironing board (one side of which was elevated on a sofa) with my head below my pelvis for fifteen minutes three times each day, playing music through headphones near the bottom of my belly to encourage my little girl to move closer to it, having my husband talk to her—again near the lower part of my belly—in the hope that she'd want to move toward his voice, and, lastly, putting an ice pack near her head at the top of my belly to persuade her to travel south to warmer climates.

My midwives told me that it was too early to worry about position. Babies are known to turn as late as the day of delivery. I, of course, did worry and I performed the exercises day after day hoping she'd move. A few weeks before my due date, an examination revealed that, in fact, she was head down again, poised for her entrance into the world. I have no idea if the exercises helped, but I breathed a sigh of relief.

About four weeks before my due date, I began taking an herbal supplement, recommended by my midwives, designed to ripen my cervix and make conditions optimal for the onset of labor. They had been predicting for some time that I was carrying a big baby and I was glad to do anything that might make my desire for a natural birth a reality. It was also during this time that I was given instructions about perineal massage, which I did daily to help stretch and prepare my perineum for birth and decrease the chances of an episiotomy. The perineum is the area around the vagina and between the vagina and the rectum. An episiotomy is the medical procedure of cutting that area to enlarge the vagina during birth. I did the massage daily, although finding a way to reach around my enormous belly was never easy. In the end, I had to have an episiotomy anyway.

My husband and I had completed our childbirth classes. We'd arranged for my niece, who is a massage therapist, to be present at the birth. And we'd packed our hospital bags and equipped our apartment with all the necessary gear. I had a very strong urge to get things in order as early as possible. This might have been the much-talked about "nesting instinct" or maybe it was just my thorough personality. Whatever the case, by the time I visited my midwives for my thirty-eight week appointment, everything was ready to go. That was a good thing, since my daughter decided she was "ready to go" that very same evening, two weeks ahead of schedule. (See Cynthia's birth story in chapter eight.)

Miriam, 34

In The Hip Mama Survival Guide, *Ariel Gore (1998) says that "the third trimester should be spent loafing, dancing, daydreaming, and following that strange nesting urge that compels you to make enough lasagna for a small army and scrub the linoleum in your kitchen with a toothbrush."*

In the final months of Miriam's pregnancy she took nesting to new heights, and when she'd exhausted all of the possible solutions for her carpet cleaning and window frame problems, she even gave herself a little time to daydream.

I was getting huge and it was the hottest summer on record in the Southeast. I stayed inside when I could, and obsessed over the preparations for the baby's nursery. We had moved into a 1925 Craftsman bungalow filled with bumps and ridges and sloping floors. The window sashes didn't quite fit into the frames, especially in the baby's room. It was these windows as well as the carpet that I focused on as my belly pulled my stomach skin tight, as I stayed close to bathrooms, nibbled small meals throughout the day, and made repeated trips to the shoe store sale rack for shoes to fit my ever-growing, swelling feet.

I decided in the emotional haze of late pregnancy that the carpet had to be cleaned, and cleaned well. I spent hours on the telephone comparing quotes from different carpet cleaning companies. Each had its own special patented process that was better than all the rest. One laid down straw. Another brought in trucks filled with powerful chemicals. Some used water, others did it dry. Who knew? I was confused, but it seemed so absolutely necessary to have that carpet deep-cleaned lest microcosmic who-knows-what might endanger my baby. It's funny how we each manage the anxiety of bearing new life. In the end, I bought a box of Arm and Hammer carpet sprinkle and vacuumed really well.

I obsessed most about the windows, filling long lists with notes about possible solutions. The frames didn't fit securely around the sashes, and warm air oozed in from the gap between. This wouldn't do! I set about learning about windows and their repair: New channels? New windows, the aluminum kind that last forever? Historical restoration so they would fit the mood of the house and neighborhood? Each possibility seemed so compelling, so necessary to the ultimate happiness and health of my baby. When a woman in my pregnancy yoga class told us how she burst into tears of hopelessness when she miscut some boards for her nursery's shelves, I nodded empathetically. I understood. There I was thirty pounds pregnant lugging around an eight-foot ladder and teetering on top as I measured for curtains, hung cafe rods, and banged in weather-stripping.

In time, the empty space became a warm and welcoming room. The crib and changing table arrived, as did the rocking chair where I would eventually sit nursing for so many hours. An old North Carolina deacon's bench was repainted fire-engine red and a quilt with primary-colored tigers and frogs and toucans hung above it. Awaiting the onset of labor, those last long days, I would sit quietly in that room, imagining.

Trudi, 32

When Trudi reached her third trimester pregnancy was really agreeing with her. She observed her body with awe as it did "what it was built to do." She also never felt "more female, more ripe, or more natural." As the final weeks approached, her excitement grew but so did a few annoying third trimester symptoms.

When I started my third trimester, I was still feeling great. That old line about having a glow was really kicking in at that time—my ripening body, combined with my increasingly active son, made me feel fabulously pregnant. When my boss asked when I thought my last day would be, I answered, "Oh, I'm planning on giving birth in your office!" I really believed that there was no need to set an end date. I was feeling so great that I envisioned myself simply finishing a day's work one day, going home, and my water breaking sometime that night. In retrospect, I see how naive I really was.

Around my thirty-fifth week, I began to realize that the third trimester, not unlike the first, was fraught with odd physical afflictions. The first to go was my feet—the swelling was such that after the half-size larger sneakers I bought toward the end of my second trimester began to feel tight, I had to resort to sporting my favorite purple Birkenstocks every day for the remainder of my pregnancy. Hello, Fred Flintstone. Next came a return to exhaustion, not dissimilar from what I felt in my first trimester. The cruel irony of the veil of tiredness, however, was that I was also hit with a fair amount of insomnia. They say that it's just training for things to come, but I think impending motherhood combined with a relatively stressful job did it to me.

The ultimate affliction, however, was stress incontinence. By my thirty-seventh week, the baby's head was in position, facing downward. A good thing, of course, but it came at a price: My son was also seemingly positioned squarely on my bladder. It seemed every time I moved with the slightest amount of physical stress—standing up quickly, sneezing, and so forth—a small amount of urine would leak out of me. In the privacy of my own home I could more readily deal with it; however, in the middle of business meetings, it was distracting, to say the least. Combine stress incontinence with a heat wave, subway rides in cars without air-conditioning, and a forty-five pound weight gain and you've got one of the more uncomfortable situations known to womankind.

Around week forty during one of my frequent trips to the bathroom at work, I noticed a weird goopy discharge in my underwear. After consulting the doctor, I realized I had lost my mucous plug, which meant, according to her, labor was either imminent or could be a way off. That, combined with the stress incontinence, was the last straw for me. I packed up some files, shared a tearful farewell with my coworkers, and told everyone that I would work from home, thinking that it would only be a matter of hours. The loss of the mucous plug was a blessing in disguise—the stress incontinence had become so bothersome at that point that I was pretty much constantly leaking some urine, or at least it seemed that way. Ultimately, it was another two weeks before I gave birth, so I actually did work from home, peeing on myself in the comfort of my air-conditioned living room.

Ginette, 31

Ginette, too, was more than ready to give birth as her twin-pregnancy neared its fortieth week. With her prepregnancy weight hovering around 100 pounds, her body was really beginning to feel the burden of the extra fifty-three pounds she was carrying around, among other things.

During my third trimester, one of my twins, Jonah, was head down while the other one, Jackson, was high and transverse or breech. They had been in these positions for most of the pregnancy. My obstetrician remained supportive about letting me try a VBAC (vaginal birth after cesarean) as long as the first baby was head down. If the first baby was breech he said it would not be a good idea.

The final months of my pregnancy had the usual ups and downs combined with some unusual complications. My back was killing me most of the time and I was out of breath all the time. It was exhausting just to go down to the washroom. At twenty-eight weeks I pulled a muscle and tore a tendon in my rib cage. Then I got the same dreaded rash that I'd experienced when I was pregnant with Joshua. (An all-over-your-body rash—in your hair, under your fingernails, in your ears, everywhere!—that drives you totally insane.) The first time around the doctor gave me a mild anti-itching cream, but it didn't work this time so I had to take steroids, the symptoms from which made me feel like I was in my first trimester.

We had an ultrasound practically every week and although it was great to see each bit of progress and change, at times having so much information made me obsess about every little thing. On one occasion when one of the babies had low amniotic fluid, I remained in a state of panic for a whole week until the next ultrasound revealed that all was well. By the end of my pregnancy I had gained fifty-three pounds, which wasn't bad considering I had gained fifty-four pounds when I was pregnant with Joshua and this time there were two in there. It seemed that I'd retained much more water with Joshua and I felt like a blimp. This time the weight seemed to be all baby.

I stopped working in my thirty-fourth week. Until then, my doctor allowed it as long as I promised him that I would lie down as soon as I walked through the door of my house after work.

At the time, my husband was working at a youth camp nearby and some weeks he was on duty twenty-four hours a day. We arranged for friends and family to come over and help me out, and my husband would sneak away whenever he could to come see us. We brought everything we needed for Joshua and myself to our bedroom so I could avoid walking up and down the stairs.

When I was thirty-five weeks pregnant, I went to see my obstetrician for my regular appointment. I was really hoping for some changes in my cervix, to indicate that the end was near, but nothing, my cervix was still closed tight. That evening my son and I joined my husband at the camp for an outing to the zoo. I walked no more than fifty feet and had to stop because I was tired, uncomfortable, and simply unable to go any further. I insisted that my husband take Joshua, and I would wait for them in the car. I remember crying while listening to the radio. The next day, I lost my mucous plug but didn't think anything of it because with Joshua I had lost it ten days before his birth.

The following evening, while my husband was at the camp, I felt one little twinge but I dismissed it as soon as it went away. My mother was nervous because I was home on my own and she offered to come and spend the night. When my husband called for what was probably the tenth time, I told him about the twinge and he went on high alert. I told him to relax since I hadn't felt a thing since then. I went to bed but couldn't really sleep that well and then at 4:30 A.M. my water broke. My water broke to start my labor with Joshua too, and it happened at the same time of the night. My first thought was "Why don't I have a towel near my bed." I called my husband, who rushed home, and by 6 A.M., with my contractions about three to five minutes apart (although not that painful yet), we arrived at the hospital. I was thrilled that my boys would soon be in my arms but was anxious about what the birth would involve. In the end, though filled with many surprises, it turned out much the way I'd hoped. (See Ginette's birth story in chapter eight.)

Nicki, 30

The physical and emotional burdens that often accompany pregnancy can be overwhelming. This is complicated by the fact that we're made to feel inadequate and guilty for expressing negative thoughts about anything related to pregnancy or motherhood. This leads us to strive for unrealistic ideals of perfection at a time when, in many ways, we have less control than ever before.

When she went into labor two months before her due date during her first pregnancy, psychologist Harriet Lerner (1998) was devastated. "I knew I had just committed the biggest screw-up in the world. The stakes had never been so high, and I couldn't even get pregnancy right."

Nicki thought she would love being pregnant and was disappointed that she didn't. Of course, there were wonderful moments but, for the most part, the experience wasn't what she'd envisioned. A number of scares during her third trimester made her even more impatient to have those long nine months behind her.

I didn't really enjoy being pregnant. I'd like to say that I did, but I didn't. The only thing I really liked about the third trimester was that it wasn't as bad as the first. For me, nothing was worse than the morning sickness. The other good thing about the third trimester is that when it finally ends, you have a baby, which, after all, is kind of the point. Pregnancy in itself holds very little appeal to me.

All in all, it wasn't so bad—none of my annoying symptoms ever affected my baby. But, at times, it felt like it was just one thing after another. Early in the seventh month I went to the bathroom and found that I was bleeding—bright red blood but not much of it. Although I was shaken, I wasn't as terrified as I otherwise might have been, as this had happened once before early in my second trimester. Nonetheless, I called the doctor and off to the hospital we went for an ultrasound. Fortunately, everything was normal and they had no explanation for the bleeding except to say that it just happens sometimes. But since they weren't concerned, neither was I, and although they didn't recommend rest, I rested the next day anyway.

Around the same time, I started experiencing the most extraordinarily itchy blotches on my breasts, belly, and buttocks. The itching was so severe I thought I would go insane. I was on a business trip 3,000 miles away from my doctor when it appeared, so I had to wait nearly a week to see her. She sent me to a dermatologist to have it checked out. He immediately identified this nuisance as a condition called PUPPP (pruritic urticated papules and plaques of pregnancy), which basically is an itchy red rash that some women get in the third trimester. It can't hurt the baby at all and generally goes away right after the birth. That was twelve weeks away. I didn't think I could take it. Fortunately, mine went away within three weeks, right about the time I caught the flu.

During the eighth month, I was still traveling for work and pretty active. By now, people would comment daily about my size: "You look like you're about to burst" and "Are you still around?" I was eager to stop working, but I still had a while to go. The third trimester felt like it would last forever. Even my husband, who had been extremely supportive and patient, was ready for this pregnancy thing to wrap up. That's why, when he started complaining of stomach pains one day I teased him about needing some attention. He wasn't laughing though. By that evening, when we were supposed to be in our childbirth class, instead he was in the hospital having an emergency appendectomy. Fortunately, he recovered fine, though he never lets me forget that I teased him.

It was around this time that I started to get a little over-emotional as well. I cried because my husband was hurt, I cried because I was fat, and I cried when I found out some other disturbing news from my doctor. At one of my biweekly exams, I asked her to look at a sore spot I had in my vaginal area. She did a test on it to send to the lab, but her experience told her it was herpes. I was in shock. I never had an outbreak before and I'd been with my husband for nearly five years. She explained that people could go their whole lives never realizing they have it. It was likely that mine showed up only because my immune system was weakened from the pregnancy. I had apparently had it for years.

I was upset enough by the stigma associated with having a venereal disease, when I learned that if the baby caught it at birth, he could be brain damaged or die. This threw me into a tailspin. I researched herpes online and in books and the more I read the more I cried. A lot of the crying was pure hormones, but the fear of hurting my baby was real as well. As it turns out, although the result of infecting a newborn with the virus is grave, the chances of doing it are very slim. I took medication to suppress it, and if there had been any chance of passing on the infection, the doctor would have performed a cesarean. I was so embarrassed that I had this virus that I manufactured excuses I would tell my parents and friends if I had to have the cesarean. In the end, it wasn't necessary and the baby was fine.

I was so tired and uncomfortable by the end of the third trimester that I sat my husband down and told him that I didn't think I could do it again. I was serious. We had always thought we would have three or four children (or at least two since I started kind of late at thirty). I was a little sad and guilty for having negative feelings about being pregnant and not wanting to go through it again, but I was sure I couldn't. However, nature, God or some merciful mental deficiency starts to blur the memory after a while. By three months postpartum, I'd already changed my mind and started to romanticize the pregnancy and childbirth experience again, just as I had before it happened. Even with a vivid recollection of the pain and discomfort and with twelve extra pounds still lingering on my middle, I would do it again and be grateful for the blessing.

Martha, 38

Much of Martha's third trimester was spent worrying. During her second, a fetal echocardiogram confirmed that her baby had a hole in his heart. Additionally, she learned that a problem with the umbilical cord could affect her baby's in utero growth. In the final months, the baby's size increasingly became cause for alarm and Martha also found herself battling preeclampsia (pregnancy-induced high blood pressure).

Most people relax after they enter their third trimester; we just waited for the next bad thing to happen. When I entered my twenty-sixth week my doctor assured me that at least now the baby would be viable. Yet, every day I thought about the hole in my baby's heart and the potential chromosomal defects. Once a day I had to lie on my side and make sure the baby was moving. At night I was getting up every hour to go to the bathroom. I had no "baby free" thoughts.

I needed to have biweekly ultrasounds to check on the fetus' development. In the thirtieth week, the baby dropped from the seventieth percentile in weight to the thirty-third. Every week he got smaller and smaller and there was increased discussion of having to deliver him early.

Then in my thirty-fourth week my blood pressure began to rise. I had doctor appointments twice a week to listen to the baby's heartbeat and monitor my pressure and his growth. If my blood pressure was high, the nurses would tell me to lie down and think nice thoughts. One time, one of the nurses came back and asked me if I envisioned myself walking the street strolling my baby. No one knew that I could not have such thoughts; that even in my thirty-fourth week I never thought I would actually hold my baby and be a mother.

In my thirty-fifth week I was told that I had to leave my job and go on modified bed rest. I was still going to the doctor twice a week and taking my blood pressure daily at home. The baby's weight continued to register below the norm and we knew it was a matter of time before I would be induced. We had a doctor appointment scheduled for my thirty-seventh week and we were fairly certain that we'd be admitted that day. The day before, a Sunday, we sat on the couch, reading the *New York Times*, acknowledging that it would be the last relaxing Sunday of our foreseeable lives.

On Monday, we drove to the hospital for our appointment, with our bag in the car. I had even packed some food "just in case." A new sonogram technician raced through the weight check and proclaimed that the baby was in the fortieth percentile. We knew this could not be true since ten days prior he had been in the eleventh. After a very stressful discussion with the director, a second sonogram revealed the weight had dropped to the fifth percentile. The obstetrician admitted us. We went to labor and delivery; a physical exam revealed that I was dilated a centimeter and 50 percent effaced. I ate a piece of cheese and waited for the obstetrician to induce me. After thirty-seven weeks of constant worry, the unthinkable was going to happen. We were going to be parents. (See Martha's birth story in chapter eight.)

Gina, 24

In some ways, pregnancy might be easier the second, third, or fourth time around, but the added challenge of caring for other children while navigating your way through the bumpy terrain of those forty weeks cannot be underestimated. Gina's third pregnancy was a difficult one and she felt badly about how little time and attention she was able to devote to her two children during her first two trimesters. As her pregnancy drew to a close, she wanted to let them know just how much she appreciated their patience and care.

Because my third pregnancy was so difficult, I was very happy when I finally reached the third trimester. I had gained a total of fifty pounds and felt huge. Sleeping comfortably wasn't easy but even more challenging was trying to get close enough to my husband to hold him during the night. Unlike the first two trimesters during which I was filled with worry, I was finally able to let go of most of the fear I'd been carrying around. I knew my daughter was healthy and I was so happy that soon this pregnancy would be over and she would be in my arms.

My two children were wonderful during my pregnancy and this meant a lot to me since I knew I wasn't the mommy I once was. I couldn't do much without feeling like I needed to go lie on the couch. I showed them how to make their beds and clean up after themselves. They helped me so much and gave me a lot of love. I would ask them how they felt about having a new baby brother or sister. My daughter was only two when my son was born and she was very jealous. This time it was different, she was seven and my son was five. I spent a lot of time during those final months trying to get them ready for the baby and prepare them for what they could expect.

At the very end of my pregnancy I was having symptoms of preeclampsia (luckily it didn't develop) and my doctor recommended that I stop working. I gave birth to a full-term baby girl eight days after that.

Surprisingly, I had more fear about giving birth the third time around. Because I'd done it twice, I should have felt like a pro. Many women told me that this time the baby would come out quickly, but

I was still scared. For some reason, I just didn't feel confident that I'd have the strength to get through the labor and birth.

The day before my daughter's birth (I was thirty-nine weeks pregnant), I decided to go online and see what other women felt like at the end of their pregnancies. I began reading about different things women had done to help induce labor and I was so eager to have the baby that I decided to try one of the things that I read about. I drank castor oil mixed with juice. After I drank it, I felt really sick and I was a little nervous that I did this without consulting anyone. I wanted to have my baby ASAP, but I knew that I had to get a hold of my emotions and relax.

That same afternoon I began to have tremendous vaginal pressure, but no contractions. I didn't tell my husband until 8 P.M. and we went to the hospital a couple of hours later. The doctor said I was having some contractions but it would still be a while, so I should go home. We left the hospital only to return at midnight when things were suddenly moving very quickly. My daughter was on her way out as soon as I started to push. The doctor wasn't even in the delivery room. One of the nurses ran to get him. My baby was born at 1:57 A.M. and I was thrilled to finally have her in my arms. My husband was wonderful. This was my third child, but it was his first and I thank God for his unwavering support and understanding throughout the entire pregnancy and during the birth.

Jenny, 36

While Jenny was preparing to give birth to her second child she was also in the process of moving out of state. House hunting, packing boxes, and trying to potty train a two-year-old were not ideal third trimester activities. As the move descended upon her, so did early contractions.

I was five and a half months into my second pregnancy, when my husband and I started contemplating the unthinkable: moving out of state during my last trimester. My husband was working on a long-term project in another state and we wanted to make sure we were together both before and after the baby was born.

In an emotional conversation, I asked my doctor whether it was OK to move during the third trimester. She said it shouldn't be a problem, as long as I didn't exert myself too much, had someone to help me pack, and was settled into my new home by the time I was seven months pregnant.

Around this time I started having a lot of Braxton-Hicks contractions. During my first pregnancy I hadn't had any until I was a
week away from my due date, but my doctor explained that during
a second pregnancy I might feel many symptoms early. She said that
many women feel contractions starting at six months. Of course, if
they ever become regular, more than four in an hour, I should call.

After many angst-filled conversations, we decided to tempo-
rarily move. This meant we needed to find housing fast, and I
needed a new obstetrician. In a quick one-day trip, during which we
left our two-year-old with a sitter, we flew to our soon-to-be home
state, met with a new obstetrician, saw four potential houses, and
returned home.

That night my contractions went on a long time. As I lay on my
bed I timed them. They were less than ten minutes apart, and continued for over an hour. They weren't painful, just a tightening feeling
in my uterus followed by a release. But because of their frequency, I
called my doctor the next day and she told me to come in.

When the doctor checked my cervix, she said it had thinned
out by about one centimeter. Apparently, this can be normal in a second pregnancy, but it can also be a sign of preterm labor. She
wanted to play it safe, so she sent me over to the hospital to be monitored. They hooked me up to a fetal monitor, and had me lie there
for an hour. No contractions showed up on the monitor, but they
asked me to take it easy for the next two days (meaning partial bed
rest).

It was too late to turn back. We had already decided to move.
So I continued packing up the house slowly but surely. A week later,
I had another incident where my contractions went on and on. I
knew that if I called the doctor, she would call me in to the hospital
to be monitored again. I conferred with a friend who had been put
on bed rest during the entire last four months of her pregnancy. We
agreed that doctors play it safe and tell you to stay in bed even
though there isn't any scientific proof that bed rest prevents you
from going into labor early.

I did go back to the hospital one more time to be monitored. I
guess I was playing it safe too. This time I felt contractions while I
was there, but they weren't showing up on the monitor. The nurse
sent me home and told me to stay in bed for a week. This is a little
rough when you're trying to pack up your whole house. I remember
sitting on my bed while my mother brought in some of the most
insignificant doodads known to man for me to sort through.

I decided that my contractions were more or less due to stress,
so I began to manifest a sort of calm resolve. I had to be calm, it

turns out, just to get through the next month. Because even after we moved, we still didn't have a house. The house we wanted to rent was on the market and while we were holed up in a bed and breakfast for three weeks (seven months pregnant and with a two-year-old who was being potty trained), we were negotiating with the owner to take it off the market and rent it to us.

Once we settled into our new house (three days beyond the dreaded seven-month cut-off recommended by my obstetrician), my contractions more or less subsided and I resumed the normal routine of a last trimester pregnancy with a two-year-old—that is, exhausting. Although I had been sure the baby would come early, I wound up going into labor the evening before my due date and delivering on my due date. (See Jenny's birth story in chapter eight.) What did I learn? If people can have full-term babies in war-torn Bosnia-Herzegovina, I could survive a state-to-state move and deliver a healthy baby girl.

Tass, 29

Getting through her pregnancy without the support of her baby's father or her family made it necessary for Tass to be stronger than she'd ever been before. As she prepared to give birth she did everything she could to take care of herself and stay positive.

The last stretch! What began as such a confusing and tumultuous experience now gave my life the purpose for which I'd always been searching. I had consistent work throughout the majority of this trimester, which helped ease my financial worries, and despite the long traveling I endured (two hours on public transport every day), I was glad to have this outside focus.

It wasn't easy to get through the holidays. I had to deal with memories of a wonderful Christmas the year before with my baby's father and knew that this year, being pregnant and without him, was going to be very different. The silence of my mother (who still disapproved of me having this baby) and thoughts of my ex-boyfriend, who was now with his current girlfriend, tormented me. I constantly apologized inwardly to my little girl for bringing her into this world without a father and I hoped that she would never resent me for this.

With the new year came a new self-awareness, maturity, and contentment. Additionally, quite a few new physical aspects of pregnancy were making themselves felt. I had now gained a total of forty pounds and although this couldn't be "seen" apart from my bump, it was making its presence known in varicose veins, severe constipation, and weak knees. I was lucky though—we were in one of the mildest summer seasons that we've ever experienced in my part of the world. I spent my days off walking, going to the beach, swimming, and of course, shopping. I had begun "nesting." It was hard at first to visit baby shops without my "partner." I would see other couples together and involuntarily tears would spring to my eyes. I forced myself to carry on. Always being of an organized nature, I made a list of all the items that I needed and slowly checked them off. I felt immense pleasure as I saw more and more ticks on my list and took great pride in getting ready for the arrival of my little daughter.

My only dilemma at this stage was who to have in the delivery room. My best friend had recently moved away so I was left with having to choose a new birth partner. I got plenty of offers but eventually decided on two of my closest friends, one of whom was pregnant too.

My ex contacted me early in the new year to discuss child support. He still felt anger and blamed me for "ruining" his life. I felt so sad that he was missing out on this glorious event. I told him that, although I had made the decision to have this baby, it was not as easy as he seemed to think.

The next time he contacted me I sensed a change in his attitude and our meetings from then on began to take a more positive route. He finally overcame his denial and started accepting the fact that he was going to be a father. He apologized for the hurt that he caused and although we were not together in a relationship I was pleased that my little girl would have a father who recognizes that she exists, after all.

I stopped working six weeks before my due date because I was sure the baby would come early. So much for a mother's instincts! My daughter arrived quite late, teaching me patience as I awaited her birth and the beautiful experience of motherhood.

I went ahead with my pregnancy knowing that it was going to be a rough and lonely time, and it was. But with the support of some very special people it didn't seem as long as it could have and, through it all, I finally found a profound sense of belonging. I definitely had moments of intense sadness, but they only lasted for a few moments as I drew on the inner strength that the pregnancy taught me. And now that my daughter Aliah is in my life, I will never be alone again.

❄ ❄ ❄

By the time we've reached the final third of our pregnancy we've grown quite accustomed to change. Our bodies have changed drastically and our daily lives are probably quite different as well. We'll be told by many, often in threatening tones, that all of this change is meant to prepare us for just how unrecognizable our lives will be once we give birth.

It's likely that approaching motherhood has also started to affect us on a deeper level as well. As our babies have developed, so have we, and in the last nine months, our views about ourselves, our lives, and the world around us, have probably undergone some major transformations. In the words of writer Bonni Goldberg (2000), "When a baby is born, so is a mother."

Chapter Four

The World of Prenatal Diagnostic Testing: Knowing Everything There Is to Know

By the time we know we're pregnant we've already had our introduction to prenatal testing. It went something like this: We walked into a drugstore, handed over $20 for a state-of-the-art home pregnancy test, went home, peed on a wand, waited a few minutes, and then, with bated breath, checked a little window to see if we'd "passed." Simple, yes, but that was just the first in a long line of tests that inhabit the world of pregnancy.

Some are routine. Urine will be tested at every prenatal appointment, and we'll all be given a glucose tolerance test around the fifth month of pregnancy to detect signs of gestational diabetes. Others are recommended to check on the health of our baby, either as standard screening devices or because age, family history, or the progress of our particular pregnancy have put us into a higher risk category. In this class, the most commonly performed are the ultrasound (or sonogram), the alpha-fetoprotein (AFP) or triple screen test, amniocentesis, and chorionic villus sampling (CVS). These tests (some more invasive than others) can provide us a variety of information about our babies. Whether we want (or need) this information, and the choices we'll make once we have it, are extremely personal decisions that warrant careful thought.

Ultrasound

The number of ultrasounds (also called sonograms) we'll have depends on the specifics of our pregnancy and the philosophies of our particular practitioners. Almost all of us will have one very detailed ultrasound around the twentieth week, when fetal growth will be measured and the brain, heart, kidney, umbilical cord, amniotic fluid volume, and placental position will be checked (and if our babies cooperate, sex can be determined as well). An ultrasound might also be recommended early on to verify dating. For some of us, ultrasounds will be frequent occurrences, perhaps because our pregnancies are considered high risk, or perhaps because our practitioners just use them more freely in their standard practice of prenatal care. Also, if you're having amniocentesis or CVS, an ultrasound will be performed during these tests so the doctor can see the precise location of the baby and placenta.

The procedure itself uses high frequency sound waves to project a visual image of your baby. After some lubricating gel (in the best conditions this goop has been warmed) is rubbed onto your abdomen, a wand (technically called a transducer) is moved back and forth across the area. As the wand sends out sound waves, a picture of your baby will appear on the ultrasound monitor (which looks like a TV screen). The test is painless, although you will often be asked to have a full bladder while it's performed and this can cause a certain amount of discomfort. At times, especially early in pregnancy, a transvaginal approach might be recommended. This involves having the wand inserted into your vagina, as opposed to placed on your belly, and has the ability to provide a much more detailed image.

There are no known harmful effects or risks associated with ultrasounds, but long-term studies are unavailable as the test is only twenty-five years old. General wisdom holds that the procedure is incredibly valuable for diagnostic purposes and should definitely be used in that regard. Unless circumstances dictate, however, there is no need for frequent, routine ultrasounds during the average pregnancy.

This procedure, perhaps more than any other, has radically changed the nature of pregnancy. Getting a glimpse of your baby as she or he rolls, flips, or just relaxes inside your uterus-turned-studio-apartment is completely amazing. You might even see it suck its thumb or wave its little hand in a gesture you just know is meant as, "Hey Mom, how's it going out there?" The baby starts to feel much more real after we've actually seen it and the image that is printed out and handed to us afterward becomes a prized possession that is proudly passed around to friends, family, and anyone who is willing to look.

❄ ❄ ❄

Jennifer, 26 Years Old

Poet and writer Anna Purves (2000) was extremely ill during the early months of her pregnancy. When she was admitted to the hospital for the second time for dehydration, an ultrasound was performed that unexpectedly provided her with some much-needed strength. As she describes it, "It is definitely a baby in there and it is fine. The technician makes a print of the picture for you to keep. He has no idea what he has done. He has allowed you, through little fault of his own, really, to see the invisible. Nine months is a short time after the fact, an endless existence during the experience. But you've seen the baby. You can make it now. You think of that psalm where they say, 'My frame was not hidden from you [God] when I was being made in secret, intricately woven in the depths of the earth.' Even then, everyone wanted to know what they couldn't know. And now you and the technician can see things that God sees all the time."

By the time Jennifer's first ultrasound was over, she was completely in love and much more pregnant than she had originally thought. Unfortunately, her second was performed under much more stressful circumstances.

When I had my first ultrasound, the notion of a baby was still quite abstract to me. I conceived while taking birth control pills so I was still getting used to the idea that I was pregnant. The ultrasound made that abstract notion into stark reality with the image it projected onto the miniature television screen that sat before me. It was amazing. The baby was now very real, and I knew I would do anything to insure its safe arrival.

I was an estimated twenty weeks along, and I was very eager to see this little person who was practicing karate moves inside of me. I had to drink thirty-two ounces of water beforehand, and yes, all those stories about trying not to pee all over the ultrasound table are true. But I held my breath and watched this picture form on the little screen, and suddenly I didn't even notice my bladder anymore. I saw a little face staring back at me. The baby's image was very skeletal, but I could see chipmunk cheeks and a little chin, and I swear the baby already had my husband's nose.

The technician asked if we wanted to know the baby's sex, and I immediately said yes. The pregnancy was enough of a surprise to me; I wanted to know what to expect at the end of it. The technician had just warned us that he might not be able to determine the sex when the baby pointed its little derriere toward the ultrasound wand. We could see she was a girl, plain as day. I admit to being a bit surprised that I was carrying a girl. I thought for sure all those powerful kicks meant I was having a boy, and a boy's name was the only one my husband and I had agreed on at that point. I looked at the little face on the ultrasound screen, and I never loved anything so much in all my life. In that moment, I perfectly understood an animal's primal instinct to protect its young.

The technician took measurements of the baby to see how "old" she was. After all his calculations, he informed us that she was twenty-four weeks and five days old. I was shocked! In the span of three minutes, I became five months pregnant instead of four. My baby was due a whole month earlier than I expected, and my maternity leave would be shorter because I now had less time to accrue the sick and vacation days that comprise maternity leave at the university where I work. In reality, I only had six months between the time I found out I was pregnant until the time I delivered. While this sounded great to my friends, it left me in a whirlwind of emotions and I didn't have a lot of time to adjust to everything that was happening. As exciting as the ultrasound was, it was also quite overwhelming to learn that the baby was coming a month sooner than we'd all thought.

My second ultrasound took place after I'd been ordered into the hospital for complications arising from preeclampsia (pregnancy-induced high blood pressure), and my doctor wanted to make sure the placenta was still functioning properly. She also wanted to view the baby's lung maturity. I was thirty-four weeks along at that time, and the baby was a giant compared to the little image I remembered from the first ultrasound. This time I could see my daughter very clearly, her every feature, and I was even able to envision what she would look like once she was born. This technician confirmed our baby was a girl, and then silently went about his job. I could see the baby moving, and I was terribly afraid something would happen to her.

My doctor informed me that my placenta was functioning well enough for the baby, though I got the impression that some things were being left unsaid. My daughter's lungs were not mature, and my doctor was uncomfortable with inducing labor until the lungs were stronger. It was almost worse to have seen my baby up close and in such great detail on the second ultrasound, because now I knew exactly what I stood to lose. I just hoped it wouldn't be the last time I saw her. Eighteen hours later, after further testing and steroid shots to mature my baby's lungs, labor was induced and my four pound, fifteen ounce daughter made her entrance. (See Jennifer's story in chapter five.)

Nell, 33

Throughout her pregnancy, Nell intuitively felt that her baby was healthy. As her twenty-week ultrasound approached, one of her main concerns was convincing her husband that they should wait until the baby's birth to find out if they had a daughter or a son. But when she arrived at the hospital on the day of the test, she found herself feeling uneasy for the first time since she'd become pregnant.

Leading up to the twenty-week sonogram, discussions about the gender of our fetus (heretofore referred to as "Nibblet") grew increasingly fervent. We'd had several sonograms previously, due to an eager sonogram technician-in-training in our doctor's office, but spotting gender wasn't an issue till now, as sexual organs don't mature typically until week twenty or so. Because both Bryan and I came from families with boys as eldest, we both kind of expected a boy. I didn't want the sonogram to reveal Nibblet's gender to us, and Bryan did. I stood on a soapbox, metaphorically speaking, and harkened back to the days when gender could only be a surprise, and childbirth a natural phenomenon. Why take away the moment of discovery? I asked. Find out the gender beforehand and all that is left at the moment of birth is anxiety about the health of the baby. Bryan countered with a shame-ridden confession: In the recesses of his heart he was hoping for a boy, and he needed time to adjust should we be blessed with a girl instead. It seemed to me that once the baby, our baby, was born there'd be no room for disappointment about gender, but Bryan held firm as the presonogram days dwindled.

We still hadn't decided what to do when the scheduled day arrived, and we were discussing it still as we walked the hospital corridor. Several couples were standing in the hallway, looking somewhat anxious. It seemed that their fetuses hadn't cooperated and various essential body parts were kept hidden from the machine. They were waiting for their unborns to wake and move. It was at that moment that I finally realized we were going in for a diagnostic test, and that we'd be finding out much more of import than the gender of our child. As we later found out, Jane, the technician, could see not only the chambers of Nibblet's heart, but even the upper lip and toes. Walking in, I realized we were about to get our first real look at our baby, and while the test might not be able to tell us that everything was OK, it could certainly tell us if something were blatantly wrong or missing. It was the first time I felt truly anxious since I'd been pregnant.

Bryan and I reached a compromise upon entering the room. We would put off the gender issue in the face of far more pressing questions. We'd have the technician write the gender on a slip of paper that could be thrown away or viewed depending on the decision we later made.

My obstetrician, quite skillful in many important respects, was never able to do much with the sonogram, and fuzzy gray pictures would fill the screen when she wielded the wand. However, Jane (our twenty-week guide) was a master. She zoomed in to show incredible detail: chambers of the heart, Nibblet's fingers and spine. As she ticked off each body part on this tour of our baby, I felt relief, that each was there, seemingly healthy and whole.

Bryan loved the sonogram, and was quite skillful at reading them. While he enjoyed feeling kicks, and would laugh when he saw an "alien" arm travel across my abdomen, there was something about the sonogram he found downright magical. While I might make out only gray static, Bryan would giggle because Nibblet was waving, or he and the technician would exchange smiles over the beauty of Nibblet's spine. That is the beauty of the sonogram. It offers a peek inside. It offers proof that the baby is moving long before you feel real movement. It suggests the depths of a hidden world. At times, especially early on, it is a fuzzy gray peek, but as both the fetus and your skills in reading the sonogram grow, it becomes possible to see surprisingly fine details. By week twenty, even I could discern the head, body, and limbs. I took the rest on faith, as both Jane and Bryan squealed with happy discoveries of the intricacies and perfection of Nibblet's body and facial features.

Bryan even went so far as to express shock over the similarity between the fetus' profile and my own. It was this, oddly enough, which precipitated our final decision about whether to find out Nibblet's gender.

After we left our appointment, full of relief, Bryan told me that we did not have to look at the paper for indication of Nibblet's gender. I looked to him, impressed and grateful that the sonogram had so moved him that he'd given up his "improper" emphasis on finding out our baby's sex. He continued by telling me that he "knew" Nibblet was a girl because of the aforementioned "resemblance" to me. Well, I thought that absurd. Additionally, for months, I'd been having dreams about a daughter, "sensed" that Nibblet was female, and thought Bryan was now trying to steal my thunder. So, in a fit of ornery self-destructive pique, I took the paper from him, opened it, and saw the little "f."

I felt numb for several minutes, and then a feeling of loss for the boy, the son, we weren't having. Loss for not having to say "it" or "they" or even "Nibblet" any longer. We could say the heretofore forbidden "her." We sat in silence for about ten minutes. Then I felt the mourning lift. We then gave ourselves over to the joy of our expected daughter.

Corinna, 32

When Corinna developed gestational diabetes (GD), her pregnancy became more complicated and closer monitoring was necessary. (See Corinna's story in chapter five.) In addition to regular ultrasounds, she had fetal monitoring once a week toward the end of her pregnancy.

When I was pregnant, I felt fortunate to have ultrasounds regularly and, starting in my seventh month, fetal monitoring once a week. Although some may regard all these extra appointments, trips to the hospital, and full bladders annoying—I found them reassuring and special.

Every time I would go in to have an ultrasound, I had to have a full bladder; the further along in my pregnancy, the more difficult this would be. But I enjoyed every second of it. Not once did I complain about sitting cross-legged in the waiting room while an emergency ultrasound bumped my time slot. Nor did I complain about drinking the two liters of water, or the pain of my baby pushing down on my full bladder. The result of these very minor and temporary inconveniences was getting to watch my baby swish around (and later, bump around) inside me. The ultrasounds were also very special to my husband. While I was lucky enough to feel our baby inside me every day, these fleeting moments in the ultrasound room provided an occasion for him to experience precious contact with our little one.

In addition to the ultrasounds, because of my GD, I also had fetal monitoring (also known as nonstress tests). This was done to ensure that the baby was still active and that the placenta was not aging prematurely, which could result in the baby not getting enough nourishment and a decision to induce labor for an early emergency delivery.

Fetal monitoring entails having two sensors strapped around your pregnant belly—one to monitor the baby's heart rate, and the other to record any kicks or movements. A monitoring machine records all of this on a long strip of paper. Most women with GD have regular fetal monitoring, and many women in labor will have the fetal monitor strapped to them to keep a close watch on the baby's progress. I would go in every Wednesday morning starting in my seventh month. Sometimes my husband would come with me, and sometimes not (it is fairly routine and not as "exciting" as an ultrasound), but I looked forward to it every week.

Because my monitoring was always done after my morning snack, my baby would almost always be active. If she wasn't (which happened twice), I would drink some ice-cold water and wait. The nurse-midwife who was in charge of the fetal monitoring had to keep me there until she had four "good kicks." While most of the time my baby would get those kicks in within the first ten minutes, once we were on the monitor for over half an hour. If my baby wasn't active enough, then the doctor would have been contacted. Happily, I never had that problem.

I can honestly say that throughout my pregnancy, (despite my GD, or perhaps because of it), I worried less about my baby than many women did with "normal" pregnancies. Because of the frequent monitoring, I knew that my baby was OK and I never sat and worried about her health.

❀   ❀   ❀

Alpha-Fetoprotein (AFP) and Triple Screen Testing

The alpha-fetoprotein (AFP) test, sometimes called the MSAFP or maternal serum AFP, is performed between the sixteenth and eighteenth week of pregnancy. Requiring only a blood sample, the AFP measures the amount of alpha-fetoprotein (a substance produced by the liver of the fetus) in the mother's blood. It screens for neural tube defects such as spina bifida (a deformity of the spinal column) and anencephaly (abnormal brain development). A low level of AFP could also point to an increased risk of Down's syndrome.

In many instances, women will receive triple screen testing instead of the standard AFP. The triple screen, which measures not only alpha-fetoprotein, but hCG (human chorionic gonadotropin, a pregnancy hormone) and estriol (an estrogen produced in large quantities during pregnancy), can assess risk for additional genetic problems and is said to be more accurate than AFP screening alone.

The procedure itself (a simple blood test) does not pose any threat to you or your baby, but it is controversial because of its high rate of false positive results when screening for Down's syndrome. Although the test can indicate risk, it is important to remember that it is not a conclusive diagnosis. A large number of women who receive frightening results go on to have amniocentesis only to find out that their baby is fine.

Many opt for this test, which is often presented as a routine screening measure, because they're eager for news about the health of their fetus. Some women decide against it because they would not terminate the pregnancy, even if a problem is found. Others, who would not terminate, no matter what, want to have as much information as possible to prepare themselves in advance.

❊   ❊   ❊

Whitney, 33 Years Old

Whitney had the AFP test during both of her pregnancies. She had no doubts about having it either time, but she and her husband disagreed about how they would handle bad results.

I had AFP screening during both of my pregnancies. The purpose of the test, which was presented as a somewhat routine screening measure, but also an optional one, was explained to me pretty clearly the first time. Perhaps because I'd elected to have the test once before, my doctor assumed that I'd want it the second time around when I don't remember it being addressed in much detail.

While I was uncertain as to what we would do with the information provided to us, I felt confident that prior knowledge of any problems would enable us to better cope with the situation on delivery. If everything was fine, the information would give us a little more peace of mind in what seemed to be a nine-month process of constant questioning and a fair amount of blind faith.

I was particularly nervous about the results of the AFP during my first pregnancy—perhaps because everything was so new and so very possible. Every test, every heartbeat check, every ultrasound presented an opportunity for reassurance or the possible detection of a problem. During my second pregnancy, having been through it all once before, I was not only more experienced, but also more educated from both books and friends. While I still thought of the AFP as a serious test, I was now much more aware of the sizable number of results that come back with high-risk readings when further testing (or the eventual birth of a baby) proves that everything is fine. So, while I was anxious for the results of the test the second time, I was also more accepting of the fact that they might raise unnecessary concerns. We were lucky enough to be blessed with good results two times and we now have two wonderful, healthy children.

If I have a third child, I'll be over thirty-five at the time of delivery. This will bring up a whole new set of worries in regard to this test since age is added to the equation when risk is assessed. I haven't yet decided exactly what I'd do if this occurs.

For me, one of the most challenging issues raised by the AFP was the question of what would happen if we did receive bad news. Preliminary "what if" discussions between my husband and myself did not even remotely result in similar views of how we would handle things. We finally decided not to discuss it until the results were in. To this day, however, it bothers me that our feelings were so very different.

Anne, 31

Anne has two healthy daughters and, for personal reasons, opted not to have AFP screening during both of her pregnancies. During her second pregnancy this decision met with some resistance from her health care practitioner.

I decided, for the second time, not to have the AFP test. With my first pregnancy, it was an easy decision. My husband and I discussed it, decided we would not terminate a pregnancy under any circumstances, and my doctor stated that if this was how we felt, there was no reason to have the test. I felt better pregnant than I had ever felt in my life and, except for some middle of the night moments of "what if?" (completely unavoidable when you are pregnant, in my opinion), never questioned my decision. My daughter was born beautiful and perfect.

This time, however, when I stated my opinion to my doctor (same practice, different doctor), she informed me that some of the problems that the AFP test screened for—such as spina bifida—could be treated in utero. She stressed that she felt that information was always a good thing, no matter what you decided to do with it. I highly respected her opinion and reluctantly made the appointment for the test two weeks later, figuring I could always cancel. I flew to the Internet to do research and made myself crazy getting as many opinions as I could—my pediatrician, the various doctors in my family (numerous), my sisters-in-law (also numerous), my mother (of course). I also reviewed all the stories in my head of friends who had abnormal results from the AFP test, did or didn't have amnios as a result (and the stress and anguish that accompanied either decision) and had healthy babies in the end. My husband and I talked for hours about the pros and cons of knowing if this baby had a disability before he or she was born, something we hadn't even considered last time.

In the end (my husband had always felt strongly about not having the test, but felt it was my decision) I decided not to have the test. Again, I would not have terminated the pregnancy and I also would not have had an amnio because of the chance of miscarriage. The chances of the baby having spina bifida were slim and this is something that often shows up on an ultrasound. My husband and I decided that, for us, knowing about a problem, such as Down's syndrome, months before the baby arrived, would not be a helpful thing for our family. I made the decision and, quite honestly, I had more middle of the night pangs of fear than last time, but our second daughter was born just as healthy as the first. I still feel strongly that my decision was the right one for me.

Katherine, 32

Katherine, like Anne, has two daughters. Unlike Anne, she chose to have AFP screening during both pregnancies. The second time, however, the test did not give her the reassurance she so desperately wanted.

The first trimester of pregnancy with my second child was miserable. At the beginning there was even some question as to whether I was pregnant. The urine test that was done in my obstetrician's office was faintly positive and although a very early ultrasound confirmed that I had indeed conceived, based on the size of the embryo, the doctor wasn't sure things were progressing as they should. Blood tests showed that everything actually was moving along fine, but it took me a very long time to feel at all confident that I wasn't going to miscarry. Also, very early in my pregnancy, my husband, older daughter, and I were unknowingly exposed to the pesticide Malathion when our neighborhood park was being sprayed. When I realized what had happened, I called a couple of hotlines and visited various Web sites, which all assured me that the amount of the particular chemical to which I was exposed shouldn't pose any harm to me or my fetus. But, of course, I was still worried.

Yet another moment of panic occurred while I was reading the label on the over-the-counter prenatal vitamins I'd been taking since I started trying to conceive. In tiny lettering it said, to my great horror, that I was supposed to be taking four pills a day when for months I'd been taking only one. Mortified, I tearfully called my mother and then the doctor. Both reassured me that people have had healthy babies for centuries without the aid of prenatal vitamins. I still felt stupid and guilty and worried. In addition to all these stresses, I felt nauseated and headachy and absolutely leaden—so tired that all I wanted to do was sleep all the time, which, of course, was not possible with our two-and-a-half-year-old daughter and my part-time elementary school teaching job.

By the time I reached the sixteenth week, I was starting to feel much better physically. When I went for my monthly appointment, the doctor gave me the sheet to take to the lab for the AFP test. She asked if I remembered the test from my first pregnancy, which I did, and if I had any questions, which I really didn't. I was a little anxious this time, because of my exposure to Malathion and my problem with the vitamins, but I hoped its results would put my mind at ease, as they did during my first pregnancy. They did not.

A week or so after I'd gone to the lab for the test, I got paged over the intercom in my classroom letting me know that my doctor was on the line. I rushed to the nearest phone, which is in the faculty room (not the sort of public place one wants to receive bad news), to be informed by my doctor that the results of my test had come back and that I was showing an unusually low level of AFP for a woman my age, which could indicate that my baby had Down's syndrome. She said that my results indicated about a 1 in 200 chance of Down's, which is usual for a thirty-eight-year-old woman, but high for someone my age. In other words, my chance of having a Down's syndrome child was three times greater than "normal." She said the only way to absolutely rule out Down's syndrome was amniocentesis, but that the risk of miscarriage from an amnio was also about 1 in 200.

The doctor said that another procedure commonly performed to check for markers that might indicate Down's is a level two ultrasound, which poses no risks to the baby. She told me to think about what I wanted to do and get back to her. Somehow I managed to teach for the rest of the day without falling apart. When I finally had a chance to go home and call my husband, I absolutely lost it. We both agreed that we wouldn't want to abort the pregnancy even if I was carrying a Down's baby. We would, however, want as much information as we could possibly have about the baby's health since we understood that many children with Down's syndrome have, among other problems, severe heart defects and intestinal difficulties. After a dreadful night of agonizing about what to do, I found myself leaning toward the ultrasound. I felt irrationally unlucky and didn't want to take even the small risk involved in amnio. Both my husband and doctor agreed that the ultrasound seemed like a good first step. If we saw any red flags then, we could reevaluate and go on from there.

The level two ultrasound was scheduled for the next week and we tried to forget about it and just get on with living, but of course this was impossible. We both kept trying to imagine what our lives would be like with a Down's syndrome child. Coincidentally, we'd both read a couple of enlightening books on the topic in recent years written by parents of Down's children—Martha Beck's *Expecting Adam* (2000) and Michael Berube's *Life As We Know It* (1998). Both books make it clear how easy it is to love children with Down's, but how various problems can complicate life. I kept playing different scenarios in my mind—of telling our families, of trying to explain to my daughter, Julia, that her sister or brother was different, and on and on.

As we walked toward the hospital for the ultrasound we encountered a large group of Down's syndrome children being taken for a walk by their teachers. As we passed them, there was an, er, pregnant silence and then I turned to my husband and said, "Now we're just not going to read anything into that," and we both laughed. When it was time for the test, the technician was very friendly and positive, pointing out all the baby's parts, which appeared to be growing as they should. Afterward we met with the perinatologist, who was more guardedly positive and suggested that we return at around twenty-two weeks, when the baby would be even more developed. At that time we would have a second ultrasound and what's called a fetal echo, a very detailed ultrasound of the heart that would be monitored by a pediatric heart specialist. Approximately half of all Down's babies, she said, have a particular heart defect, which could be seen with this procedure. If both the second ultrasound and the fetal echo looked good she said the chance of our baby having Down's syndrome would be much closer to what it should be for someone my age. So, the news was good, albeit limited, but I could not, as yet, put my anxieties to rest.

We had to get through a few more weeks of waiting and unfortunately, these coincided with the Christmas holiday, which we spent with my family. My husband and I decided not to tell our parents and sisters, not wanting to burden them when there was nothing they could do. It was hard not confessing our worries, but several good friends knew of our situation and were very supportive and upbeat, which helped a lot. I would put it out of my mind for hours or even a day, but the anxiety kept coming back, even though part of me knew it was irrational to worry so much about what were essentially pretty good odds that everything was fine.

A few weeks later, the day finally arrived, and we went in for the second ultrasound. Thankfully, the results were good again and the fetal echo also showed no problems. Without an amnio, this was as much information as we were going to get and it seemed very positive. Our chances of having a Down's baby were now something like 1 in 350 and we were told to relax and enjoy the rest of the pregnancy. Both of us certainly relaxed a lot, but I knew doubts would occasionally creep into my thoughts as I anticipated the baby's birth. In fact, when Eleanor was born nine days early on a hot, sunny Saturday afternoon, the first words out of my mouth were, "Does she have Down's syndrome?!" The nurse looked at me like I was crazy and said, "No, sweetie, she's perfect." And, thank goodness, she is.

Looking back, despite all the anxiety it caused, I'd probably take the AFP again. Had Eleanor had Down's syndrome, advance warning about any health problems would have been invaluable. The fact that she didn't and that my husband and I both wasted a lot of psychic energy worrying isn't the fault of the test, which is just, after all, a screening. The test is intended to let you know your chances and, when I think now about how truly small the chance was that our baby would have Down's, I actually feel a little silly for having worried so much. But perspective is almost impossible to maintain when thinking about one's child and, of course, that's one of the great things about being a parent.

❅　❅　❅

Biochemistry and Ultrasound Nuchal Membrane Assessment (BUN)

The efficiency and effectiveness of prenatal diagnostic tests continues to improve and in the next several years it's likely that new and better options may exist. One such possibility may arise out of a current study whose purpose is to provide a noninvasive first trimester screening that can accurately assess our risk of carrying a baby with Down's syndrome or other chromosomal abnormalities. Sponsored by the National Institute of Child Health and Human Development

(1999), this study is being conducted at numerous centers throughout the United States and Canada.

Called Biochemistry and Ultrasound Nuchal Membrane Assessment or BUN, this screening measure promises to be more accurate than the current AFP/triple screen test and less invasive than amniocentesis and chorionic villus sampling (CVS). BUN, which is performed between the tenth and fourteenth week of pregnancy, combines three factors to determine the likelihood of genetic disorders: maternal age, a blood test (which measures the amounts of two proteins found in the blood of pregnant women), and a nuchal translucency ultrasound (which examines the space behind the fetus' neck for excess fluid, which can signal problems). Those conducting this study (in which 100,000 women will participate) cite a detection rate as high as 90 percent (National Institute of Child Health and Human Development 1999).

※ ※ ※

Karen, 36 Years Old

Karen's excitement about being pregnant was tempered as she struggled to make a decision about diagnostic testing. She didn't feel comfortable opting out completely, but she wasn't willing to subject herself to tests that were unreliable or invasive.

My husband, Steve, and I are ecstatic first-time parents-to-be. Ours was a planned pregnancy, and when I was just thinking about trying, nearly six months before we conceived, I called two obstetricians from the practice I had joined a year earlier to see if there was anything I should be doing or not doing in advance. It was from them, both women with children, that I had the first indication that what I wanted to embark on was, besides a joyous experience, one that would make me "high risk."

For the first time since I had thought about getting pregnant, I became alarmed. Even at age thirty-six, I never once considered that my being pregnant would throw me into any greater hazard than the average woman trying to expel a large human baby out of a relatively small hole. Pregnancy always seemed natural to me, a no-brainer, as long as I could conceive.

Maybe my attitude is attributable to the fact that most of my friends are beginning families after age thirty-five and they have all had mostly healthy pregnancies. I may feel more relaxed about childbirth because my mother was an early Lamaze pioneer, birthing all four of her children using Lamaze's techniques and as few drugs as possible. I was lucky that she sent me on my tentative pubescent way by giving me only the most positive images of her experiences.

I've also always been very in touch with my body. I've been a professional dancer as well as a generally curious explorer of my own body's functions. I remember the day I found out that I could actually chart my ovulation by measuring a few observable signs. I was outraged that I hadn't been taught this at age fourteen.

So, for me, birth was quite simply something to be done with minimal amounts of intervention and at home, if possible. Why bother with a hospital unless something was wrong, and why am I made to feel that something is wrong just by telling someone my age? I feel wonderful. After my obstetricians told me that I was high-risk, they advised me to have a look at the hospital that I'd be giving birth in, because I would be giving birth in a hospital. I thanked them and promptly began to search the Internet to find midwives who would give us a home birth. As if it were meant to be, I located a two-woman practice a block from our home. From that point forward, I have no longer felt at risk. I am treated as the healthy woman that I am.

Except, of course, that even the midwives are obligated to give me the facts: that women over thirty-five have an increased probability of having a baby with a chromosomal disorder. After giving me these facts, they naturally need to tell me about all the tests that I have at my fingertips, tests to stamp out or confirm the possibility of this or that defect. What happened to trusting birth, my body, and the process of life? I found myself actually fighting knowledge. Yes, in light of statistics, I did want some kind of assurance that things were OK—I didn't want to be in denial—but I also wanted to keep my faith, and I didn't want notions of risk and fear of the unknown to dominate my thoughts. Having an amnio was repugnant to me. Here was an invasive test that had as much chance of causing a problem (miscarriage) as coming up with a positive result. The bottom line was: What would I do with the information? A year ago, I might have said I'd terminate anything that wasn't perfect. Today, I no longer feel so certain, and after tracking a heartbeat and seeing our creation move, I can't imagine it.

Our genetic counselor told us that most severely defected babies don't make it; that the majority of the ones who are born with defects go on to lead semi-independent, even fulfilling lives. I turned to Steve and asked him what he would do if we had a baby with a problem. When he replied, "I'll love whatever we make," I was closer to deciding against amnio, but I still wanted that nod that would indicate that everything was OK. I knew that some of my hesitancy about amnio stemmed from having to wait so long to have one, and even longer for the results.

As we were about to leave the counselor's office, she reminded us about the triple screen (AFP) test, which helped some women to decide. This didn't appeal to me, however, because age was factored into the assessment, which increased chances that I would be deemed at a higher risk.

The counselor then told us about a study that was being done on a new screening test called BUN (National Institute of Child Health and Human Development 1999). With the noninvasive measurement of not two but three elements, this test is as high as ninety percent effective in estimating the risk of Down's syndrome and Trisomy 18, and it can be done in the first trimester. I liked the idea of being part of a study, and the numbers were certainly encouraging. A low-risk result would put me at as much ease as an amnio would, and if we were categorized as high risk, I could reevaluate whether to have an amnio at that time.

As my pregnancy was fourteen weeks along, I was meeting the test's cut-off by a hair. We first had the ultrasound, during which the technician measured the nuchal translucency, or the space between the skin and spine of the baby's neck. One indicator of a possible chromosomal disorder is a large amount of fluid there. After that, my blood was taken and was then dropped onto a card to measure various hormones and proteins. We were told that in ten days they'd have a result and would call me.

I admit that my mind raced over those ten days at various times. But because the test had been done relatively early, had been noninvasive, and because I wanted to feel confident, especially after having seen our baby's lively form on the ultrasound, I was pretty calm. After ten days, one of the study's investigators called to say that I had been measured as being at low risk for carrying a Down's syndrome baby, from the 1 in 270 expected for pregnant women my age to 1 in 360. My risk for carrying a baby with Trisomy 18, a much less common defect, was 1 in 10,000. That was enough information to make me feel comfortable that all was well.

The investigator encouraged me to have the AFP test at sixteen weeks, since it tests for neural tube defects, which the BUN does not. However, Steve and I decided to forgo the AFP and amnio and to consider another, more detailed ultrasound at twenty weeks, more for our own interest than to make sure everything was OK.

To dance through the amount of information available to us about the status of our growing fetus was something of an obstacle course. How could we best balance the facts of statistics and wanting to do what we could for our fetus, while still maintaining a sense of organic health and a firm faith in ourselves and our ability to handle any outcome? While wanting to know what we were at risk for, but by sticking with noninvasive means to calculate that risk, we felt we reached that balance. Hopefully, by the time our children are having babies they will be able to know even more, sooner.

❀ ❀ ❀

Chorionic Villus Sampling (CVS)

Chorionic villus sampling (CVS) is usually performed between the ninth and twelfth week. Like amniocentesis, CVS can detect genetic abnormalities including Down's syndrome, Tay-Sachs disease, and sickle cell anemia. It does not, however, diagnose spina bifida. The fact that this test can be done very early in pregnancy has made it increasingly popular. Before the test, a meeting with a genetic counselor will provide information and answer questions. The procedure involves having a long thin tube inserted into the cervix through the vagina to take a sample of chorionic villi (small finger-like projections on the placenta), which will then be tested for genetic abnormalities. In some cases, due to the particular placement of the placenta, the procedure will be performed through the abdomen with a thin needle. A local anesthetic might be used. An ultrasound is done simultaneously to guide your doctor. As with amniocentesis, there are risks involved, including a small chance of miscarriage and infection, so the decision to undergo this test is not one that is ever taken lightly. Some women experience vaginal bleeding afterward, so taking it easy for a while is always a good idea, even if just to recover from the emotional strain that will inevitably accompany the experience.

❀ ❀ ❀

Marie, 41 Years Old

When an amniocentesis revealed devastating news, Marie made the difficult decision to terminate her second pregnancy, which was already eighteen weeks along. This time, she felt strongly about having a test that could be performed at an earlier stage.

I got pregnant for the first time at the age of thirty-six. All of my friends of a similar age were having babies at the same time. All of them were having amnios so it was a no-brainer that I would have one too. The procedure went great, no pain or discomfort, and no cramping or problems afterwards. I was told I was having a healthy baby girl, which I did.

My second pregnancy was two years later. I again decided on an amnio. After all, I was now thirty-nine and would be forty at the time of delivery. I knew I needed the peace of mind an amnio would bring.

My second pregnancy was quite different from my first. I had misgivings about it from the start. My progesterone level had been low so I had to supplement. Plus, I was freezing all the time. I would be wearing three layers of clothes and still be cold. This was very unusual behavior for a person living in a warm climate, even in the winter.

The amnio experience was also quite different. As the doctor inserted the needle into my abdomen, I had a contraction and the needle could not reach the amniotic fluid. I was forced to lie on the table with a needle in my stomach until the contraction passed. It seemed like an eternity. When the procedure was over, I had a lot of pain at the site where the needle went in. Further, I couldn't shake the fear that something was really wrong with the baby. When the call came a little over a week later my worst fears were realized. At eighteen weeks, I learned my baby, whom I had already felt moving around, had Trisomy 18. My husband and I knew nothing about this chromosomal abnormality, although we were told it was much worse than Down's syndrome. We quickly learned the awful truth through the Internet. It was doubtful I would even carry my baby to term, or, if I did, it would likely be stillborn. For those that lived, the severe genetic defects kept them from having any real quality of life. We read that many babies born with this condition didn't live to see their first birthday.

Because my husband and I could not see bringing a child like this into the world, we considered termination. We also felt it would be extremely unfair to destroy our daughter's quality of life for a child who would in all probability have none. So, at eighteen and a half weeks, I proceeded with the termination process.

A second trimester abortion is extremely painful, both physically and emotionally. It is something I never want to face again. When we met with my obstetrician afterward, he suggested that we give some thought to CVS for our next pregnancy because it could be done earlier, and if there was a problem, it would be caught in the first trimester.

I got pregnant for a third time, at the age of forty. I knew I would have to decide if I wanted CVS rather quickly, so I immediately started trying to find out all I could about the procedure. My source of information was the Internet. I checked out several "parenting" boards that discussed prenatal diagnostic testing and read everything I could. Unfortunately, my third pregnancy resulted in a natural miscarriage at about six weeks—I felt my body just wasn't ready to support a new pregnancy—so no CVS was needed, but I continued to research the procedure.

Happily, four months later I was pregnant again and I was once more thinking of CVS. I learned that the miscarriage rate for CVS was higher than for amnio. Further, there was some suggestion, not supported by any hard evidence, that CVS could cause shortened limbs. Unlike an amnio, CVS was used only to diagnose chromosomal abnormalities. A different test would be needed to diagnose a potential neural tube defect. Further, unlike the amnio, CVS could be done either by inserting a catheter vaginally, or by going through the abdomen. Also, CVS was not accurate for diagnosing "mosaic" chromosomal abnormalities. This meant that if some but not all of the cells showed a Trisomy problem, then CVS was considered inaccurate and an amnio would be needed to determine whether there was a problem.

As much as I respected my own doctor, I knew he had never before performed CVS and I certainly did not want him to learn on me. Therefore, I began to research the doctor to whom I was referred by the genetic center, through which the test would be arranged. Fortunately, I already knew of him by reputation. He was considered an excellent doctor, although everyone agreed his bedside manner was not the best. I learned that he was very experienced with the CVS procedure and that his miscarriage rate was only slightly higher than the amnio rate.

One thing I didn't learn in my research is that there are some pre-CVS tests you have to undergo. For example, I had to have an ultrasound to confirm my dates because CVS cannot be done any sooner than ten weeks from your last menstrual period. In my case, my CVS was scheduled for a date, it turned out, when I would be only nine weeks, six days, so I had to put it off for a week. Also, I had to have "vaginal samplings" taken to confirm that I did not have any sexually transmitted diseases because of the possibility they could be transmitted to the fetus during the procedure.

After I went through the initial testing, my husband and I met with the genetic counselor. Due to my extensive research, I pretty much had all the information available, but I did learn that if the baby was positioned right, the doctor always performed the test vaginally, which was a relief. After my last amnio, I really did not want him going through my abdomen. We signed the consent forms, and confirmed our date.

The actual procedure did not last very long. Before the CVS, another ultrasound was performed to reconfirm dates and to pinpoint the location of the placenta. Then we waited for the obstetrician. As forewarned, the doctor did not have a great bedside manner. He was very professional, greeted us, and got down to business. That was fine with me. I wanted the test over.

There were three people in the room other than my husband and myself: the doctor performing the procedure, the ultrasound technician, and the genetic doctor. The test was performed with me in the same position as I would have been for a pap smear. My feet were in stirrups and a speculum was inserted. Then the doctor completely swabbed me out with a Betadine solution. I felt him doing this, but it was not painful. After that, the doctor inserted the catheter into the vagina, through the uterus, and to the placenta where he started trying to extract the tissue. I watched the whole procedure on the ultrasound screen. It did get a little frightening because it looked like the doctor was so close to the baby. The ultrasound technician assured me he really wasn't. He was only in there for a few minutes, then he removed the catheter, and emptied the contents into a dish.

While the ultrasound was being performed, the genetic doctor had set up her equipment. As soon as the fetal tissue was removed, she examined it to make sure there was enough to conduct the test. The doctor only has two chances to get the necessary amount. If he doesn't get it on the second try, you are out of luck. In my case, there was not enough tissue the first time so he had to do the procedure again. The second time he went in I did feel the catheter. It really wasn't painful, just uncomfortable. He quickly made his way to the placenta, extracted the tissue and emptied it into the dish for the genetic doctor to examine. The second time there was enough.

Initially I was on bed rest following the procedure and then on limited bed rest and light activities for the next couple of days. I had a little achiness, not really cramping, and absolutely no spotting.

At about 4 P.M. the next day, we received a telephone call from the genetic doctor with the preliminary results. She told us everything looked fine at that point but they would not know for sure for another week or two. She also said it looked like it was a little girl.

We received final results about nine days after the procedure. The genetic counselor called on a Friday evening. She confirmed that we were, indeed, having a girl. She also said there was no sign of a Trisomy 18 problem, as before, or of Down's. They tested about sixty-plus cells. There was one cell that had a problem but the doctor said it was just a tissue remnant and nothing to worry about. Apparently, when cells are grown for the time period necessary for this test, little anomalies can result. The genetic doctor was very reassured by the test and I later found out that my doctor was as well. I chose to accept both of their opinions and not worry about the anomaly.

I had an AFP test during the fifteenth week of my pregnancy and a level two ultrasound not long after that; I was reassured by these results as well. The final reassurance came when my beautiful, healthy eight-pound daughter made her way into the world several months later.

Lynn, 42

Lynn wanted a test that could be performed in her first trimester before anyone other than her partner knew she was pregnant. She was still getting used to the idea of pregnancy when she made the decision to have CVS.

First, you look at the charts. Chromosomal abnormalities zoom skyward with advancing maternal age. You think you're crazy for conceiving a baby after the age of forty. You're shocked that you got pregnant without even trying. You're embarrassed to be embarking on a twenty-something adventure when your hair is turning gray. You feel old. You feel scared. You feel guilty. You're afraid to feel happy.

The road ahead was not on your map. You're drowning in anxiety, while the nausea builds and your breasts ache to bursting. You don't want the world to watch your belly rise until you know the fetus is OK. You learn that with CVS, doctors can test the genetics before anyone knows you're pregnant. Certainty in the first trimester has the sweetest appeal; you can wrestle the future in the private embrace of your partner.

Your doctor's office schedules the procedure. They send all their patients 100 miles away; they say it's the best place for the test. And it's a scary test! Miscarriage rates are higher than what they are for amnio. There are terrifying risks of damage to the limbs as they develop. How can you untie that impossible knot (finding out if your fetus is OK might do unspeakable things to it)? Can this be real? You cry, you ache for sleep, you try to learn more from friends and friends of friends.

You get lousy information: false positives; false negatives; residents performing this delicate procedure; conflicting, terrifying information; things that can't possibly be true. At ten weeks, you have a preliminary ultrasound. There's nearly no fluid so early, so the ultrasound wand goes up the vagina instead of over the belly. The image is clear as a bell. The fetus is real, it's moving, and, thank god, there's only one. The CVS docs want to confirm gestational age, but you just stare in amazement. How could something just one inch long cause so much fear and nausea? One more week to wait.

Sweetheart trundles you off to the big city medical center. Bright lights, kind counselors. You sign the consent form where it says "Mother." Sweetheart wonders why. Then *he* has to sign where it says "Father." Shocking adjustment! Another ultrasound (this one over the belly with your kidneys full of pee). Jelly on the wand, and the image looks like algae. Somehow the sonographer sees all. The placenta looks solid to the untrained eye, but those in the know call it chorionic villi. Maybe a cervical approach, maybe abdominal, says the technician. The fetus hangs out in the middle of the road.

Doc comes in the door. He's short of stature and head of the department. He's sure an abdominal approach would be easiest, given the fetus, the placenta, and the lay of the land. He plays no favorites between the belly and cervix; the research strongly favors whatever's easy. He laughs when you tell him you heard residents do the procedure. Hah hah! We don't even let attendings do this. Doc assures you that limb deformities aren't a risk (if the doctor is experienced and the fetus is ten and a half weeks). "No! Stop!" You sit bolt upright. "I'm not ten weeks!" In unison and amazement, everyone present stares. Two ultrasounds and serious calendar counting have preceded you to this moment. You admit defeat, lie back, and pretend it's dentistry. With a mouth full of thousand-dollar crowns, you're sure you've been through worse.

The belly's bathed in Betadine, your navel's a deep red pool. New towels, new needles, everything is stripped from plastic wrappers. If infection is a cause for miscarriage, then you feel worry-free. NASA couldn't be this sterile. Novocaine needle, close your eyes. Next needle, close your eyes. Another device sucks up the cells. Definitely close your eyes! Minor pain for a minute and a half. Doc counts the cells he's collected; when he reaches twenty, it's safe to stand up and get dressed. Home to rest. No cramping, no fever, no fluids discharged.

You're so reassured by the abdominal approach (glad the choice was obvious, and glad the cervix was untouched). But waiting is hell. Paranoia, fear, and anger. Phone calls, worrying, terror. The cells grow slowly, in their own sweet time. Then it's all good news. The counselor announces on the telephone: "Forty-six chromosomes, nothing extra, nothing missing." Twelve weeks into pregnancy, you know you'll never sleep again. You're going to have a baby!

Sandra, 36

Like Lynn, Sandra's CVS was performed through her abdomen because of the placement of the placenta. In her case, the procedure was much more uncomfortable than she expected.

There's no denying it. Being pregnant over the age of thirty-five puts your baby at risk for some very bad diseases. Knowing this, and knowing I would be almost thirty-seven at the time my second child was born, my husband and I decided to opt for CVS to identify any chromosomal problems or other genetic diseases.

Frankly, I suspected that I would terminate my pregnancy if I discovered that our baby had a chromosomal disorder. I felt that taking such action earlier in my pregnancy, as opposed to later when you can feel your baby inside you, would make the whole experience less heartbreaking.

I felt nervous making the appointment with the genetic counselor and even more so at eleven weeks gestation when we met with her to go over our baby's genetic risks. We discussed lots of numbers. My odds of having a baby with chromosomal abnormalities? 1 in 200. My odds of miscarrying due to the procedure itself? Nearly the same. For such a personal issue, the math made the discussion oddly impersonal.

Our visit included a nuchal translucency screening: a high-resolution ultrasound and examination of the nuchal area—the space between the skin and the spine behind the fetus' neck. Combined with the mother's age, the results can determine an adjusted risk for Down's syndrome. Seeing my baby's movements for the first time was truly wondrous, and I couldn't stop smiling as I gazed on this new life inside me, floating contentedly in its amniotic cocoon.

The doctor told us that from the measurements, it was still difficult to determine if the baby had Down's. The baby's odds of having a genetic abnormality were now, just a tiny bit less.

"Do you still want to go ahead with CVS?" the doctor asked. "You can take a week to think about it, or choose to do amniocentesis later." My husband and I debated a few minutes about whether the procedure was a good idea given that the statistics of miscarriage from CVS were about the same as my risk of having a child with chromosomal abnormalities. Yet I felt that I had to know that everything with our baby was all right, and chose to continue.

At the beginning of my appointment, my husband and I had watched a video of women having CVS and amnio, and talking about their experiences. The film did not discuss how painful the test could be (it did mention cramping), nor did it point out that a pelvic CVS can involve poking through the patient's stomach for several minutes.

The procedure began with a nurse wiping my belly with a topical anesthetic cream. I told the doctor that I was closing my eyes but to tell me what was happening. He inserted a needle into my abdomen to make room for a narrow tube to extract a piece of my placenta. The extraction was terribly painful for about three minutes. A stranger was digging around in my stomach, and I was sure I was going to lose the baby.

I looked down and saw dried blood in places, and felt very sad and exhausted, both emotionally and physically. No heavy lifting for two days, the doctor cautioned. Tell that to my two-year-old, I said, trying to feel upbeat. Fortunately, my husband stayed home for the next forty-eight hours to help care for our daughter.

After a couple days had passed without any complications, I felt fairly confident that our baby was OK. Eleven very long days later, the geneticist called. "Great news," she said. "You have a healthy baby. Do you want to know the sex?" "Yes!" If others were going to know whether we were having a boy or a girl, I certainly wanted to be included.

I found out that day that we were having a baby boy, who will probably be named after one of his grandfathers. My husband and I were thrilled to be having a son, while our daughter seemed to be more interested in being a big sister than having a baby brother in her life.

Would I do CVS again? I'm not sure. The procedure was risky and quite traumatic. But it felt great to know that our son was going to be just fine.

❋   ❋   ❋

Amniocentesis

Amniocentesis is most commonly performed between the sixteenth and eighteenth week, although sometimes it is used in the later stages of pregnancy to determine fetal lung maturity if, for some reason, the baby needs to be delivered early. Before the procedure, you'll meet with a genetic counselor who will take a look at your history and that of your family, tell you what the test can determine, and explain how it will be performed.

The test involves having a long hollow needle inserted through your abdomen wall into your uterus to withdraw some of the amniotic fluid that surrounds the fetus. An ultrasound is performed simultaneously to guide the doctor as the needle is inserted. The fluid contains fetal cells which, when cultured and examined, can detect a variety of genetic disorders including Down's syndrome, Tay-Sachs disease, and sickle cell anemia. The test can also detect neural tube defects and determine the sex of the baby. The procedure is relatively quick and most doctors will recommend that you take it easy for approximately twenty-four hours afterward, during which time you might experience mild cramping and, more rarely, amniotic fluid leakage. It takes between ten days to three weeks to receive the results.

Because the test is not without risk (there is a slight chance of miscarriage or infection), it is only advised in certain situations. An amnio will probably be recommended if you are over age thirty-five, if you have another child with, or a family history of, a particular genetic disorder, or if you or your partner are carriers of a particular disease. Additionally, if your AFP (alpha-fetoprotein) screening has put you at a higher risk for carrying a child with a disorder, this test might be suggested.

❋   ❋   ❋

Emily, 35

During her pregnancy Emily suffered from hyperemesis, a condition that causes severe nausea, vomiting, and even dehydration in pregnant women. She was extremely ill and her day-to-day life was unrecognizable. She knew early on that she wanted an amnio because of her age, and the results allowed her, for the first time in her difficult pregnancy, to relax.

Learning the news from my amniocentesis was the single event of the early part of pregnancy that made the pregnancy more "real" to me. After a rough four months of vomiting, dehydration, and sleepless nights, upon hearing "It's a girl!", I suddenly felt there was a human being inside of me, not just an alien. It also helped to be told "everything's OK." I started to relax into the pregnancy for the first time. I had chosen to do an amnio because of my age and because I wanted to know as much as I could about the baby's health. (I was relieved, in fact, that being the magic maternal age of thirty-five meant that my insurance would pay and that my doctors advised the procedure.) I wanted any kind of reassurance that this mysterious process that felt so out of control was actually proceeding as it should.

The procedure itself was tolerable—while physically uncomfortable, the pain was minimal. It's certainly not something I would willingly choose to do every day—sort of somewhere in between going to the dentist and minor surgery. But even though I did choose to do it, I wasn't prepared for how violent and intrusive it felt to have a needle stuck in my pregnant belly. Fortunately, I was distracted from this emotional intensity during the procedure by my husband's unconscious nervousness. His task was to provide a hand to hold in case I needed to channel my physical discomfort somewhere. Because he was in direct view of the needle about to enter my abdomen (and I was not) he provided a sort of early warning system—just before the needle entered my belly he squeezed my hand (rather than the other way around) causing me more pain than the amnio itself.

Then there was the waiting. Ten days or so. Forget you ever did the test. Put it on the back burner. Go about your daily life. It was all so bizarre. Then the phone call came. Had the news been troubling how would I have dealt with it? I have no idea. All I know is that I was willing to take the risk of facing that dilemma.

Jenny, 36

While pregnant with her second child, Jenny felt strongly that she didn't want or need an amnio. The statistics about the chances of women over thirty-five carrying a baby with a disorder did not sway her, nor did the opinion of one of her health care providers.

Although I was past the so-called "safe age," I opted not to have amnio. Since I had had a healthy daughter just two years before, I didn't feel it was necessary to go through what had been described as a painful procedure, which has certain risks associated with it. I figured my mother had three kids when she was in her mid-thirties, before there was such a thing as amnio, with no complications. And, how much could my body really have changed in two short years? And, even if I did have an amnio, and got abnormal results, I didn't know what I would do about it.

I was a little nervous about telling my obstetrician my decision, because I thought she'd try to change my mind. But that was far from the case. She told me that the AFP (alpha-fetoprotein) tests are very accurate now and that if my blood work turned out well, she would be satisfied. In fact, she said, *she* didn't have an amnio when she was pregnant with her third child and she was well over thirty-five. As it turned out, my AFP test put my chances of having a baby with Down's syndrome at the same odds as a thirty-one-year-old. I was relieved to find out I could safely skip amnio. My doctor did suggest that I see an ultrasound specialist, to insure that the fetus was closely examined, and I did. That particular doctor happened to be an amnio specialist as well, and he filled my ear with his pro-amnio point of view, which I could have done without. All in all, I am thrilled with the decision I made regarding the amnio, and my pregnancy resulted in the birth of another healthy baby girl.

Sheila, 33

For Sheila, there was no question that she would have an amnio. She was completely comfortable with her decision, but the procedure itself took her by surprise.

I knew even before I became pregnant for the first time that I would have an amnio. My sister, a doctor, had shown me the recent medical literature, which demonstrated that the risk factors were not that different between a twenty-nine-year-old and a thirty-five-year-old, and since I would be thirty-three when I delivered, I figured that difference was basically nonexistent. In addition, I knew of someone who had had an amnio that had strongly indicated Down's in her second pregnancy despite the fact that her first pregnancy had been perfect, and there was no history of genetic problems in the family. So all in all, an amnio seemed the way to go.

All of the pregnancy related literature that I read simply stated that a slender needle is carefully guided through the abdomen into the amniotic sac. What no one tells you is that in order for the needle to break through, it needs to be jabbed with significant force. Now, this would not have been a particular problem for me except for several things. First, as I had some fibroids, I needed to lie at a 45-degree angle during the procedure for them to have a good entry angle, which was very awkward. Second, I have extremely strong reflexes and am always nervous that medical procedures will involuntarily jerk me into a strong reaction; as a result, I tend to be very tightly wound, bracing against this possibility. So when that unexpected jab came, my body left the table by about a foot. Needles went flying, and I was terrified I'd hurt the baby. Of course, as the fetus is quite small at that point, and they are inserting the needle a long way from wherever the baby is, that was not a problem.

The doctor tried again. This time the needle appeared to go in. After what seemed like a really long time, with a lot of uncomfortable poking around, no fluid was being drawn. Finally, they realized that the outer wall of the sac had tented around the needle. So, once more, they jabbed the needle in. By this time I was used to it, everyone was calmer, and it went in fine. A little while later, it was all over. It had been uncomfortable, startling, and not at all what I'd expected, but in the end it wasn't that bad, and I was very glad I had done it. To my great good fortune, everything came back fine, and I later gave birth to a gorgeous and wonderful baby girl.

Dakota, 45

After two miscarriages Dakota was elated to be so far along in a pregnancy. However, her age made her chances of carrying a baby with a chromosomal abnormality very high. Knowing that she and her husband had agreed that they would terminate the pregnancy should they receive bad news, she was filled with fear as the testing day neared.

Because I was forty-five when I became pregnant, it was mandatory that I should have an amnio. Since my husband was also a man of a certain age (fifty-two), the doctors indicated that amnio was absolutely essential because Down's syndrome and other age-related problems are not only transmitted through an older mother but also an older father! Who would have thought such a thing?

I was feeling physically very well, so I put the thought of the amnio out of mind for a while. As the time approached, however, I began dreading the upcoming test. We had decided that if there was anything wrong with the baby, we wouldn't have it. I felt that as much as I longed for a child, I couldn't care for one with severe (or even "mild") physical and mental problems. I also knew that my husband wouldn't support me in having a child with problems. He would most likely leave me. He already had two children from a previous marriage and he wasn't crazy about having another one, most assuredly not an unhealthy one. We both had agreed that we would go for the amnio, but as the time neared, I most especially was afraid.

I will forever be grateful to my husband because he was so loving to me on that bleak December morning. That time of the year is so dark, and that winter it snowed mountains and was cold a lot. There were no lights in any apartments in the whole of West End Avenue, except ours. I shiver as I remember the edgy reluctance I felt trying to get ready.

My doctor will always be in my pantheon of good guys. I put on the robe and lay down on the table. The ultrasound machine was hooked into a huge monitor with a replica of ET draped on it. The doctor greeted us warmly and introduced us to the lady technician. I transfixed my eyes to the monitor, and, amazingly enough, another ET-ish creature came into view. I looked at it and began weeping. I just couldn't stop. I felt such a relief, such a crazy pleasure and such a pity for the little thing. Its legs were obstinately crossed and no amount of prodding made it undo them so the doctor and the technician couldn't tell its sex.

Mercifully the doctor kept saying that the baby looked healthy and after he drew the amniotic fluid easily, he said it looked like vintage champagne. He seemed very satisfied with the exam. (When the results arrived, they confirmed this good news). I was still crying, softly, I might add, because I felt that no one wanted to see a grown woman cry over a test. The worst was over.

❄ ❄ ❄

However we might feel about the role of diagnostic testing in pregnancy, there is no doubt that over time, the number and variety of these tests will only continue to grow. As the world we live in becomes more scientifically advanced and technological, so will pregnancy. Whether we feel violated by even the suggestion of procedures that seem invasive and unnecessary, or whether we embrace every new test eagerly in our desire to know as much as we can about the heretofore unknown, there are, and will continue to be, a host of decisions to be made in this fairly new, but obviously permanent, realm of pregnancy.

Chapter Five

When Problems Occur: Dealing with Pregnancy Complications

Pregnancies rarely are perfect and many of us will have to deal with one complication or another while our bodies are engaged in the rigorous work of growing a baby. Some are relatively mild and pose no significant risk to mother or child. Others are more serious. Some will be fleeting while others will affect our entire pregnancy. We'll be routinely tested for early indications of some of these conditions, including preeclampsia and gestational diabetes. But others, preterm labor and hyperemesis among them, are only discovered when we start to experience symptoms.

Our bodies change so radically during pregnancy that it can be difficult to know which symptoms are considered normal and which might be cause for concern. Most of us will, at one time or another, fear the worst only to learn that those sudden pangs were actually something as trouble-free as gas pains. Others of us might find ourselves in the throes of preterm labor without knowing it. Our health care practitioners will give us a good sense of what kinds of symptoms should raise red flags. When in doubt, a phone call is always a good idea.

When complications do arise, it can be both physically and psychologically draining. Even at its best, pregnancy brings a wide and wild range of emotions, and when something goes wrong this only intensifies. It's difficult to find anything positive about a frightening pregnancy experience, but the fierce maternal love that springs forth from just such moments is often the source of much comfort and sustenance.

Preterm Labor

Preterm labor is labor that takes place any time before the thirty-seventh week. After that, a pregnancy is considered full term. Of women who experience preterm labor, some will be affected quite early in their pregnancies while others will show no signs until their third trimester. As with many other pregnancy-related complications, the cause of preterm labor is often a mystery although certain factors (including previous preterm labor or carrying more than one baby) are known to put you in a higher risk category. There are a variety of treatment options recommended to stop the progression of this early labor, including simply lying on your left side and drinking lots of water, full-blown bed rest, and IV fluids to assist in hydration. In some cases drugs will be administered. The goal is always to keep the baby inside you as long as possible. The earlier preterm labor is diagnosed and treated, the better.

Some preterm labor symptoms include menstrual-like cramping; uncomfortable tightening of the abdomen; pressure in the lower abdomen, groin, or thighs; low, dull backache; and an increase in clear vaginal discharge.

Dealing with preterm labor can be scary and unpleasant. Long periods of bed rest, side effects from the medications used to stop contractions, and the constant fear of delivering your baby too early are just some of the situations that can make life very difficult for those of us who have to cope with this problem.

❊　❊　❊

Amanda, 31 Years Old

When Amanda started to feel pain and pressure in her abdomen and lower back during her second trimester, she had no idea that she was experiencing preterm labor. From the moment she was diagnosed until her first child was born seventeen weeks later, her life was almost exclusively devoted to ensuring that her baby did not arrive early.

I went into premature labor at twenty-three weeks, just two days after my husband and I found out we were having a baby boy. We had a name picked out and were excited to settle into the pregnancy, confident that things were progressing normally.

I was at work when I began to feel some unusual twinges, some slightly uncomfortable pains, in my barely rounded belly. My colleagues who'd been pregnant assured me everything was fine and the sensations I was experiencing were normal. Who was I to argue? This was all new to me, so I accepted that this must be what it feels like to have a twenty-three-week-old baby inside me. "Maybe he's just pressing on something in there," I thought.

I had a long, uncomfortable day at the office, and by the time I got home, my lower back, too, was really hurting. I tried desperately to make myself comfortable, and even stood on my head in hopes of getting the baby to shift his position and relieve the pressure on that internal organ I thought he might be sitting on. I went to my pile of pregnancy books and looked up every complication I could think of but nothing seemed to match my symptoms. I remember seeing preterm labor listed in several tables of contents, but its major symptom was always "cramps." I was feeling a lot of pressure in my lower back and a rhythmic pain in my abdomen. These didn't feel like cramps to me. Looking back, it seems ridiculous that I didn't immediately associate a "rhythmic" pain with contractions. I went to bed and slept fitfully, and finally called my doctor the next morning. That "rhythmic" thing tipped her off right away and I was told to get in a cab and meet her at the hospital immediately.

At the hospital, I was hooked up to a fetal monitor that showed I was having pretty serious contractions. After receiving two liters of IV fluids the contractions didn't abate in the least. I was given a shot of terbutaline that worked, but only for a little while. After another shot, and another brief respite from contractions, I was given a pill form of the same drug. The pills made me terribly ill, and the contractions returned. Things were getting worse, and very scary. After being in complete denial for about twenty-four hours, I began to understand that I might be losing this baby. It didn't seem possible.

I was next given magnesium sulfate intravenously. I vomited immediately and felt very bad. My head ached, I was horribly nauseous, and I was so, so sad. The sonograms I received every few hours were particularly upsetting. The baby looked so alive and healthy—and he was. It was his environment—my body—that was threatening to shut down and end his life. How could I be doing this to my sweet boy? The thought of losing him was devastating.

The magnesium sulfate, despite its crippling side effects, worked. The problem was, because I was only twenty-three weeks pregnant, I couldn't stay on it for long without putting the baby at risk. When it was stopped after about twenty-four hours, the contractions started again.

The next drug we tried was nifedipine, which finally stopped my contractions for good. After two days in the hospital, I was sent home, drug-free, and a fetal monitor was delivered to my house. I would put the monitor on my belly twice a day and transmit the readings to a nurse who would call me back to tell me how many contractions I was having during that hour-long monitoring session. It was very comforting to have the monitor and to have a nurse to talk to twice a day. I did make a few more emergency trips to the hospital, even though my monitor showed that everything was normal. But when I'd feel something unusual, I'd want to ensure everything was OK.

I stayed in bed for six weeks. I was told to drink a lot of water and that my subway commuting days were over. I considered taking a cab to and from work every day, but my doctor advised me to stay home for the remainder of my pregnancy—four months. Amazingly, I carried my son a full forty weeks, and he came into the world just two days shy of his due date. We still don't know what caused my preterm labor or why my pregnancy was normal and healthy from that time forward. I have fibroid tumors that grew dramatically during the pregnancy. Perhaps they were the culprits, but it's hard to say for sure.

Gina, 24

Gina struggled with preterm labor in all three of her pregnancies. Her first child was born eight weeks early and her second and third pregnancies required close management to prevent this from happening again.

I have three children and something went wrong during each of my pregnancies. It was very hard for me to live with the high-risk label that I'd been given, but I think that the thought of losing my babies made me cherish them even more when they were born.

During a first pregnancy it's often difficult to know what aches and pains are normal and which ones signal a problem. I certainly didn't know that the light cramping I was experiencing the night before my daughter was born, during the thirty-second week of my pregnancy, was a sign of preterm labor. I just decided to go to bed. The next day, however, when I was getting ready for my baby shower, the cramps started getting worse. I called my doctor and she said I should come to the hospital immediately! When I got there I was already two centimeters dilated and was told that my daughter was on her way. She arrived four hours later.

After my daughter was born they rushed her out of the delivery room. The doctors told me that she was being transferred to another hospital with a very good neonatal unit where she could be treated. Born two months premature, her lungs were not fully developed and she was having trouble breathing. I was alone in the room after they left and I started to cry. I was overwhelmed with fear. The first time I saw my daughter I wept and wept. She was only three pounds, three ounces, and she looked so tiny. The nurses assured me that she would be OK and that soon she would be home. And three weeks later she was released, weighing five adorable little pounds, a month before anyone expected she would be well enough to leave the hospital.

When I was twenty weeks pregnant with my second child I went into preterm labor again. I was hospitalized overnight and when I was released I was told to rest. My schedule was grueling and it seemed impossible to slow down. I was under an enormous amount of pressure. Between work, school, and mothering my two-year-old daughter, my body was definitely beginning to show signs of exhaustion. But I had so much to take care of that, of course, I didn't heed its warnings.

In the seventh month of my pregnancy, while taking an exam in school, I went into preterm labor again. I was rushed to the hospital where I was told I would have to be on bed rest for the remainder of the pregnancy. I was put on medication that made me feel worse and that made my hands tremble. I couldn't even hold a cup. When I was able to stop taking the medication, I rested. Two months later my son was born, full term and healthy.

During my third pregnancy I was sick all day and night well into my second trimester. Then, once again, in my twentieth week, I experienced preterm labor. I sobbed in the hospital because I could not deal with being in bed for the rest of my pregnancy. I was put on bed rest for a week and, after that, I made sure I slowed down. Although I was not put on medication, I had to maintain a strict schedule. I was to rest as much as possible.

It was hard not to feel depressed and inadequate but my husband and children were wonderful, and thinking of my baby always made me feel better. I am a believer in the power of positive thinking, and I was determined to conquer my negative feelings and learn from the experience. Living in such a restricted manner wasn't easy and I was tired of not being able to do things for myself or be there for my family as I usually was. I was willing, however, to do whatever it took to give birth to a healthy baby, which I did. I welcomed my third child, a daughter, into the world after nine full months of pregnancy.

※　※　※

Hyperemesis Gravidarum

Hyperemesis gravidarum is a condition that causes severe nausea and vomiting in pregnant women. Much more serious than "morning sickness," hyperemesis can also result in dehydration, changes in body chemistry, and hospitalization. If not monitored carefully, this affliction can be harmful to both mother and baby. Women who suffer from hyperemesis are often too ill to get out of bed and some of them will vomit more than ten times a day. Many lose a great deal of weight due to their inability to keep food in their bodies, and they frequently need to be nourished with intravenous fluids.

The treatment varies according to the severity of the case and in some instances medication is necessary. Although theories exist about the causes, which include carrying more than one baby, inflammation of the pancreas, and psychological factors such as stress and depression, the truth is that no one can really explain why and how it occurs. Women who have had hyperemesis, however, are said to be at a higher risk to experience it with subsequent pregnancies.

In a fascinating article on nausea, in which writer Atul Gawande (1999) provides one of the best accounts of hyperemesis to date, it becomes clear just how little is known about this mysterious condition and the ways in which it should be treated. Detailing the pregnancy of a twenty-nine-year-old woman, carrying twins, who was suffering from an extreme case of hyperemesis, Gawande describes the confused reaction of the doctors she'd consulted:

> "Some doctors kept telling her that in another week or two she'd turn the corner. One doctor asked if she wanted to go back to New York (she was currently living with her parents in Virginia), and she had the distinct impression that he just wanted to get rid of her. Another seemed to believe that she wasn't trying hard enough to eat, as if the nausea were under her control. Their frustration was palpable. Later, they suggested that she see a psychiatrist."

Rachel, 30 Years Old

Many women who've suffered from hyperemesis confirm that health care providers are confounded by this illness and don't take their complaints about its severity seriously. This was definitely true for Rachel. After more than two months of constant vomiting (at least once an hour, twenty-four hours a day), she was finally admitted to the hospital (for the first time) and treatment was begun. It would still be a long time, however, before her condition stabilized and she could resume some semblance of her old life.

I always knew that if I was lucky enough to become pregnant, my highly tuned stomach would immediately let me know. I have always experienced life through my stomach. As a child, I would feel nauseous whenever the teacher called on me in class, as a high school junior I arrived at the Scholastic Aptitude Test (SAT) late because I had the runs, and as a liberated twenty-something New Yorker, I discovered while riding a city bus that the pill made me vomit.

I was already throwing up for several days before I got a very faint positive reading on my pregnancy test. Still, to make sure, I called my friend to see if I was pregnant. I wanted to know if it was possible to feel nauseous only a few weeks after conception. "No way," she confidently told me. "You wouldn't be nauseous for at least a month." But I've always been a firm believer in my stomach and it was, in fact, telling the truth.

When I went for my first obstetrician appointment, I was six weeks pregnant and vomiting constantly, two or three times an hour, twenty-four hours a day. My doctor hardly looked up from the examination when I complained that I was "really, really nauseous." His silence seemed to be telling me "of course you're nauseous, it's the first trimester, what did you expect?" He told me what everyone else told me: "Try to eat crackers in the morning and always keep something in your stomach."

So, being a good girl, I diligently ate saltines before getting out of bed in the morning and constantly lined my stomach with easy to digest starchy foods. Unfortunately, the more I ate, the sicker I got. By the eighth week of my pregnancy all I seemed to be doing was throwing up, but still the doctor told me to ride it out. He promised, "You will soon be back on your feet and feeling fine." At this point, I had moved into my parents' apartment for twenty-four-hour bed-side care. My husband came with me and so did our cat. I was back in my childhood bedroom, sharing one bathroom with my parents.

As soon as we arrived, my mother sprang into action. Under her watchful eye, I lay on the couch clutching my vomit bowl while she nervously hovered over me, instructing me every few minutes to eat another saltine or sip some water. After a few days of this, I was no longer able to tolerate even a saltine. I was still planted on the couch and could no longer move. I was now wearing my mother's pink polyester muumuu, which hung loosely over my churning stomach. Even when I reached for the remote, I would swoon from nausea, and if I tried to stand up, there would surely be an "up-chucking" of whatever saltines my mother had lovingly forced me to eat. I tried to lay perfectly still on the couch. This, I knew, was my only hope.

After watching me deteriorate for a few more days, my husband called the doctor. He tried very hard to explain how awful I looked, but still the doctor wasn't concerned. Then my mother stepped in. No doctor is a match for a concerned Jewish mother. The doctor was told that we were coming to the hospital and finally he had no choice but to agree.

When we got to the emergency room someone finally recognized that I was, in fact, "sick." I was completely dehydrated and might have lost the baby if I hadn't been hooked up to an IV of sugar and water. This was my only treatment.

I was released from the hospital three days later, still green with nausea, but, in the words of my doctor, "ready to return home." Before I left the hospital, a nutritionist was sent to my bed. Once again, I was told that the solution to my problem was to eat. She gave my mother the name of some liquid shakes and suggested I try orzo and chicken broth. I resumed my motionless position on the family couch.

A few days later, I was in the hospital again. This time they understood that my nausea would not simply go away. Again I was put on an IV, which the doctor assured me was all I needed to keep my baby and me alive. Even so, I was still vomiting my guts out and to make matters worse, my vomit was now green. We talked about adding an antinausea drug to my intravenous drip (in retrospect this seemed like the logical thing to do), but, at the time, I was spooked that I would be hurting the baby. Although medical evidence did not confirm this, the doctor never encouraged me to take medicine. His silence on this subject seemed to be telling me, "Be strong, after all, it's only nausea." Strangely enough, my mother agreed. She reminded me that my pregnancy would soon be over, but "any medicine I took could potentially destroy the life of my child." This was enough guilt to make me continue my nauseated march to the second trimester.

I was sent home after arrangements had been made for a twenty-four-hour home IV. I soon learned that I had "very bad veins." The nurses would "stick" one vein after the next, trying to establish an IV line. Inevitably, however, the needle would "infiltrate" the surrounding tissue and have to be removed. This is common with women in my condition. The dehydration somehow makes the veins disappear. I had been stuck by needles so many times that the nurses had simply run out of "good veins."

I was now nearly three months pregnant and only getting worse. It was Thanksgiving and my family huddled in the kitchen trying to make an odorless dinner. By this point, I was too sick for the public couch and had permanently stationed myself in my childhood bedroom. All noises, odors, and light were oppressive. I spent three motionless days in my dark and quiet bed, getting up only to go to the bathroom. It was clear that I needed medicine. Guiltily, I allowed them to attach a second drip bag of antinausea medicine to my IV and I started to feel better.

Unfortunately, a few days later, the visiting nurse came to the conclusion that there was no choice but to insert a catheter that would create a permanent line for the IV. This procedure would be performed at home on my parents' king-size mission bed. I was told to lie flat and still while the nurse changed into a surgical gown and prepared a long needle to insert into my arm. My mother summoned up all of her courage to look protectively on from the bedroom doorway.

The nurse confidently inserted the needle into what appeared to be an enormous blue vein at the center of my arm. But, of course, the needle "infiltrated" again and again until finally she had to give up. The next day, I was admitted to the hospital for a third time. Now, the doctor told me, a surgeon would have to use an ultrasound to insert the catheter. To make matters worse, sugar and water were no longer enough for the growing fetus. Fats and lipids would have to be added to my IV.

The young girl in the bed next to mine, also suffering from my condition, had such a bag. It was filled with thick white goo. This was too much for me. I begged the doctor to give me twenty-four hours without the IV and a chance to eat some solids. Perhaps the goo bag next to my bed was inspiration, or perhaps the extreme part of my battle with hyperemesis had run its course. Whatever the case, miraculously, the next day, I held down some toast, then some tea, then some potato. Within two days, I was released from the hospital. The girl in the bed next to mine miscarried on the day I was discharged. I'll never forget that.

From that point on, I slowly started to feel better. I continued to carry around my vomit bowl for the remainder of the pregnancy, but eventually, I felt well enough to walk around and, shortly thereafter, return to work. When I was still vomiting in my ninth month, people assured me that this was the sign of a "strong, healthy fetus," and with such a fighter, "she will surely be a girl." They were right.

When my daughter was born, the first words I heard were: "She's perfect. Enjoy her."

❋ ❋ ❋

Preeclampsia

Preeclampsia (also called pregnancy-induced hypertension or toxemia) is pregnancy-induced high blood pressure. Approximately 5 to 10 percent of pregnant women will be affected by this condition, the causes of which are still unknown (Eisenberg, Murkoff, and Hathaway 1991). It is known, however, that preeclampsia usually occurs in first pregnancies, and women with diabetes, chronic hypertension, or who are carrying more than one baby might be more likely to develop it.

Preeclampsia is often discovered during routine prenatal appointments when blood pressure is monitored, weight is checked (sudden excessive weight gain can be a warning sign), and urine is tested for protein. In other cases, the first symptoms will reveal themselves directly to you. These include swelling of the hands and face, headaches, and blurred vision. Preeclampsia can be very dangerous to both you and your baby so it is important to take your practitioner's recommendations seriously, even though you might be feeling fine when the diagnosis is made.

Treatment options depend on the severity of the particular case. They include varying degrees of bed rest, either at home or in the hospital (ideally while lying on your left side), and, in more advanced cases, medication will be administered to prevent possible seizures. Additionally, you and your baby will be closely monitored for the duration of the pregnancy. Along with frequent blood tests, ultrasounds, and fetal monitoring you'll probably be asked to check your blood pressure several times a day at home.

The only real "cure" for preeclampsia is to deliver your baby. But the less pregnant you are, the less desirable that is. If your condition or the condition of your baby deteriorates, however, and it is determined that delivery is the safest option, a decision might be made to induce labor.

Living with this condition can be very frightening; but with the right monitoring and treatment, the outcome is usually always good and, in the majority of cases, blood pressure returns to normal levels soon after delivery.

❋ ❋ ❋

Jennifer, 26 Years Old

Jennifer was diagnosed with preeclampsia at the beginning of her third trimester and her pregnancy became quite complicated as a result. She lived in fear of every new test result and was terrified of the possibility of delivering her daughter early.

Up until my seventh month, I thought my pregnancy was pretty normal. Even though it was my first and I didn't have anything to compare it with, it seemed to be going smoothly. I felt strong and healthy (albeit rather wide), and I was having a great time decorating the nursery.

I was just entering the third trimester when I suddenly seemed to grow out of all my maternity clothes overnight. At my last check-up, the scale had informed me that I had gained a total of twenty-three pounds after twenty-nine weeks of pregnancy, which my doctor said was right on target for a petite woman like me. Now here I was, standing in the middle of a pile of discarded maternity tops that no longer covered my bulging belly. I was disappointed, but I figured that's what happens in the third trimester—I bought bigger clothes.

I didn't give this sudden weight gain a passing thought until I woke up one Sunday morning to see that my feet had swelled to the size of footballs. I immediately panicked and called for my husband, whose eyes widened when he saw the swelling. It looked as if someone had used a bicycle pump and filled them with air to the point of explosion. I looked up "swelling" in *What to Expect When You're Expecting* (Eisenberg, Murkoff, and Hathaway 1991) and read that swelling of the ankles and feet is nothing to be alarmed about, especially if unaccompanied by other symptoms. It also said that swelling in the hands and face are quite another matter and, if this occurs, a doctor should be notified immediately.

Because the swelling was only in my feet I decided to wait until Monday morning to call my doctor. When I woke up the next morning I could barely put my shoes on and I called my doctor as soon as her office opened. The nurse asked me all kinds of questions: Was my vision blurred? Did my head ache? Were my hands and face swollen? Was there a sharp pain under my ribs? No, I answered, my feet were just huge. The nurse told me to stay off my feet as much as possible and to visit my doctor at my scheduled appointment the following week. She said to call her if I started to see spots or if my hands started swelling, but that what I was experiencing was rather normal in July. My swollen feet were annoying, but I stopped worrying so much after this conversation.

At my next appointment, the nurse weighed me and then weighed me again. Then she brought in a different scale from another room to weigh me. I couldn't believe my eyes—I had gained almost twenty-five pounds since my last visit three weeks ago. She then took my blood pressure and mentioned it was a bit higher than usual. She analyzed my urine sample and left to find the doctor. When my doctor came in, she said there was a trace amount of protein in my urine, which told her I was exhibiting symptoms of preeclampsia. The first thing that popped into my mind was a television episode of *ER*, when a mother with preeclampsia came into the emergency room and, after a terrifying delivery, had a seizure and died. I became very nervous as my doctor explained she would be watching me closely, because preeclampsia could become very dangerous very quickly. She also said that the only "cure" was delivering the baby. I was thirty-two weeks along at that point.

I continued to work since I couldn't really afford time off without pay, and I didn't really think I was very sick at that time. On the advice of my doctor, however, I stayed in bed every evening and weekend. I was still gaining about five pounds a week, and walking from my car to my front door exhausted me. As my blood pressure crept higher, I was given blood tests to monitor my liver and a twenty-four-hour urine culture. The culture involved collecting my urine over a twenty-four-hour period, then bringing it to a lab. I was naturally drinking about a gallon of water a day, and my doctor wanted to see how much of that was being retained by my body, as well as check the protein content of the collected urine. When the results reached the doctor, she called me and ordered me into the hospital immediately. The protein content was high and I was only passing half of the water, making it clear that my kidneys were in danger. "We may need to take the baby," she said. My heart plunged to the floor. I was only in my thirty-fourth week.

In the hospital, I was not allowed to get out of bed except to go to the bathroom. I was put on blood pressure medicine, but my pressure stayed extremely high. I endured a week of five blood tests a day, an amniocentesis (to check the baby's lung maturity), an ultrasound (to check if the placenta was functioning properly), two steroid shots (to force the baby's lungs to grow faster), and painful antinausea shots in my hip to combat the intense nausea that the steroids caused. I was also given a second twenty-four-hour urine culture. The tests were not nearly as agonizing as the waiting. One minute the doctor would plan to induce labor, and then five minutes later she'd decide to wait. I didn't really comprehend that I was getting very sick; all I understood was that my body could poten-tially hurt the baby, and I was terrified the baby would die because of me.

On my sixth day in the hospital, my doctor came in and said they were going to wait (yet again) to induce labor. Two hours later, after analyzing my second urine culture, she said she planned to induce in half an hour. My urine culture had over 10,000 units of protein, and she was worried about kidney failure. I was hooked up to three IVs: one with Pitocin to induce labor, one with saline for hydration, and one with magnesium sulfate to relax my muscles and stabilize my blood pressure. Being on the "mag drip" was horrible. I had no muscle control at all. I couldn't see with my glasses or hold my head up, my speech was slurred and slow, and my brain seemed like it was full of cotton. I felt like a fish out of water, flopping about and scared out of my mind.

I was given an epidural when I was dilated to four centimeters to keep my blood pressure down (contractions equaled stress). I slept for most of the next eighteen hours, when suddenly I felt a deep pressure in my abdomen. The nurse and my husband helped me sit up and "push," and thirty minutes later a baby girl popped into my doctor's arms. The neonatal specialist was right next to me, checking over my wailing daughter. Even in my drugged state, I remember the relief I felt when I heard her cry.

My daughter was five weeks early and weighed four pounds, fifteen ounces. She spent an hour in the neonatal intensive care unit and was then placed in the regular nursery. She developed jaundice but was otherwise in perfect health. I had to stay on magnesium sul-fate for twenty-four hours after she was born, so I missed out on the immediate bonding experience. My doctor explained that the two weeks following delivery were the most critical for me, as I was vul-nerable to having a stroke, so I was to keep taking the blood pres-sure medicine. She also prescribed a diuretic to help reduce the edema. I went home four days after my daughter was born.

Over the next four weeks, my blood pressure normalized and the water weight slowly drained away. At my six-week post-pregnancy check-up, my doctor couldn't tell I had been sick at all and I haven't taken any blood pressure medication since. I have had no lasting effects from the preeclampsia other than an intense fear of becoming pregnant again. I feel I was extremely lucky and am in no hurry to tempt the fates. I am utterly amazed by my daughter every single day, and I am just so grateful we both survived.

Nell, 33

Nell's pregnancy was free of complications until she was three and a half weeks away from her due date. What she and her obstetrician thought was a stomach bug turned out to be a form of preeclampsia called H.E.L.L.P.(Hemolysis, Elevated Liver enzymes, Low Platelets) that makes itself known mainly through abdominal pain, nausea, and sometimes vomiting. Blood pressure is not usually elevated with this much less common variation, but blood tests do reveal low platelet counts and elevated liver enzymes.

My pregnancy had been rather blissful. I lived in a fourth-floor walkup, and taught school, so it was an active pregnancy, which I supplemented with a prenatal yoga class. With the exception of a mysteriously sore tailbone that caused some inconveniently located pain, I really sailed through the lion's share of the pregnancy with minimum discomfort. So, when I woke up three and a half weeks before our due date with stomach pains, I figured it was simply what was coming to me—an inexplicable illness, gas pains, which were my due as a pregnant woman. It did occur to me to question whether it might be a contraction, but whenever I'd asked what labor would feel like I was told, "Oh, you'll know when you're in labor. You'll recognize a contraction!" Then, the person speaking would nod sagely, with a slightly condescending smile. So, that night, despite the occasional stomach pain, I curled up into a yoga-inspired "child's pose" and tried to get back to sleep.

A week later I again woke in the middle of the night with the same sharp pain. During the intervening week, I'd been told that contractions often feel like stomach cramps with an accompanying backache, so I tried to figure out whether I felt any back pain. While contemplating this, it seems my whimpers woke my husband (as I'd hoped) and to his sleepy inquiry I told him (rather sharply) that no, I was not in labor, I simply had gas pains, again. My back didn't hurt, only my stomach. I had my weekly doctor's visit scheduled for later that day, anyway, and would he rub my back because it felt tight. I didn't fall back to sleep.

Monday morning we took the subway to my doctor's office. On the train, I felt a sudden wave of queasiness and threw up the orange juice I'd just consumed. (It was the first food of my day—I hadn't been feeling hungry.) This was the only time I'd thrown up since I'd been pregnant. I was also tired from my lack of sleep the previous night, and, to ensure that I presented as pathetic a picture as possible, I threw up again once we reached my obstetrician's office.

My doctor didn't seem too concerned, though she thought it prudent to take some precautionary blood and urine tests. She mumbled something to herself about preeclampsia, but it was under her breath, and she seemed as willing as I to believe that my symptoms were related more to a stomach bug than pregnancy. She checked routinely for any signs of labor. (The baby, lovingly nicknamed Nibblet, was beautifully positioned but hadn't dropped further from the previous week, and my cervix was still only minimally dilated.) Then I had some blood taken. Needles make me pass out, usually. Well, not pass out, but they do make me light-headed, and I hate blood tests. It was one of the factors that led me to an approach of natural childbirth. I figured I could take the pain of labor, but I really wanted to avoid any IVs or epidural needles. Anyway, after the appointment, Bryan went to work and I went back home, where I ended up kind of miserable, not hungry, my stomach still hurting, and desperate for sleep. I was to call the office the next day if I didn't feel any better.

Tuesday came, and I still felt rotten. I began to feel a bit worried that I still had the stomach bug. I really wanted to be healthy for the delivery. I called the office as soon as it opened at 9 A.M. The results were not yet back and the nurse said she would call when they were available.

It was not until 4:45 P.M. that I got a call from the doctor's office. The blood results were inconclusive, and they wanted me to come back up to the hospital for additional tests. (My obstetrician's office is located in the lobby of the hospital.) The nurse advised that I bring a book to read because the test results could take a while coming back. So, I brought a mystery and a book on pregnancy. I called Bryan and told him about the new testing. We arranged for him to meet me at the hospital. On my walk to the subway, I passed a drugstore, and, on a whim, picked up a toothbrush.

Bryan and I had had several discussions about the difficulties we faced in getting to the hospital from our apartment. Under the best of traffic conditions, it's a thirty-minute trip. Under the worst, it can stretch to nearly ninety. We hatched a plan to rent a hotel room in the city when I went into labor, so we could pass the early part of labor in relative comfort. We also talked about the most reliable car service companies should it start in the middle of the night. I didn't think about any of this as I walked to the train.

Suffice to say that the subway train was rerouted several times on my way uptown. I changed trains three times, after agonizing delays with stalled cars. I passed some of the time reading about preeclampsia. The book said that if it was caught early it wasn't particularly dangerous, that the "cure" was to deliver the baby, and that, in its later stages, magnesium sulfate would likely prevent any seizures or coma. I wondered at its relevance to me, however, as I didn't suffer any of the apparent symptoms: elevated blood pressure, protein in urine, or water retention and bloating. It was after 6:30 P.M. when I reached the hospital. Bryan had worn a path in the pavement from pacing.

We arrived at labor and delivery, where they were to take the blood. In the triage room, the nurse and resident hooked me up to an external baby monitor and took my blood pressure. It was much higher than normal. I attributed this to my hellacious subway journey, and asked the nurse to retake it some minutes later. It was still elevated. The nurse wanted to put in an IV. I explained that my doctor had agreed that I wouldn't have to have an IV unless it became medically necessary. The nurse pointed out that they could take blood through the IV needle and I wouldn't need to be "stuck twice" if I then needed an IV. I told her I didn't mind the sticking. She expressed astonishment. They sent in another resident. She looked at me intently. The condition they were testing for would necessitate my having an IV. I should put it in now to prevent complications. My husband nodded with her. They put in the IV. They took blood.

Meanwhile, I was being monitored for contractions. It seemed that they were six minutes apart. So much for gas pains! So much for recognizing a contraction! Bryan and I hung out awaiting test results. Then the resident returned with the news that I had preeclampsia (so much for symptoms!) and that my obstetrician was heading to the hospital. It seemed that we were to deliver the baby that night. I was glad I had a toothbrush. I was a bit disappointed I had nothing else. So much for music in the delivery room.

I knew that my birth experience would likely involve a few surprises, but I had no idea that everything about my pregnancy and plans for delivery could change so quickly. (See Nell's story in chapter eight.)

Jeney, 29

Jeney felt fine, and was still exercising four times a week, when slightly elevated blood pressure and protein in her urine were discovered during a routine prenatal appointment. A few days later, during the thirty-first week of her pregnancy, she was officially diagnosed with preeclampsia.

When my pregnancy began, I had been doing aerobics six times a week and dieting rather severely for about six months. My husband and I had reason to believe that he was sterile and, therefore, that we would never have children. We had accepted this as fact for more than ten years. The first symptom of pregnancy I experienced was that I started to feel sick any time I went more than two hours without food. I did a home pregnancy test that indicated a positive result before I even set it down, so I made an obstetrician appointment, which, three days later, confirmed I was pregnant. The pregnancy was determined to be eight weeks along at my first ultrasound and the reality that I was going to become a mother was beginning to sink in. I had extremely mixed emotions. I was, of course, thrilled to be pregnant; however, after so many years, my husband and I were comfortable childless.

The pregnancy progressed normally until my fourteenth week, when I had severe pain in my right side and a 102-degree fever. My doctor wanted me to come in immediately. She took one look and sent me to the nearest emergency room. Once there, it was determined that I needed to have my appendix taken out. Of course, the first thing I wanted to know was how this would affect the baby. I was told that an alternative anesthesia would be used for the safety of the fetus, but otherwise the pregnancy would not be at all affected by the surgery. As promised, the appendectomy went smoothly and we sailed through the next three months with no complications. I "passed" all the various tests administered during that time, including the alpha-fetoprotein (AFP) and the glucose tolerance test. Thankfully, it looked as if the appendicitis scare would be the dramatic highlight of the pregnancy.

Then, at thirty-one weeks my weight suddenly jumped eight pounds in two weeks, my blood pressure was a little high, and there was a trace of protein in my urine. The obstetrician drew some blood on a Friday and sent me home with instructions to rest on my left side for two hours every afternoon and evening. Although I felt good at this point and had been working full time and exercising four times a week, I did as I was told during that weekend. On Monday morning my obstetrician called and asked me to come to the office as soon as possible to discuss my blood tests.

I left my office that day thinking that I might have to give up my workouts and cut back on work a little. Over the weekend, I had researched high blood pressure during pregnancy and knew what preeclampsia was, although I had no clue that my condition had reached that level. When I arrived at my doctor's office the nurse practitioner told me that my test results were really worrisome and that they wanted a second batch of blood to test. They also wanted to admit me to the hospital immediately. I was stunned. I told her that I felt fine and that I had been following the instructions I was given three days earlier. Despite that, she said that the results of my blood work looked too bad to not put me in the hospital. I cried all the way home to pack a bag; my husband was shocked to find out I was somehow ill.

As I was signing in to the hospital, I heard a nurse say I was there for suspicion of pregnancy-induced hypertension, and that's when I found out how serious my condition was. Once admitted, a doctor, who I did not know but who was from the same practice as my obstetrician, came in and told me that I needed to be on strict bed rest and that I was going to be given steroids to help develop the baby's lungs. In his opinion, it looked like I would not carry the baby for more than another few days. I kept thinking how unfair it was that my son would have to fight for survival before I had even held him.

Four days later, after repeated blood tests and weight and protein monitoring, they declared I was safe to leave the hospital. My blood pressure had been running at 130/70, which was still a little high for my prepregnancy average, but my lab results showed no other sign of preeclampsia. My sudden decrease in activity had worked and my liver and kidney functions had returned very near to normal. I was told, however, in extremely harsh terms, that strict bed rest was imperative and that if I didn't lie on my left side for the remainder of my pregnancy, I would lose my baby. "Eat lying on your left side and take a sponge bath if you need to, but don't get up." The doctor's instructions, which could have been worded in a more comforting and supportive way, terrified me and made me feel like my world had come to an end. I was too healthy and active for this to happen, I had projects to complete for the baby, and it was the holiday season.

From that point on, I monitored my blood pressure at home and would watch as it went up to dangerous levels every time I sat up, then immediately lower as soon as I lay back down. The obstetrician saw me twice a week and ran nonstress tests on the baby once a week. I also had ultrasounds every three weeks to verify that the baby was still growing at acceptable rates. Every visit included warnings from the doctor that eventually the blood pressure would force us to induce, earlier rather than later was the prediction. My blood pressure would go through the roof at every single appointment because I was terrified that the baby was in jeopardy. I cried every day. I would lay on my sofa waiting for the next kick or squirm to let me know that the baby was OK, while my blood pressure slowly increased from the 130/70 range to 150/90 by the time I was in my thirty-sixth week.

My doctor told me that if we got to thirty-six weeks and my blood pressure was deemed too high, they would induce labor, both for my and the baby's safety. When one of my nonstress tests didn't go so well after that milestone, I was readmitted to the hospital immediately. The labor and delivery nurses monitored the baby's movements and heart rate constantly, and, two days later, I was sent home. Everything was OK with the baby, but my blood pressure was higher than ever.

I was certain my blood pressure would go down if I went home and relaxed. I don't handle hospital environments well and I was terrified that they were going to force me to have the baby before he was ready. Shortly after I got home, my blood pressure came back down, as I predicted. Little did I realize that over the next month I would visit the hospital six more times (on four of those occasions I was admitted) before I delivered my baby. At every doctor's appointment my blood pressure would go up while I waited to be sent to the hospital for one reason or another and it would come back down as soon as I was home. I had been told at thirty-two weeks that the pregnancy would not make it to forty, but, by maintaining strict bed rest and eating a lot of high-protein foods, I managed to keep my baby inside me for forty weeks and five days before labor was induced.

My son, John Spencer, was face up and was delivered via cesarean. They let me labor for fifteen hours. I'd dilated to five centimeters before the doctor came in and said that things weren't progressing. She offered me a cesarean, and after all the baby and I had been through, I agreed wholeheartedly. Even though my high blood pressure had dominated my life for the past months, the only effect it had on the delivery was that a nurse monitored it twice an hour to insure that it wasn't going too high. John Spencer weighed six pounds, six ounces. His Apgar scores were 8 at one minute and 9 at five minutes. He was, and still is, healthy and has shown no ill effects from the preeclampsia.

I've been to the doctor several times since the birth. My blood pressure still hasn't returned to my prepregnancy level, although it has returned to a level that is considered to be within the normal range. The medical professionals have no explanation for why my blood pressure increased at thirty-one weeks and they tell me that there is nothing I could have done differently to prevent it. If I were thinking of getting pregnant again I would seek information from a variety of sources in hope of finding a way to avoid developing this condition again. Because there is no sure way to do so, I would be very reluctant to consider having another child. Conveniently, my husband and I have no plans for more children at this time.

Maggie, 31

Maggie has two children and is pregnant with her third. She was diagnosed with preeclampsia during her first two pregnancies and she knows that it might return this time, especially since she suffers from chronic hypertension.

I have two wonderful children and am now thirteen weeks pregnant with my third. I had preeclampsia during my first two pregnancies and, although there are no signs so far, I am fearful that it will strike again.

It was during the twenty-fourth week of my first pregnancy, during a routine appointment, that my doctor diagnosed pre-eclampsia. My blood pressure was elevated and there was protein in my urine. I was told to keep my eyes open for any symptoms, of which I suffered a few in the following weeks. I became extremely swollen—not just my hands and feet, but all of me. I also began to suffer from migraine-strength headaches, and I was generally feeling very uncomfortable. At the time, I worked as a sales person in a department store. By my thirty-second week, however, I had to leave my job because my legs would become so swollen during the work-day that I could hardly stand.

I was feeling inadequate, fat, and ugly. I didn't know much about preeclampsia and its potential complications so instead of focusing my energy on the seriousness of my condition, I just became more and more frustrated with myself. I rely a great deal on faith and I was confident that God would see me through and everything would be fine. Although this might sound naive, when I learned just how serious my condition could be, I realized that the only other option was constant fear, and I didn't want to live in that state.

The preeclampsia worsened dramatically when I received word of my grandmother's death during my thirty-seventh week. I had a headache that became unbearable and I started seeing "spots" in front of my eyes. Out of concern, my husband took me to my doctor and I arrived at his office in a cold, clammy sweat, with a pounding headache. My blood pressure was 218/110, putting me at risk for a seizure, and I was sent to the hospital immediately. The sense of urgency was lost on me. I just remember feeling so tired that all I wanted to do was sleep. They finally got my attention when they told me that I could begin having seizures at any moment and that both my life and the life of my child were at risk.

At the hospital I was given Dilantin, an anti-seizure and blood pressure medication. I was told that once I was out of risk for seizure, they would induce labor. It was vital that I delivered the baby as soon as possible. Fifteen hours later, at 7 A.M. they started Pitocin. I wasn't dilated or effaced at all so we were starting at square one. Once the Pitocin kicked in, they broke my water. I was hooked up to lots of equipment including numerous monitors, both internal and external, and an EKG machine. The contractions were really unbearable so I was given a little Demerol to take the "edge" off.

Nine hours later, I was ready to deliver. The delivery went pretty smoothly, given all that had happened in the previous twenty-four hours. I gave birth to a very healthy little boy at 4:38 P.M. As is often the case with preeclampsia, my blood pressure went right back to normal shortly after the delivery so my postpartum treatment was minimal.

The situation was a bit different with my second pregnancy. Preeclampsia didn't set in until my thirty-second week and I didn't have anywhere near as much swelling. I still, however, had terrible headaches. I had an office job then that kept me off my feet so I was able to continue working. I was relieved to have what seemed to be a more mild case and assumed that everything would go more smoothly because of it. Nothing prepared me for the labor and birth I was about to experience.

I went into labor the day before my due date. I went to the hospital because I thought my water had broken but was sent home after they determined that the fluid leaking out of me was not amniotic fluid. While I was there, they took my blood pressure and although it was high, the nurse sent me home before the doctor had the chance to give orders for a nonstress test (which checks the baby's heart rate in relation to its movements to see if there are any signs of distress). By the time we got home, there was a message on our machine from the hospital scheduling me for a nonstress test at 7 A.M. the following morning. I went into labor about four hours before I was supposed to have the test.

I wanted to stay home for as long as possible so I could move around freely and not be confined to a bed. After about three and a half hours, my contractions coming eight minutes apart, we decided to head for the hospital.

When we arrived, I was hooked up to all the various monitors and given a nonstress test that showed that the baby was doing fine. They also checked my blood pressure, which was high again, although not as high as with my first. I was, however, given Dilantin as a precautionary measure. My labor slowed down and they started giving me Pitocin to speed it up. Labor moved along fine after that and, six hours later, I was wheeled into the delivery room.

The pushing was awful. The cord was wrapped around my daughter's neck and every time I pushed she would start to crown but the cord would pull her back in. I remember not being allowed to push for every contraction; I had to breathe through every other one, which was really difficult. When this happened, my blood pressure would spike. I was at stroke level, exhausted, out of breath, and ready to give up (in more ways than one). They were about ready to do a cesarean when, as a last ditch effort, my doctor used a vacuum extractor to help pull my daughter out. They had clamped and cut the cord while she was still inside me and when they pulled her out she had no breath sounds and was purple. The neonatal crash unit was there and they took her immediately and administered CPR. I remember not hearing anything. It was the longest, most horrifying wait of my life—not knowing what was going on or whether my baby was going to be all right.

Finally, after what felt like forever, I heard a faint little cry and then a more robust one. She was fine. They brought her over to me so I could see her, but only for a little bit. She was tiny and beautiful and I felt so blessed that we'd survived the whole ordeal. I knew from that moment that she was a very strong little girl. My blood pressure was still pretty high, so they took me to a room and gave me some medication to try and get it back to normal. Eventually it stabilized and we were able to leave the hospital two days after my daughter's birth.

As I write, just beginning the second trimester of my third pregnancy, the fear of preeclampsia is very real. I have been told that I do have chronic hypertension and that even though preeclampsia is most common during first pregnancies, there is still a chance that I might experience it again. I am very careful to watch my salt intake and not let myself become too upset or stressed out. Because of the difficulties I had with both of my previous deliveries, I am seriously considering the option of a cesarean this time around. I'm five years older than I was the last time, my second birth experience was much worse than the first, and this time I began the pregnancy with higher blood pressure levels than before. All of these things weigh on my mind as I anticipate the birth. All I can do, however, is take good care of myself, and, in turn, the baby, and pray that everything works out fine.

❊ ❊ ❊

Gestational Diabetes

Gestational Diabetes (GD) occurs when pregnancy hormones interfere with the effectiveness of insulin in a woman's body and higher than normal glucose levels result. The condition can be detected from routine prenatal urine tests (although some sugar in your urine does not necessarily mean that you have or will develop GD) and, more conclusively, with a glucose tolerance test. This test, usually performed during the fifth month of pregnancy (unless there is reason to administer it earlier), requires that your blood be taken both before and after you ingest a special glucose drink, which comes in a variety of flavors and tastes a lot like flat soda. It is estimated that approximately 2 to 4 percent of all pregnant women in the United States are diagnosed with GD (Verrilli and Mueser 1998).

Although living with GD is a challenge in many ways, complications that can result from this condition are usually easy to prevent with the proper treatment, which includes daily blood glucose monitoring, a special diet, exercise, and, in some cases, insulin injections.

❊ ❊ ❊

Corinna, 32 Years Old

Corinna's pregnancy changed dramatically after she was diagnosed with gestational diabetes. Terrified of the diagnosis and what it would mean for her day-to-day life and the health of her baby, she went through an extremely difficult period before she was able to find the strength to take control of her situation.

The first trimester of my pregnancy was filled with a lot of stress and emotions. I was in my tenth week when my doctor discovered sugar in my urine during the routine prenatal urine test that is performed at every appointment. I was sent for a one-hour glucose tolerance test (GTT) and then a three-hour, and, based on the results, I was diagnosed with gestational diabetes. To say that I was emotional over this would be an understatement. I felt guilt (Did my diet cause this?), anger (Why is this happening to me?), and fear (What is this going to mean for my baby?).

To make matters worse, I had a fear of needles. The idea of checking my own blood sugar using needles terrified me. My doctor referred me to a diabetic clinic at the hospital, which set aside one day a week for pregnant women. During my first appointment, I sat dumbfounded while the nurse and the dietitian explained how to check my glucose levels. I couldn't believe it! They expected me to do this! I couldn't. I wouldn't. I would sit and bawl at the idea of stabbing myself with the little needle to check my glucose level. My husband was supportive and "stabbed" himself in sympathy to show how easy it was. That only made me cry harder. I wouldn't even try.

I went to see my regular doctor. I begged her to help me find an alternative. She gave me the one piece of advice that started to change things for me. She said, "Ultimately you don't have to do anything. It's up to you. We can only say what is best, but the decision is yours." That statement empowered me and shortly thereafter I started testing my blood sugar. Then I began to test it without crying. Then testing at work (with other people around), and from there it got easier and easier.

The diet was never a problem. Yes, it took some trials and errors to figure out what I could eat and in what portions. I was learning that testing my blood sugar wasn't so much a punishment, but a source of valuable information that helped me to modify my diet. As I started feeling better and my anger faded, I began to educate myself. I found every bit of information I could on GD. I soon learned that my guilt was unfounded—there was nothing that I did to cause it (just as there was nothing I could do to stop myself from getting it). I learned that GD was a result of pregnancy hormones interfering with the production and effectiveness of the body's insulin. I learned about the various effects that GD could have on my baby and me: I could have a large baby (resulting in a hard labor and possible cesarean), a prematurely aging placenta (this is very serious since the placenta is the life force for the baby), or a hypoglycemic baby at birth (if the baby's body is compensating for its mother's high glucose levels, he or she may produce an overabundance of insulin, then when removed from the mother's glucose supply, the baby may require extra). There was also the possibility that my child might contract juvenile diabetes in its early teens.

By the time I was in my fourth month I had begun to take my GD very seriously. I strove to perfect my glucose readings and my diet had never been healthier. I went for walks during my lunch hour and if my numbers were high after dinner, I'd walk around our building before bed. I learned that saving some of my chores until after dinner would help my glucose readings.

As I rounded the corner into my sixth month, I started feeling tired and my glucose numbers became harder to control. Meals that had previously been fine would now give me high readings. My diabetic registered nurse and dietitian said that around the thirtieth to thirty-sixth week of pregnancy, the hormones from the placenta increase, making the diabetes more difficult to manage and perhaps this was happening earlier for me. When I spoke with my obstetrician about my levels as well as my increased fatigue, she told me to stop working immediately. I was feeling so tired that I was more than happy to follow her orders.

Being at home, I was able to take longer walks and make better meals. This resulted in better glucose numbers. Additionally, during these last months I was having fetal monitoring (nonstress tests) once a week. This was done to ensure that my baby was active and moving and that the placenta wasn't aging prematurely. I would lay with the sensors on my tummy, listening to my baby's heartbeat. It's one of the most soothing sounds in the world.

As my pregnancy progressed into the seventh and then eighth month, my numbers again became difficult to manage. I was then referred to a diabetic doctor. Even though my glucose levels were no longer in the "optimum" range, they were not quite in the insulin requiring range either. As my baby grew (and I was getting bigger as a result), my pelvic bone ached (making walking a chore), and sleeping was becoming very uncomfortable. I was also constantly adjusting my meals. I found that milk had become a big offender. I could not have any milk after lunch. If I had even half a glass of milk with dinner, my after dinner number would be high and my morning fasting number would be high as well. I also discovered that a former "safe" meal (spaghetti with tomato sauce) had become off-limits. Instead of tomato sauce, I began to make spaghetti with butter and cheese.

During the last month of my pregnancy my husband and I decided to move to a bigger apartment in our building. All of the packing and the stress of the move were not good for me, and my glucose numbers were high as a result.

I had an ultrasound in my thirty-ninth week to check the approximate size of the baby, which estimated that my baby weighed almost ten pounds. Because of this, my obstetrician decided to induce my labor. A large baby, one of the possible side effects of this condition, is one of the biggest fears of women with GD because of the increased possibility of a cesarean birth.

On the day following my estimated due date, I went to the hospital to have gel applied to my cervix to stimulate labor. I was sent home afterwards. I wondered if labor would begin while my husband moved our belongings from our one-bedroom apartment to our new two-bedroom apartment down the hall. When nothing happened, I went back to the hospital for more gel. My father was over helping out and we picked up food for dinner. After we ate, I went back to rest while they went back to moving.

My father went home at 9:30 P.M. and my husband continued moving until after 10 P.M. When he began getting undressed, exhausted and looking forward to a night of sleep in our new bedroom, I changed his plans. My contractions were coming roughly every four minutes. We couldn't phone anyone (including the hospital) because our phone hadn't been connected yet, so my poor husband got redressed and off to the hospital we went.

I refused the offer of the wheelchair when we arrived at the hospital. I wanted to keep walking. Not only did it help me deal with the contractions, but it helped keep them regular. When we finally made it to labor and delivery, the doctor on duty asked me to change into a hospital gown and wait as he was with another patient. It was at this point that I threw up my lovely dinner. The doctor sent me straight down to the laboring room.

I labored throughout the night. At some point in the early morning, my water broke in the shower and a few hours later I was four centimeters dilated. It was time for an epidural. The doctors had a hard time giving it to me because my spine curves in an odd way. It took several anesthesiologists and a full day of laboring before the epidural worked. The first epidural simply didn't take, the next one only gave limited relief, and the third, finally, was perfect. It was fantastic! I couldn't feel any more contractions, the Pitocin was increased to keep my labor going (my contractions had slowed down during the period before the epidural started working), and I was dilating well.

My GD showed up in the most unusual way during the second day of my labor. It was determined that I was in need of nourishment and was given a glucose drip that elevated my blood sugar and made it necessary for me to have periodic insulin shots.

When I finally began to push, it became apparent that my baby's shoulder was stuck. I was rushed into the operating room just in case I needed an emergency cesarean. This was the most frightening part of the entire labor. It was scary going from the dimly lit, comfortable laboring room into the bright and sterile operating room. Happily, despite the preparations and precautions, my obstetrician was able to bring my daughter into the world with the help of forceps.

When they placed my daughter on my chest, everything was forgotten. The glucose tolerance tests, the four daily glucose checks, the strict diet, the stress of balancing meals, even the labor. All forgotten. All I knew was the love for my daughter who lay on my chest, crying.

And she was healthy. Catherine Alice weighed in at eight pounds, fifteen ounces; a full pound lighter than the ultrasound estimate. Her Apgar scores were 9 and 10. She did not have hypoglycemia (low blood sugar, common with newborns born to GD moms), nor jaundice. She and I learned to breastfeed very quickly. I can't express in words how much I love her.

Angela, 28

Unlike Corinna, Angela wasn't diagnosed with gestational diabetes until the beginning of her third trimester. In her case, diet alone was not enough to keep it under control.

When I was twenty-eight weeks pregnant, I was diagnosed with gestational diabetes. I wasn't too surprised because different types of blood sugar problems run rampant in my family. For two weeks, I was on the special gestational diabetic diet and testing my blood sugar numbers at home four times a day by poking my finger. At first, it was a novelty. I got my own special foods that nobody else could have and I got to eat practically all day long. On the GD diet, one has to eat small meals every two to four hours to keep the blood sugar levels even. My blood sugar numbers were continually too high and getting higher so I decided that the diet was a joke and I tossed it aside.

I went back to my regular eating habits for a week and kept monitoring my blood sugar. The numbers were still high, of course, but not as high as while on the diet. I thought I was doing great and had the problem beat. That is, until I told my doctor. He put me back on the diet and warned me that if I had one more high number within a week, I'd be put on insulin. Every blood sugar number that I took that week was too high and by the time I was thirty-two weeks pregnant I had a bottle of Humulin U (insulin) in my refrigerator.

I thought I wouldn't have a problem giving myself shots because I'd given insulin shots to my grandma for years and I'd been poking myself with the lancet pen to check my blood sugar numbers for weeks. There was a big difference. First of all, it wasn't my grandma I was poking, it was me. Secondly, I couldn't actually see the needle on the lancet pen so the device didn't look like anything I should be afraid of. The first time I actually "shot up," I got everything ready with my leg skin pinched and the needle ready to stab. I kept moving the syringe up and down, like I was saying, "One for the money, two for the show, three to get ready and here we go," but it didn't go in. I got the tip of the needle close to the skin, but some cosmic force stopped it just in the nick of time.

Something seemed inherently wrong with my holding a needle to my own skin with any type of willingness to stab. I thought I had my brain completely convinced that it wasn't a problem, but I still couldn't get my hand and arm to cooperate. I took a deep breath and remembered the instructions I'd read in a GD book that said to keep the syringe at a 90-degree angle. I did that and just went for it. What a big surprise. There was absolutely no pain at all! In fact, it was much less difficult to give myself the insulin shot than it was to check my blood sugar numbers with the lancet pen.

My baby girl was born three weeks early and very healthy. During labor, I had to check my blood sugar every hour with a nurse standing by to record the results. When Samantha was born, her little foot was lanced every hour for the first eight hours to check her glucose numbers. Sometimes a baby will get used to the high sugar levels in the womb, and after the birth, when it's suddenly gone, the baby's levels drop too low. Luckily, we didn't have that problem, but it was hard to see my little girl go through that.

Wendy, 31

Wendy also had to deal with diabetes during her pregnancy but she did not have gestational diabetes. Early in her first trimester she was diagnosed with Type II adult onset diabetes, a condition she will have for the rest of her life. Unfortunately, this was not the only complication she would experience during her long nine months of pregnancy.

I was diagnosed with polycystic ovarian syndrome when I was twenty-five years old and knew that getting pregnant might be difficult or impossible without fertility drugs. When my husband, Chuck, and I decided we were ready for a family, I went off the medication I was taking for that condition, and my birth control pills, and we tried to conceive naturally, which we were lucky enough to do after eight months. When I took a home pregnancy test and discovered it was positive, I was in complete shock. I didn't believe the results until I went to the doctor and had them verified. I was ecstatic.

I went to see my obstetrician for the first time when I was eight weeks pregnant. During the appointment I mentioned that I'd had problems in the past with elevated blood sugar (at one point being diagnosed as borderline diabetic). Upon learning this, she decided to give me the glucose tolerance test, which is usually administered around the fifth month of pregnancy, immediately. My blood sugar level rose to 348 during the test and my obstetrician referred me to an endocrinologist who would manage my insulin administration throughout the course of my pregnancy.

I did not have the kind of diabetes that is specific to pregnancy but was diagnosed with Type II adult onset diabetes, which, unfortunately, I will have for the rest of my life. I suspected that I had diabetes because I was tired a lot and thirsty all of the time, although I wasn't positive because these symptoms are also common to early pregnancy. I also found myself feeling sluggish after I ate anything sweet, which raised a red flag in my head. But to be honest, I was in a state of denial about the whole thing, not really wanting to learn the truth.

In addition to the endocrinologist, I saw a diabetic counselor who showed me how to give myself injections and to test my sugar levels four times a day with a machine called an Accu-check reader. After drawing a drop of blood from my fingertip with a lancet, I'd put it on a digital test strip that fits into the machine, which measures the glucose level. I recorded these levels in a book and shared it with my doctor weekly so my insulin dosage could be adjusted. I was injecting myself with insulin three times a day. I also went to a dietitian who helped me manage my diet to keep my blood sugar level in check.

I was constantly worried about my baby after I learned about the various problems that are associated with untreated diabetes, including missing fingers and toes, spina bifida, and heart irregularities. I saw a specialist and was given ultrasounds every month. I was terrified at every one of these appointments, never knowing if I was going to hear bad news, and feeling as if no one was being sufficiently encouraging. It took a lot of time and energy to deal with the diabetes and I felt lucky that my other first trimester symptoms were minimal.

When I was in my sixth month, the baby was quite active and I was feeling more confident about its health. It seemed that things were finally settling down when I had to deal with one of the most difficult events of my life. My mother, who had been battling cancer for two years, died. The fact that she wouldn't be there for the rest of my pregnancy and the birth of my baby was incredibly difficult for me. She fought hard to stay alive so that she could see my baby and I was devastated that she didn't make it. It gave me some comfort to think that she was watching over me from above, but I missed her terribly.

And then came the preeclampsia. In my thirty-third week, my hands and ankles swelled up and did not get any better after a night of rest. At first it was mild, but it progressively got worse. For two weeks, I took two-hour lunches so I could go home and lie down in the middle of the day. I was trying to convince my doctor to continue to let me work full time since it would have been a major financial burden to stop at that point. She agreed to let me try these two-hour rest periods as a compromise.

Unfortunately, it didn't appear to help much. The swelling was at its most extreme the day following Thanksgiving after I'd been on my feet a great deal preparing the holiday dinner. I went to the hospital for my scheduled nonstress test the following evening (these were being done weekly due to the diabetes). While I was there, my obstetrician examined me. She prescribed blood pressure medication and advised complete bed rest. From my thirty-fifth week onward, I couldn't work and I could only get up to use the bathroom, get something to eat, and go to doctor appointments.

I was just beginning my thirty-seventh week when, during my usual visit to the obstetrician, my blood pressure was so high that they decided to induce labor right away. I was admitted to the hospital at 4 P.M. and they started giving me Pitocin through an IV. The contractions were extremely mild and they stopped completely when the IV was shut off that night. They started administering Pitocin again the next morning and kept increasing it throughout the day. One of the hardest things about my labor was not being able to move because of the fetal monitor that was attached to me to watch the baby's heartbeat.

By late afternoon, they broke my water and installed a head monitor on the baby. Her heartbeat was jumping around quite a bit, and that concerned the doctor. I remember thinking that I just wanted this whole ordeal to be over. When the pain got so intense that I couldn't stand it anymore, I asked for, and received, an epidural. Shortly after that, I was checked and was nine centimeters dilated. At that point, the obstetrician discovered that the umbilical cord was wrapped around the baby's neck and I was told that, due to all the circumstances, an emergency cesarean section would be the safest way to deliver. I was wheeled into the operating room and given general anesthesia because the epidural had not had enough time to work.

With my husband by my side, my daughter, Daria Kay, was born, three weeks shy of her scheduled due date. She weighed six pounds, three ounces, and was eighteen and a half inches long. She was the picture of health! I was allowed to see her briefly, for the first time, later that evening after I woke up from the surgery. She was beautiful and had a full head of dark brown hair. I felt cheated that I did not get to see her birth but the situation was complicated and scary and I know the measures taken were necessary.

❋   ❋   ❋

Incompetent Cervix

Incompetent cervix is a condition in which a cervix is softer and weaker than normal and, as a result, might open prematurely during pregnancy. This problem, which usually manifests itself in the second trimester and is estimated to occur in 2 percent of pregnancies, can lead to preterm birth or the loss of the pregnancy (Eisenberg, Murkoff, and Hathaway 1991). As with many other pregnancy-related complications, the causes of incompetent cervix are not always clear, although there are some factors that have been linked to it, including exposure to the drug DES in utero (prescribed decades ago to many of our mothers to prevent miscarriage) and prior trauma to the cervix. Symptoms include feelings of heaviness or pressure in the pelvic area and increased vaginal discharge (with or without blood).

Diagnosing this condition can be tricky and often occurs only after a woman has lost a pregnancy in her second trimester, usually without experiencing labor. However, in some cases an ultrasound image showing a short cervix might also lead to diagnosis.

If you do suffer from this condition, you will likely be treated with cerclage, a simple surgical procedure with a high rate of success that involves having your cervix stitched closed. This is usually performed around the twelfth to fourteenth week of pregnancy. In most cases, the stitches will be removed a few weeks before your due date and labor often begins shortly after that. Depending on your situation, varying degrees of bed rest might also be recommended for the remainder of your pregnancy.

❋ ❋ ❋

Carol, 34 Years Old

As is often the case, Carol didn't know she suffered from incompetent cervix until she lost her first baby. She was relieved to learn there was a treatment available that could prevent this from happening again, but her subsequent pregnancies required a great deal of strength and courage nonetheless.

I have been pregnant three times and was treated for incompetent cervix during each pregnancy. The initial time was during an emergency procedure while I was in premature labor with my first baby. My obstetrician unsuccessfully attempted closing my cervix by means of purse-string stitches known as cerclage. In light of my history, my doctors decided to perform planned cerclages in my next two pregnancies, which successfully held my cervix closed until my babies had, at least, reached viability.

Incompetent cervix took me by complete surprise the first time. It had been a wonderful pregnancy up until the loss of my baby. I had not experienced the discomfort of morning sickness, I'd gained the recommended amount of weight, and I generally felt very healthy and happy. I still remember how exciting it was to feel the baby move for the first time, reminding my husband and me that we were really on our way to becoming parents. But my perfect pregnancy came to a sudden end during my twenty-second week.

I'd been having some contractions for about a week and, having never been pregnant before, I just assumed they were the harmless Braxton-Hicks contractions I'd read about. I mentioned them to my doctor and he, too, thought they were Braxton-Hicks. Then one morning, getting out of bed, I discovered that my mucous plug had dislodged, which I knew was a sign of trouble from having read my pregnancy books so thoroughly. I'd read that the mucous plug can slip out just prior to the onset of labor and that it is usually pink in color since it contains a small amount of blood.

The enormous amount of slippery, unmistakably pink mucus on my toilet tissue left no doubt in my mind that my pregnancy was in jeopardy. I drove myself to the hospital and, much to my surprise, the doctor determined that I was four centimeters dilated and the amniotic sac had partially descended through my cervix, something he referred to as "hourglassing." I was given two options: They could attempt an emergency cerclage even though there wasn't much cervix to take hold of, or they could keep me tilted (with my head below my feet) for as long as possible. I was also told that the baby needed at least eight more weeks inside to have a chance at a decent start in life and that if he was born that day, chances were great that he would not survive for more than a few minutes.

My husband and I chose the emergency cerclage. They tilted my body long enough to get the amniotic sac back into my uterus so the doctor could begin the procedure. He made a brave attempt, but my contractions got worse as my cervix was disturbed, pushing the amniotic sac out again so that it accidentally broke during his stitching. My son arrived stillborn about an hour later, weighing one pound, two ounces and measuring twelve inches in length.

During this tragic event, my husband and I were in complete shock. It seemed like a bad dream and we just wanted it to end as soon as possible. Feeling drugged and sick to my stomach from the pain medication only added to my torment. The nurses provided excellent physical care as well as much-needed emotional support for both my husband and me. They offered to wrap our baby in a blanket and let us hold him, take hand and footprints of him, as well as a photograph. This was all so overwhelming that we initially turned them down. We were so distraught that we just wanted to get out of there so we could start forgetting about the awful experience we'd just lived through.

To this day, I feel lucky that we reconsidered their offer and decided to hold our baby so we could say good-bye. We also had his hand and footprints made. He was so small yet so perfectly developed right down to his tiny fingernails. His eyes were still fused shut, his hair had barely begun growing on his scalp, and he was quite red skinned and bruised from his breech birth, but he was so very, very beautiful to us. We still declined the picture, and I regret that decision because I would love to have such visual proof of my first son's existence. My husband, on the other hand, still prefers his own mental image to a photograph that would show all of our son's bruises and his parchment-thin skin.

I was discharged the same night and remember being so exhausted that I couldn't even bring myself to think about what I'd just been through. My first instinct was to just go to sleep. By the middle of the night, however, the grief took hold and I was completely overwhelmed by the deepest, most empty feeling I'd ever known. Early in the morning I had awoken to the happy feeling of my baby's kick, and the same night I had gone to bed with him gone forever. This was quite a jolt for a happy young couple excitedly expecting their first child.

The only positive thing about this awful experience was that it served to alert us (and our doctor) that I had an incompetent cervix. Luckily, there were treatment options that could be used for future pregnancies. My doctor reassured us that with an early cerclage and careful monitoring, I could carry a baby almost to term. He told us to expect bed rest at some undetermined point in my pregnancies, as well as the need to take the medication Brethine to calm my uterus. Brethine is really an asthma medication that calms smooth muscles in the body and, when used during pregnancy, it acts to calm an irritable uterus. The doctor's words gave us hope and confidence. After a few months we began trying to conceive our next child.

I became pregnant rather quickly and although I did not have any fears while trying to conceive, as soon as I found out that our next baby was indeed on the way, I panicked. Seeing a positive pregnancy test made me just as joyful this time, but a little black cloud quickly gathered over my shoulder as I began to mark the weeks of my pregnancy on the calendar. I had to stop at week twenty-two and cry, and every week after that, I prayed for success this time around. Once again, I had a mostly wonderful first trimester with no morning sickness and a hearty appetite. Because I had the same cravings and aversions as with my previous pregnancy I suspected I was carrying another boy. This may have been "old wives" type thinking, but my prediction came true.

We had our first scare at nine weeks when I spotted a little brownish blood and had mild cramping, but the doctor said it was most likely due to the placenta growing. In spite of his reassurance, we were very nervous about what the future held.

In my thirteenth week, the doctor placed a cerclage in my cervix and the procedure went well. My biggest complaint was the nausea and vomiting I suffered later as a result of the anesthesia they used. The doctor said light bleeding would be normal for a few days, but if it got heavy to call him immediately. He instructed me to stay off my feet for several days and take the antibiotics he prescribed. Having a cerclage gave me some peace of mind, but it was not to last for very long.

In my seventeenth week, the doctor discovered that my cervix, although not at all dilated, was 90 percent effaced. He ordered immediate bed rest and I began taking Brethine and antibiotics. I also used a home monitoring service daily. Twice a day I would strap a monitoring device around my belly for an hour to determine whether I was having contractions. The recording was then sent over the phone line to an office staffed with nurses who would call me once they received it. They would ask me general questions about how I was feeling and how much I felt the baby moving. I was allowed five contractions per hour, but if I exceeded that, the nurse would tell me to drink some water, which also calms the uterus, and monitor for another hour. If I still had more than five contractions, I was told to go to the hospital. Many of our scares during that pregnancy journey were the result of too many contractions. Luckily, each time this happened, I was sent to the hospital where a shot of Brethine calmed my uterus down and I was sent back home. My cervix never dilated.

Happily I made it to my thirty-fifth week without giving birth (the doctor had set thirty-three as a goal) and was able to discontinue bed rest. A few days later, my cerclage was removed. I loved being up and around after so many weeks of lying on the sofa. I finally felt like a "normal" pregnant woman. As the days wore on my contractions intensified and it seemed very strange to actually be in a position to welcome them.

By the end of my thirty-sixth week, they were regular and close together and I was admitted to the hospital. Several hours later my wonderful little son arrived safely. He weighed six pounds, four ounces, and was nineteen and a half inches long. My husband and I were absolutely overjoyed, especially in light of the tragedy we had lived through the year before and all the weeks of stress and worry we'd endured to bring this baby close to full term. His birth was a dream come true!

When my son was almost three years old, I became pregnant with my daughter. We had been trying to conceive for several months without any success. When my husband accepted a job that would involve lots of overtime and a cross-country move, we decided to postpone a new baby until our lives settled down somewhat. Mother Nature had her own ideas, however, because just one week before our big move I discovered I was pregnant. My deepest feelings were of joy and happiness about the new life I had inside me. But that joy was greatly tempered by worries about how we would manage another high-risk pregnancy in an unfamiliar city with the added complications of finding day care for my son and my husband's long working hours.

I quickly found an obstetrician in our new town and explained my pregnancy history. He agreed that an early cerclage would be a wise course of action and performed the procedure during my thirteenth week. Again, I recovered without any heavy bleeding or infection. In spite of the positive outcome of our last cerclage, I was still very nervous during this pregnancy, and the further I progressed, the more worried I became.

This doctor also had a different method of checking the condition of my cervix, which made me uneasy. Whereas my previous doctor checked my cervix every two weeks by means of a standard internal exam, this doctor preferred checking by means of vaginal ultrasounds every five to six weeks. I knew that my cervix could change very quickly and without much warning, and I was not happy that so much time passed between ultrasounds. Additionally, caring for my active son all day without my husband around was becoming stressful. Fortunately, my cervix appeared long and firm at my fifteen-week ultrasound; I also discovered that I was carrying a girl. This was exciting news because I really wanted at least one daughter.

My cervix was still in great shape at my twenty-week ultrasound and it was then that I began to relax, somewhat. I even started thinking that maybe this pregnancy would be entirely different from the first two and that I would carry to thirty-eight weeks or longer. I still begged my doctor for precautionary bed rest because I frequently had cramps and I wanted my husband to be able to provide "doctor's orders" to his employer that would recommend he reduce his work hours. I felt even more confident after my son began attending day care, relieving me of the daily physical burden of caring for him, and I began taking a light dose of Brethine. My next ultrasound was scheduled for twenty-six weeks, but, to my great surprise, I never made it that far.

During my twenty-fifth week I noticed a small amount of pinkish mucus on my underwear and, having been through this before, suspected that it was part of the mucous plug. I was admitted to the hospital that night after my doctor discovered that I was two centimeters dilated and that a little "button" of amniotic sac was showing through the small opening in my cervix. This news brought back all the fear and pain of my first loss and I was terrified.

Labor was held off for five days with magnesium sulfate, which acts in a similar fashion to Brethine but is much more intense in its effects. It made me feel extremely hot, jittery, and unable to focus my eyes well. I also received a few injections of steroids to help mature my daughter's lungs. I lost more and more of my mucous plug during this time.

I had barely accepted the fact that I would be hospitalized for several weeks when my body insisted on going into labor and delivering my daughter. I started spotting increasing amounts of blood and contracting at consistent fifteen-minute intervals. The nurses turned up my magnesium sulfate dosage a couple of times, but the contractions would not stop. In fact, they started coming closer together and the bleeding became quite heavy. It was a Sunday evening and the on-call doctor was not on the premises, but when the nurses recognized a "point of no return," they told him to come quickly.

It was a night of extreme pain and terror for me. I was so very, very frightened for my daughter. As my labor continued, she began showing signs of distress. Her heart rate was taking longer and longer to come back up to its normal level after each contraction, and the contractions kept getting closer so that neither she nor I were getting much rest in between. Finally, the on-call doctor arrived and ordered that I be moved at once to the delivery room. I don't remember much of this because I'd just received a shot of Demerol, but my husband said everyone started to move very quickly. If the doctor had come a bit sooner I would have had a cesarean delivery (which is preferred with premature births since it spares the baby's delicate head the trauma of vaginal delivery), but it was too late for that now. My water broke as I was placed on the delivery table, and then everyone yelled, "Push!" My daughter was born after the second push and she cried immediately—something my thirty-six week son had not even done.

Miraculously, she was also breathing on her own and did not need the assistance of a ventilator. She did, however, need supplemental oxygen given at high pressure to keep her lungs partially inflated. Her neonatologist later told us that only 5 percent of babies as premature as she was could breathe so well. My daughter came into this world weighing one pound, fifteen ounces, and she was fifteen inches long. I had completed twenty-six weeks and three days of pregnancy. After the placenta was delivered, the doctor checked my cervix to find out if any damage had occurred since they failed to remove the cerclage before the birth. Everything looked fine and he concluded that the knot came untied with all the pressure and the stitches just fell out.

For the remainder of the night I was mostly out of it, maybe from the Demerol or maybe from the emotional upheaval, probably from both. However, I can recall vividly the dream I had. I dreamt that I had lost my daughter, just like I'd lost my first son, and I was extremely sad and felt a sense of intense failure. That night, my husband also dreamt that we'd lost her. The next day, with great trepidation, we met with the neonatologist who gave us encouraging news about her condition, but was careful not to paint too rosy a picture since she still had a long way to go.

I had a difficult emotional time during my daughter's stay in the neonatal intensive care unit (NICU). It was depressing coming home without her in my arms and having a postpartum body without a baby to care for and cuddle. The empty feeling from the sudden end of my first pregnancy returned. Both times my body did not have the chance to reach those final pregnancy weeks when a woman's hormones prepare her mentally and physically for her baby's birth. Whenever I went about familiar daily activities, like housework or taking care of my son, it felt like my pregnancy had been nothing but a dream and this son in front of me was my only child. Taking care of him reassured me that I was a successful mother, although I felt like a failure whenever I thought of my daughter.

When I visited her in the hospital, it was very difficult for me to feel like her mother at all. The nurses were the ones caring for her every need and I was scared to even touch her. She was an extra-sensitive premature baby and did not like to be touched or talked to. The nurses even put a sign over her little bed reminding everyone to be very quiet around her. This made it very difficult for me to interact with my little girl. I was able to hold her a few times, but only for very short periods since she would become unstable quickly. Added to this emotional turmoil was the constant stress and worry about her condition. At one point, she developed an infection in her lungs that brought on pneumonia. This was my bleakest time during the entire NICU ordeal. I was so worried that she would die, and so depressed, that I barely got myself out of bed in the morning. I went about the day like a zombie, barely managing to care for my son. Many times the only thing I could do was just sit and hold him on my lap. I did not even have the energy to read him a book.

Eventually my daughter's pneumonia cleared. Over the next several weeks, she grew stronger and acquired the reflexes necessary for life outside the womb that all babies develop in the month prior to birth. During this time, I was allowed to feed and clothe her and change her diapers. It might seem strange, but she still seemed like someone else's baby. All that fear of losing her, the lack of nurturing contact when she was too sensitive to touch, the depression from postpartum hormones, and the many NICU stresses, all added up to a critical delay in our bonding.

When she finally came home from the NICU we were able to slowly get used to each other and the bonding process began. She had been in the hospital for two and a half months, and she came home about three weeks before my original due date. She needed supplemental oxygen and a monitor to measure her blood/oxygen saturation and heart rate. It was awkward moving about the apartment with her attached to wires and tubes, but we somehow managed for the few months she needed those aids. As she grew bigger and stronger with each month, life gradually returned to normal for all of us. Looking at my daughter today, you would never guess that she had been a micro-preemie! At two and a half years of age she is just like any other happy, healthy toddler!

As we battle our particular symptoms, endure the necessary treatments, and worry about the health of our babies, those of us who experience pregnancy complications will often find ourselves feeling guilty, inadequate, and betrayed by our bodies. Fear, sadness, and anger are also likely to creep into the picture. As is often the case in difficult circumstances, however, we'll be able to call forth a surprising amount of strength and courage, while we do whatever we can to protect the life inside of us.

Chapter Six

Exercise, Nutrition, and Weight Gain: Living with Our Pregnant Bodies

Whether you're an aerobics queen or a couch potato, a healthy eater or a disciple of Kraft macaroni and cheese, a daily weight checker or a woman who doesn't own a scale, during your pregnancy you'll find yourself spending lots of time thinking about exercise, nutrition, and weight gain.

Women's National Basketball Association (WNBA) star Sheryl Swoopes worked out and played five-on-five basketball throughout her pregnancy (All 2000). Vicki Iovine (1995), on the other hand, devotes eleven pages in *The Girlfriends' Guide to Pregnancy* discussing the reasons why women should say no to exercise during those long months. As for nutrition, some of us will find it difficult to eat anything, especially in the first trimester when even the smell of certain foods turns our stomach. Others will eat at Taco Bell more during those early months than they have in their entire lives.

Stepping on the scale at the beginning of every prenatal appointment will definitely be more traumatic for some women than for others. But everyone will find themselves amazed by the sometimes erratic and unpredictable weight gain patterns that pregnancy brings. Our old bodies become nothing more than a memory as we watch our breasts swell, our bellies grow, and stretch marks appear in places we had no idea could be stretched any further.

How we eat, exercise, and put on weight during pregnancy will be unique to our particular body. It's certainly not a bad idea to set some goals as long as we realize that this body is no longer completely our own.

❄   ❄   ❄

Jennifer, 26 Years Old

Jennifer, an avid exerciser, was committed to maintaining a reasonable, yet serious, exercise regimen throughout her pregnancy. For various reasons, this plan was abandoned by the time she reached the halfway mark.

Before pregnancy I was a typical, self-absorbed, midtwenties gal who was determined to keep my slender figure after getting my first desk job. Diet Coke and salad was my usual lunch, and the gym served as my second home (work, of course, was my first). I was in the entertainment business, and I was focused on staying trim, trendy, and efficient.

Eight months after I was officially hired, I found out I was pregnant. Because I'd gotten pregnant while taking birth control pills, the news came as quite a shock. I was not happy (although it did explain why I suddenly couldn't lose five pounds of water weight). A baby was not supposed to be part of my life plan yet, and all I knew of pregnancy was that I'd have to give up Diet Coke and take some enormous daily vitamin. I had no idea how to begin a diet or exercise routine that was fit for a baby.

Until my first appointment with the obstetrician, I studied the exercise/nutrition chapters in *What to Expect When You're Expecting* (Eisenberg, Murkoff, and Hathaway 1991), which I loved. I decided to keep going to the gym and just use lighter weights. I also lowered my aerobic intensity, usually choosing to walk around an indoor track or to swim (water is much easier on tender pregnant breasts), and I gave up abdominal crunches. I wanted to be strong for delivering the baby, and most literature said exercising was good for both mother and child.

I tried to follow the book's suggested diet plan, but my body had its own idea of what I should be eating. It seemed my body instinctively desired certain foods, such as protein, fruit, and dairy (after I visited my obstetrician, I added prenatal vitamins and calcium supplements to my plate). I found myself eating food I normally didn't prefer, such as peanut butter, tuna, and cheese, and I seemed to be hungry all the time.

I had to eat something every two hours, whether it was cheese and crackers or half a watermelon. I had no control over the hunger or food choice. Lunch could be a half container of cottage cheese, four scrambled eggs, or six oranges. By my second trimester I was inhaling hamburgers and eating bread by the half loaf. I did my best to eat healthfully, and not once did I drink caffeine (my proudest feat). My diet mostly consisted of red meat, cheese, peanut butter, and fruit—most of which I hadn't allowed myself to eat for years.

I grew out of all my pants about a month after I discovered I was pregnant. My waist grew wider, to the point that it was almost even with my shoulders, before my belly grew outward. My behind grew wider as well, and for a while I thought the baby had taken up residence there. Around the middle of my third month, strange aches and pains started occurring. The bottoms of my feet became incredibly tender. It felt as if I had walked barefoot for days over sharp rocks. I finally had to buy expensive tennis shoes with air cushions in the soles. I stopped walking for exercise because my feet just couldn't take it. Ligaments began to stretch with my growing uterus, and weight lifting became uncomfortable.

When my hands started going numb in my fourth month (a pregnancy-induced carpal tunnel syndrome), I simply gave up exercising altogether and it didn't bother me at all. With those second trimester hormones flowing, I felt I could take on the world. By my twenty-ninth week of pregnancy, I had gained almost twenty-five pounds, which made me very nervous. The book said that twenty-five pounds was about the most weight you should gain for the whole nine months—I still had three to go. My doctor assured me that this was normal with my small frame, but I was starting to worry that I would never stop eating like an elephant, nor would I stop looking like one.

Some of the side effects of pregnancy were annoying, but I didn't really start to get uncomfortable until I entered the third trimester. A sudden and sizable weight gain in my seventh month made me feel lethargic and huge, and although it seemed odd to me, I had no idea that it was anything more than a typical late-pregnancy phenomenon. It certainly made it more difficult to get around, and I spent a lot more time on the couch. In my thirty-first week of pregnancy, I woke up to enormously swollen feet. It was then that my doctor diagnosed the beginnings of preeclampsia (see Jennifer's story in chapter five), which explained the unusual weight gain and the swelling.

I was now an additional twenty pounds heavier, and, under my doctor's orders, I spent every evening and weekend in bed or on the couch. My body seemed to replace its appetite with an unquenchable thirst, and I continued to gain weight rapidly. I was finally ordered into the hospital during my thirty-fourth week, and on the day my labor was induced, the scale reported that I had gained a total of sixty pounds.

Although I haven't resumed my prepregnancy figure, in many ways I do resemble that carefree girl from long ago. Well, I resemble her as long as I don't wear a swimsuit. I just look more like a woman and less like a cast member of *Friends.* There are days when I feel very unhappy about the ten extra pounds I carry around and the way the pregnancy has shifted my weight. I'm sure if I had the time and energy to pursue it, I could come close to getting my former body back. At the same time, however, I try very hard not to obsess about my body's imperfections because I don't want my daughter to grow up the way I did—thinking she has to be thin and buff to be happy. So, for now, running after my two-year-old is enough exercise for me and I think adding macaroni and cheese to my lunch menu now and then keeps me young. These days, there is more to my life than having a sculpted body, and I'm glad.

Sandra, 36

We all begin our pregnancies with noble ideas about eating right. Once the first trimester kicks in, however, our bodies might give us strong signals about food and we have no choice but to listen. A generally health-conscious person, Sandra has a two-year-old daughter and a son on the way. Although her ideas about nutrition stayed the same, her eating habits during each pregnancy were very different.

This is my second pregnancy, and you might hate me for writing this, but I've barely exercised, my eating habits are atrocious, and I've hardly gained any weight. However, I wish I felt more fit and ate more healthfully, as I did during my first pregnancy. I have no qualms about the weight gain part.

During my first pregnancy, the need to exercise and eat well was paramount. I was an aerobics fanatic before I got pregnant, and continued about four times a week with low-impact and step aerobics classes as well as prenatal yoga throughout that pregnancy. Working out and building up a good sweat felt great, even as my belly swelled. I felt like a big-bellied Amazon, strong and very large.

As for my eating habits, I noshed on fruit and ate lots of yogurt for calcium because I don't like milk. I had aversions plenty: meat, fish, and poultry made me nauseous. I got my vitamins from bean and rice burritos and falafel sandwiches whenever I could. I was far from perfect, however. Pizza was a diet staple and I knew where every Ben and Jerry's ice-cream store was in my town. Hey, ice cream and pizza are loaded with calcium, right?

Overall, I gained thirty pounds during that pregnancy, mostly in the last couple of months. Since I'm five foot, eight inches tall, and a few pounds heavier than I should be, I was pleased that I didn't put on more.

Did my attempts at a healthy prenatal lifestyle pay off? At thirty-eight weeks, I gave birth after a tough delivery to a beautiful daughter who weighed six and a half pounds. And I managed to get back to my prepregnancy weight within two months.

With this pregnancy, I get my workouts chasing my two-year-old daughter. I spent the first trimester exhausted and nauseous, and asking my husband to come home early so I could go to bed at 7 P.M. I'm currently midway through this pregnancy, and still find exercise hard to schedule in my daily routine—I work a couple of days a week and any spare sitter time is often devoted to errands and phone calls. I'm now trying to do prenatal aerobics and yoga at least twice a week, and walks on other days. I know exercise makes me feel great, and it's important for my health and the health of my baby.

Nutrition has also been a problem. Instead of craving peaches, melon, and yogurt, I seem to be craving sweets and pizza all of the time. I'm trying to reign in those impulses. But every time I tell myself I shouldn't eat refined sugars or too much fat, I immediately desire a chocolate chip cookie or two.

My weight gain this time parallels my first pregnancy. I've put on less than ten pounds so far, but I'm sure my body will pack on what it needs toward the end. Sometimes, I feel terribly guilty about how I'm treating my body and the growing baby inside me this pregnancy. Yet I'm trying to do the best I can, and have come to embrace that. While I may not look like an Amazon on the outside, I know, deep down, she lurks within.

Sheila, 33

Like Sandra, Sheila's body reacted quite differently to her second pregnancy and her approach to exercise changed as a result. She was, however, diligent in her practice of certain key exercises, including the infamous Kegel, which involves tightening and relaxing the muscles in your vaginal and perineal area over and over and over and over again. After all, it doesn't matter if you've visited the gym every day of your pregnancy, the Kegel is the only exercise that tones the muscles in your pelvic floor. This can lead to fewer tears and episiotomies during birth, and it can enhance sexual pleasure as well. Additionally, it will help prevent urine from leaking out of you during a sneeze or cough, and this is a very good thing.

With my first pregnancy, I was determined to stay reasonably fit, and, in fact, I began the pregnancy in great shape, having recently prepared for a ski trip. The funny thing was that the first time I got on a treadmill after I knew I was pregnant, I panicked. I thought the baby was going to fall out! Despite all the supposedly rational brain cells in my skull, I couldn't shake this feeling, and got off the machine with my heart thumping. Then I reached the "extremely tired, somewhat nauseous" part of the pregnancy, and it was all I could do to function, let alone tone.

When I started to feel well enough to exercise a bit, all of the prenatal classes I located had inconvenient schedules. It seemed like they either assumed that pregnant women did nothing other than arrange their lives around exercise classes or that moms-to-be only wanted to exercise once a week. Further, I was terrified of trendy exercise videos because I don't believe those tapes are vetted by doctors.

Then a friend of mine at work passed on a tape that her obstetrician had given her a few years back, which she had never used. It carried the American College of Obstetricians and Gynecologists' seal of approval, and I asked my obstetrician about it, who said it was fine. The tape was laughably "affirming" and very early 1980s California, but darn if it didn't stretch and strengthen me in the right places. I got hooked on it and found my body stiffening up if I didn't do it every few days.

Meanwhile, my weight gain was steady until the beginning of the third trimester, when I went on a bagel binge and experienced a sudden surge, but overall I was still OK. I was having a lot of leg and hip cramps at night, and the exercise helped, although maybe some of the hip pain was a result of the exercise—who knows? Toward the end of the third trimester, I began experiencing a lot of Braxton-Hicks contractions, those fake ones which can be a bit debilitating when you're walking down the street. My doctor told me to take it easy. This meant that I couldn't do any of that purposeful last-month walking, the kind that is supposed to be so helpful in inducing labor.

In the end, I gained thirty-five pounds, went two weeks past my due date, and labor had to be induced. Unfortunately, the one exercise no one mentioned to me until the childbirth class I attended one month before my due date was the Kegel, which is essential, but is kind of hard to begin in month eight. Kegel-ing many, many times a day helps to tone the muscles in your vaginal area to strengthen them for delivery. Whether it was because of a lack of Kegels or because it was my first baby—and the baby was big—I had the "mother of all episiotomies" (no pun intended). Ouch!

Nine weeks after delivery I started a postpartum exercise class twice a week, which was great. Do not be misled: I am not nor was I then an exercise freak, but this type of Mommy and Me class was very helpful in getting an appropriate routine started. As with almost everyone I know, all but the last five to ten pounds came off easily and the rest came off after a year.

I became pregnant again two years after my first child was born. I was in reasonably "returned" shape. What shocked me was how I started to show almost immediately, even though I hadn't gained that much weight. The muscles, however, remember pregnancy and it seems like they just collapse. I wanted to wait until I was three months along before telling people that I was pregnant, but it became apparent much earlier. It was sort of embarrassing and unnerving at the same time. I eventually met someone else who was also pregnant with her second child, and she—although certifiably svelte—was having the same experience.

The second time around my whole body seemed to relax much more, so as my ligaments started loosening up in preparation for birth, I had all sorts of problems with my back and other body parts. If this happened with my first pregnancy, I certainly didn't feel it the way I did during my second. It led to a lot of early discomfort. Luckily I experienced some relief by exercising, using a belly belt (a contraption that wraps around your body and supports the weight of your pregnant belly), and the general settling in process.

Unfortunately, I couldn't use my miracle video because we have only one TV and my two-and-a-half-year-old had control of it. Besides, it's frankly embarrassing to hoist your ungainly frame around in mixed company. I had to put up with my husband's jibes (for which he was suitably punished) the first time I was pregnant, and now, I didn't feel like putting on a show for my daughter. Anyway, between work and my daughter, I was just too tired. Before I went to bed at night, however, I did some of the more essential exercises, like pelvic tilts and, oh yes, those Kegels, which I now knew about. When I delivered my nearly nine-pound baby without an episiotomy, I knew my little nighttime ritual paid off. For some reason, I didn't experience Braxton-Hicks contractions with my second pregnancy, but maybe that was because I wasn't exercising so much, who knows?

I survived a hellishly hot summer during which I could barely move, let alone exercise, but once the weather cooled a bit, right before my due date, I suddenly perked up and was able to walk for exercise again. I walked a lot the few days before I went into labor, and, unlike the first time, I delivered a week early. Hallelujah!

On the weight gain front, I didn't do anything drastic one way or another and I, once again, gained thirty-five pounds. My baby was bigger, but he also came three weeks earlier than my daughter had. From my experience and from talking with friends, it seems that unless you become obsessive, the body naturally knows how much weight to gain, and, typically, you will lose it all within a year.

Post second baby, I rejoined the gym and hired a personal trainer. I see her once a week. She helps keep exercise fun, and the commitment motivates me to go to the gym a few times a week. This has enabled me to more easily lift my children, sleep restfully, shed tension, and, generally, hold it all together a little better.

After my children were born, I found myself more accepting of my body—I was less focused on the fine points, and more content with the overall picture. After sharing my body with someone else for nine months, I was so happy to get it back that I embraced it, faults and all, with a fuller appreciation of all that it can do, both inside and out.

Whitney, 33

Trying to get back in shape after her first pregnancy consumed more of Whitney's time and emotional energy than she was comfortable with. She was determined to approach that aspect of pregnancy differently the second time around.

Throughout my teen/young adult life I struggled with my weight. I was never what many would call overweight but at five foot one it doesn't take many extra pounds to make you feel/look a little too "healthy" or "womanly." For about three years prior to getting pregnant I'd enjoyed a time of healthy fitness. I had developed a regular exercise routine and a free-weight program that resulted in a toned look to which I had grown quite attached. When I became pregnant with my first child I was in the best shape I'd ever been. I was excited to be pregnant, but I was also anxious about how my body would change and how I would take the weight off once the baby arrived.

During my first pregnancy, I watched what I ate but did not obsess about it. I have a big sweet tooth and I did try to keep that in check. The only foods I really craved at the beginning were oranges and garlic Chinese chicken, and I ate them both regularly. In my case, food aversions were much more common than cravings and there were certain foods I couldn't go near, including grilled chicken, red meat, and plain vegetables. I tended to want foods that were either pretty heavily spiced or completely bland.

Pasta was a food I was very drawn to because it settled my stomach and was completely inoffensive. Despite the fact that it is a high-calorie food, it became a staple in my diet. I made a conscious effort to eat more vegetables but found I could only tolerate them when they were hidden in the garlic chicken or something spicy. My biggest challenge was trying to constantly keep food in my stomach because when I did, I experienced much less nausea.

I exercised pretty regularly, particularly in the beginning, although I decreased the cardio intensity, gave up sit-ups, and went less intense on the weights. Even working out three to four times a week, I still managed to gain thirty-three pounds on my ninety-eight pound body. I definitely felt big and, even more annoying, I felt thick everywhere. The weight gain wasn't localized—it was on my butt, my upper arms, my face, you name it. I handled this all fine during pregnancy, but postpregnancy it hit me very hard.

Because my daughter was breech, I ended up having a cesarean ten days before my original due date. To my disgust, when I left the hospital three days later, I had only lost ten pounds and I still looked pregnant. On top of that, I couldn't really return to my usual workouts until I recovered from the surgery, which would probably take around six weeks.

Four months after my daughter's birth I was still carrying around eight extra pounds. My husband hired a personal trainer for me to help boost my spirits and motivation. It's not that I was upset by the pounds themselves, but I wasn't even close to fitting into my regular clothes, especially if they buttoned around the waist—I was really tired of living in leggings and long shirts. Two months into my new regime of 5 A.M. workouts, I was exhausted although much more toned. I still had about four extra pounds, but my clothes were once again fitting around my waist. I stopped nursing my daughter about two months after that and the last few pounds came off pretty quickly, without much extra effort. I then gave up the 5 A.M. routine and started sleeping again.

When my daughter was ten months old I was fitting into almost all of my clothes and my stomach was even starting to come around. This happened just in time for pregnancy number two! I was thrilled to be expecting another baby and I was determined not to, once again, make myself crazy about weight. Losing the weight from my first pregnancy was very difficult emotionally. This time, I wanted to avoid that by not gaining as much weight and by not being so focused on losing it.

My goal was to keep my weight gain in the twenty-five to thirty pound vicinity by watching my food (and snack) intake carefully. I ate healthy, but reasonably. I continued to exercise with a slightly higher intensity than during my first pregnancy, maintained my weight routine, and did sit-ups throughout my first trimester. At the end of my pregnancy, I was happy to find that my weight gain was exactly where I wanted it to be—twenty-five pounds. I was sure I'd be back in my clothes in no time. Boy, was I wrong!

I dropped all but seven pounds or so within the first six weeks and there I sat for a while. In another couple of months I was back to my prepregnancy weight, but my body was very different and my clothes still didn't fit. This time, however, I didn't stress about it.

As I write this, my second child (who I weaned a month ago) is eleven months old and I'm definitely getting closer to wearing more fitted waistbands as well as my old bras. In the back of my mind, I still wait for the return of my old body, but part of me has accepted that I may never get back to the shape I was in before. Whether it's because of a wider rib cage, larger hips, or just the effect that nursing two children has had on my breasts, I realize that this may be as good as it gets. When I look at my two wonderful children, I know, without question, that's good enough for me!

Renee, 32

A very athletic person by nature, Renee was in the position of having to curtail some of her usual activities during pregnancy. Opting out of some of her favorite pastimes was, for her, one of the most challenging parts of being pregnant.

I have always been an active person (going to the gym four to five times a week, rollerblading, biking, skiing, etc.) and my eating habits have consistently been healthy with perhaps an overly conscious effort toward staying thin. Because of this, it was difficult to limit my activities and watch the numbers on the scale rise during my pregnancy.

In my first trimester, my low energy level and my fear of overexertion kept me from working out very much. When I reached my second trimester, my energy returned and I felt more comfortable that my baby was safe and I wouldn't have a miscarriage. I went to the gym about four times a week, lifting weights and using cardiovascular machines, such as the Stairmaster and treadmill, for the remainder of my pregnancy. I ate nutritious foods and my diet included no caffeine, no sugar substitutes, and no alcohol, although in one area I definitely indulged—sweets. I don't know if that was due to pregnancy cravings or if I was just more willing to let myself enjoy dessert during that time.

Luckily, my pregnancy was rather uneventful, with no complications, no major aches or pains. But it did require some major lifestyle and self-image adjustments. There were many occasions when I wasn't able to participate in activities that I enjoyed because of the risk factors involved. Even though I felt well enough to ski or bike or rollerblade, I heeded my doctor's advice, showed restraint, and didn't do any of these things.

Another source of frustration was not having any control over what my body looked like. It was hard for me to believe that my bulging belly would return to its original state. On the positive side, though, it was nice not to have to worry about sucking in my stomach. Even though I was anxious about losing the weight I gained (twenty-four pounds in all) and regaining my abs once the baby was born, I did grow accustomed to my changing body and I even managed to find some cute maternity clothes to wear.

Cynthia, 36

Cynthia has always trusted her body and while she was pregnant she learned to appreciate and respect it in a wholly new manner. As it grew, she was amazed at its transformation and sense of purpose.

My body told me what to do when I was pregnant and I listened to it very carefully. It told me when to eat and what to eat and it sent rather strong signals when it wanted to move around and when it wanted to stay put.

Of course, thinking about the little being growing inside of me, I tried to eat healthfully as I imagined every step of her embryonic development. But when my body would shy away from certain healthy foods and instead long for something very salty or very sugary, I'd trust it, knowing that it had some grand design to which I could only acquiesce.

My main source of exercise during those long nine months was walking. My subway commute to work included many city blocks and many flights of stairs. I endured this journey through my entire pregnancy and, at times, it was truly exhausting. At other times, it felt great. Sometimes I'd take additional walks on the weekends, and I also did prenatal yoga at home (with the assistance of a video) a few times a week.

Although I've never been one to obsess about weight issues, there have certainly been times when I thought my life would be greatly improved if only my thighs and butt were a bit smaller. I think it's impossible to live in America and not feel this way. Interestingly enough, though, while I was pregnant and impressively putting on the pounds, I actually loved my body more than ever before. I spent a great deal of time studying it as it grew, and I loved its roundness, its shapeliness, and the way my skin seemed to glow and soften as it stretched itself over my very pregnant form. It was clearly a body with a purpose, looking strong, determined, and even beautiful. It helped that my husband loved my new look and that our sex life was enhanced by it as well.

There were times when I'd wonder what I would look like postbaby and just how quickly those extra forty pounds would disappear. Fortunately, these thoughts did not consume me. As I write this, sixteen months after my daughter's birth, my body is no bigger (in fact, it's even a little smaller) than it was prior to my pregnancy. Its shape is certainly a bit different and it bears some telltale signs of pregnancy, childbirth, and breastfeeding. But I wear those signs proudly as I delight in the strength, power, and history that they represent.

❋ ❋ ❋

Pregnancy often forces us to listen to our bodies in a brand-new way. It tells us when to eat and it lets us know what it is craving. It grows and it stretches as we stand by and wonder what it can possibly do next. This amazing process can teach us a lot about our relationship to patience and control, and these lessons will certainly come in handy as we begin our lives as mothers.

Chapter Seven

Missing Children: Coping with Pregnancy Loss

Pregnancy loss crosses all of our minds soon after we become pregnant. For some of us the thought is fleeting, coming and going at various times, but never occupying a primary place in our consciousness. For others, it's a steady fear that grows along with the realization that there is very little we can do if something were to go wrong at this early stage.

Losing a baby is devastating. In addition to sadness, anger, shock, and even a sense of failure, most women who have miscarried will tell you that they feel misunderstood. The degree and volume of the grief involved is rarely acknowledged and hardly supported. Statistics will be thrown about, reassurances made, and positive predictions for the future will abound, but none of this makes the loss any easier.

In describing her experience of pregnancy loss, writer Helen Schulman (1998) says, "You have children—not in the world inhabited by other people but in the private world of your own heart—you have children you will never get to mother. They are secret children, like those children you read about, confined to an attic or closet. No one but you recognizes their existence, you yourself don't even know their form, their genders, the shape of their noses, the color of their eyes, and yet the strength of their souls flutters inside your heart like a caged bird's wings."

❋ ❋ ❋

Liz, 26 Years Old

Although both of Liz's pregnancies ended in first trimester losses, she still considers herself a mother. She feels intense love for the two babies she conceived and they will always be an important part of her life.

I have wanted a baby since I was fourteen years old. When my husband and I decided we were ready to begin a family, it never occurred to me that I might face problems. None of the women in my family ever had any difficulties in terms of fertility or pregnancy loss. I assumed that I would conceive, carry a child, and give birth nine months later.

Our first child was conceived after four months of haphazard trying. I was overjoyed. It is the kind of happiness that is quiet and deep, and intensely personal. My body was not my own anymore. I was sharing it with my child, and that child was immediately as much a part of me as I was of it. We were connected in a most primal way. I was in love with my baby from the moment I looked down and saw two lines on the home pregnancy test.

After about three weeks, I had some scant, light brown spotting. My midwife told me it was probably nothing to be concerned about as long as it remained brown. (The general wisdom seems to be that brown is old, and therefore not a part of the pregnancy.) That night, the brown became pink and I called the doctor who works with my midwife. He suggested having an ultrasound to ease any fears. The next morning I went for the test. I cannot express the unimaginable joy I felt at seeing my child floating around inside me. There was a picture of my child, only six weeks and five days old, its beating heart represented by a quick flicker. Had the technician told me I could stay all day to watch that beautiful image, I would have lain on that table for the next eight hours. I was happier than I ever thought a person could be.

That night I tried to allay my deep feeling that something was wrong. Although the technician and doctor found nothing suspicious, and told me spotting and bleeding are more common than is talked about, I "felt" that something bigger was happening. The next day I had slight but constant cramps, and called the midwife for reassurance. She asked me to come in to the office and subsequently sent me to the hospital for a higher level ultrasound. Again, we saw a seemingly healthy pregnancy. My child was alive with a rapid heartbeat, and looked well. The technician measured the baby as six weeks and five days again. No one thought this was alarming, however, as the machines were different, and maybe our dates were off. I was sent home and told to relax, with the reassurance that everything was fine.

The next seven hours would change my life irrevocably. I began bleeding and cramping. I knew this was wrong. The bleeding was very heavy and very red. I called my doctor who advised me to meet him at the emergency room. Before the exam I was told to empty my bladder, but I was afraid to go to the bathroom. I knew that if I relaxed enough to urinate, I would lose my baby. My doctor told me that I must empty my bladder, however, and so I did. I began crying, as I knew this was the end. He then did a painful internal exam and told me he would classify my pregnancy as "threatened" and that I should call his office in the morning to schedule another ultrasound. I told him I knew it was over, as I was pretty sure I'd already miscarried moments before into the toilet. I was sent home. That night I had very little bleeding and no additional cramping. Though a part of me knew it was over, I was afraid that I still had more to endure physically. My doctor told me that I might experience contractions before "expelling" the "product," but the only pain I experienced that night was emotional.

The next morning, I had an ultrasound that showed an empty uterus. Just like that, every dream, every hope, all that joy, was dashed away. I had never felt worse in my life. In my mind, I had failed. I had failed my child, I had failed my husband and family, who we had told right away, and I had failed myself as a woman. I was failing at the one thing that women all over the world, from generation to generation, seemed to do so easily. I did everything right. I'd been on prenatal vitamins since before conception, I hadn't smoked, and I was careful about food and sleep. I had done all I could to provide a warm and safe environment for my beloved child, and, just like that, it was gone. That night, I experienced the most intense cramps I'd ever had. One thousand milligrams of ibuprofen didn't touch the pain. My mother suggested that I was having the contractions the doctor warned me about. I used guided imagery to relax, and concentrated on breathing through them. This was especially painful as there was to be no happy end to this pain, just more bleeding and clotting.

There was no funeral; no palpable loss to anyone but me. I was completely alone in my grief. As much as my husband and family tried to comfort me, they couldn't really understand my pain. No one could comprehend the enormity of what I was feeling then, and what I continue to feel, a loss as profound as the love that had come before it.

Four months later I found myself pregnant again. This time I was fraught with worry from the moment I tested positive. I was terrified. No twinge went unnoticed, no spot of fluid unchecked. I was a mess. I had an ultrasound done at six weeks because I was again having some light brown spotting. Once more, we saw a tiny flickering heartbeat and a baby growing inside me. And again I was in love. My heart was full of fear, and hopes, and prayers that this time I could make the goal.

One week later, before a trip overseas, I had another ultrasound. This time it was to reassure me that all was OK before I left for ten days in Italy. There is no way to describe the devastation I felt when there was no heartbeat to be seen. Without warning and without any outward signs, my baby had died. Once again, I was a failure. This time my doctor performed a D&C (dilation and curettage), and I left for Italy four days later. Fetal tissue testing revealed a genetic disorder that occurs by pure chance. I was told that I'd been struck by lightning twice and it was all chalked up to bad luck.

As of this writing, my husband and I are still trying to conceive a healthy child. I am brokenhearted and confused on a daily basis by where life has taken me. It hurts me deeply when people imply that since my losses occurred so early, they should be less difficult to deal with. Losing a baby, no matter where you are in a pregnancy, is shattering. I cannot imagine loving anything more than I loved my tiny babies. It is a love I cannot even begin to explain.

There is not a day that goes by that I don't mourn them, their potential, and our lives as they should have been. There is not a day that goes by that I don't miss their tiny private presence in my life and body.

There are days when I am successful in my attempts to live moment to moment, and days when I can think of the pregnancies fondly. Sometimes I feel hopeful, sometimes I feel intensely depressed. I still cry, I still mourn, and sometimes I still feel like a failure. "Nature taking care of itself" is not a term that comforts me. I am angry at what I've lost and who I've lost. But every day that passes seems like a step in the right direction, a sign that I am stronger than this, and one that gives me hope that we will someday conceive a child who I carry to term. Hope is what sustains me through the dark days, and through the seemingly unbearable grief.

Though the world does not know it, I am a mother, and for that I am forever grateful. I try and honor my babies and the impact they've had on my life in private ways. Simultaneously, I nurture my longing to be pregnant again and to carry the next baby to term, in spite of my fears. The love that I feel for my two babies is much greater than the grief.

Shannon, 25

Shannon always had a strange feeling about her second pregnancy. Nothing could have prepared her, however, for the emotional and physical turmoil she'd experience when it ended in loss.

In retrospect, I'm not sure I ever felt secure about my second pregnancy. My first son, Andrew, had been so easy to bring into the world that I wondered if I would be that lucky again, so soon. We had decided that we would try to get pregnant again once Andrew was weaned and one year old, but we didn't expect that we would be pregnant two weeks after my first postpregnancy period, which happened on Andrew's first birthday. We welcomed the chance to have another child, but, in all honesty, I think we weren't prepared to have two children under the age of two. A visit to our obstetrician, however, confirmed the positive home pregnancy test, and we mentally began preparing ourselves for a new baby. Everything seemed to be moving along normally: I had indigestion and some nausea, cravings were plentiful, and all was well. At my ten-week visit, we heard a strong heartbeat at 172 beats per minute (bpm), which I recorded to play for my husband later. As I said, everything was, by all appearances, normal.

Then one Wednesday morning I woke up and the first thought in my mind was "I'm going to lose the baby today." I had had some lower abdominal discomfort the night before, but I wrote it off to round ligament pain. When I stood up, I felt a slight gush of fluid; in the bathroom, I saw that it was indeed blood. I called the answering service for the obstetrician's office at 6:30 A.M., and the obstetrician on call—the only male on the staff of four—called me thirty minutes later and told me that he could squeeze me in at 10 A.M. to see what was going on. It didn't help matters any that he said if I was actually miscarrying, there really wasn't anything they could do about it.

This wasn't supposed to be happening—we'd heard the heartbeat. I was already at thirteen weeks and five days. We had just sent out our Christmas letters, telling friends and family the good news. I called my aunt, who happened to work at the hospital as the head of the radiology department, and she said she could do an ultrasound before my visit, to "take a peek" as she put it and to reassure me that everything was actually fine. We loaded our son into the car and drove to the hospital, wondering how we'd be feeling when we returned home later that day.

My aunt met us in the waiting room and led us back for the ultrasound. She slowly moved the instrument back and forth over my abdomen for a few minutes before turning to us and saying, with sadness in her voice, "I'm sorry, kiddo, but I don't see a heartbeat." Rob and I burst into tears, with Andrew wondering what was going on. Once we composed ourselves somewhat, my aunt gave us the news that we had never expected: "I don't know how to tell you this, but there are two in there." I had been carrying twins and didn't even know it until they were gone. She told us that they only showed growth to about ten weeks, five days ... a few days after I heard the heartbeat for the first and final time. I called my mother from the exam room and gave her the news, and then I got ready to go for my appointment with the obstetrician, already knowing what I would be told there.

After performing a pelvic exam and giving me brief condolences, the obstetrician told me that I had three choices: have a D&C that day, wait and see if everything would resolve itself naturally, or give it until the following Monday and then schedule a D&C. I opted to go naturally, and I asked what I could expect. The obstetrician gave me very little information; he told me that it would be like a heavy period and to call if there were any problems. Problems? Isn't it a problem to be having a miscarriage at all? As my husband and I drove home, we happened to pass a funeral home; we agreed that, even though this experience was excruciating, we would rather it happen this way than to bring a baby home for a day and then have to bury it. God has His reasons for doing what He does, and this was no different. So, I went home to wait.

And wait ... and wait ... I had some spotting, but nothing extraordinary. My mother came to stay with me during the day because I'd been told that it was possible that I would hemorrhage and that I should have someone available to take me for medical attention, if it became necessary. I felt like everyone—my mother, my husband, the obstetrician—was sitting around, watching me, and waiting. I tried to keep busy by baking Christmas cookies for the housewarming party we had planned and were going through with on Saturday.

How long would it take? I was frustrated to read on a miscarriage bulletin board on the Internet that miscarriages sometimes took weeks to come to completion; why was there so little information out there? My obstetrician had told me next to nothing, the pregnancy books I had only discussed how to know if you were having a miscarriage and what to do—nothing about what it would be like, how long it would take, how it would feel. I turned to the Internet to try and get some semblance of information from women who had been there not that long ago.

On Friday, I had cramps similar to a very difficult period and I hoped that it was almost over. I was sitting at the computer, reading an e-mail from one of the members of the Internet bulletin board, when—I remember the exact time, 1:28 P.M.—I felt two small pops in my pelvic area. I stood up and blood began coursing down my legs, soaking through my sweatpants. I ran to the bathroom, and after I had sat on the toilet for five minutes, the blood so profuse it sounded like I was urinating every five seconds, I asked my mom to call the obstetrician.

The doctor on call this time was a woman, and she expressed sympathy for what I was going through and asked how I was feeling. She told me to collect any large pieces of tissue in a Ziploc bag, and if the bleeding didn't ease up in the next ten minutes I should head over to the emergency room. As my mom kept an eye on the clock, she went upstairs to get me clean undergarments and pants, and she put my son in the car. From the bathroom, I called my husband and told him to meet us at the emergency room (ER).

I put myself back together, picked up my Ziploc bag, and worked my way into the kitchen to get my shoes on. At one point, I knelt down on the floor to stop myself from passing out, and when I got to my feet I left a brief note on the table telling my husband and my son that I would always love them; I wasn't sure I would be coming home from the hospital when all was said and done, after all.

We reached the ER in half an hour, and I was taken back into a very crowded area, helped onto a bed, and told that someone would be with me soon. I waited as I continued to gush blood all over the table, watching the clock as the cramps came regularly—just like labor had been. It's hard to remember what happened when the obstetrician came and told me that I would indeed need a D&C, although I really only needed the "C" (the curettage), since I was already dilated. She explained the process and asked what kind of anesthesia I would prefer—when I heard that a vacuum would be used, I knew I did not want to hear the sucking sound, even though I knew the babies were already dead. I opted for general anesthesia. I was given an IV, my husband came, I had blood drawn, and I couldn't have anything to drink, even though it had been hours since lunch. In all, I waited for three hours before being brought to the operating room (OR).

Everyone in the OR was very kind. I remember the transport nurse being extra careful as he wheeled me through the hall, and the various staff of the OR making every effort to extend sympathy and make sure that I was comfortable. The procedure itself was the shortest part of the whole ordeal: The surgery began at 6 P.M. and I was home by 8 P.M.

I wore my identification bracelet throughout the next day; I called it my "badge of courage." It was so painful to tell our housewarming guests, our neighbors, and our friends that we were no longer expecting in June, and to get Christmas cards in the mail giving us well wishes for our pregnancy. A few times a week I would go into the extra bedroom, the one that would have been the new baby's, and cry as I realized that the room was going to stay empty longer than we had thought. The first few weeks were the worst. Many nights, Rob and I would just curl up in bed and cry.

But, again, in retrospect, I have to say that I think a part of me might have known all along. I remember that as I "talked to the baby," I usually addressed my words heavenward rather than toward my abdomen—somehow, I felt that his or her spirit wasn't a part of the little body inside me yet, which was consistent with our religious belief that a spirit isn't joined with the body until the point where the mother feels movement. I wouldn't have wished this on myself—or anyone else, for that matter—but, thinking about it, I really would have had a hard time handling three children at home under the age of two. I believe that, for reasons I may not fully understand in this life, God knew that the pregnancy was not going to be to our benefit if it was allowed to continue, and in His mercy He let it end sooner rather than later. I might feel a twinge of sadness when my due date rolls around, but I hope I can keep it in an eternal perspective.

As I write, I am pregnant again now entering my twenty-first week. Pregnancy after a miscarriage is a strange beast: On the one hand, once you're given the go-ahead to try again, it's the only thing you hope for, dream of, and think about until it happens. But once it happens, every day is filled with worries and doubts about its chances for survival. A woman may only have a 5 to 25 percent chance of miscarriage (depending on which statistic one reads), but, after all, I was in that 5 percent not that long ago so it is difficult to find comfort in the statistics. One of the pregnancy books I read, when discussing pregnancy loss, made an analogy to people who have been struck by lightning: The chances of their being struck again are slim, but they still get nervous whenever there's a storm. You never get to have that rosy innocence of a previous pregnancy, if there was one—you know how easy it is to lose a baby, to be pregnant one day and not the next, with no baby to show for it.

Our obstetrician told us we should wait until I had a menstrual period before trying again; it was only later that he explained that the first one didn't "count," and that it was the second one that would indicate the time to begin again, if we wished. My husband and I talked it over, and we read about the subject online. After my first period came and went, we decided to leave matters up to God once again.

On the day that I expected my period to come and it didn't, I ran to the store for a two-pack of pregnancy tests. I waited until I was two days late, but both tests came back negative. When my period was a week late, a friend suggested I try again. I waited until my son was down for a nap and tiptoed into the bathroom to retest. Two lines! I saw two lines! Instant joy, exhilaration, laughter—and I ran to the phone to give my husband the news. Oddly, that was the day that—for the first time in my life—my father decided to stop by after work and bring me flowers, for no other reason than that he'd never done it before. I almost blurted out, "But how did you know?" when I saw him at the door, but I managed to contain myself.

Almost immediately thereafter, the worry set in. Every day was torturous; every pain was cause for alarm. I decided to change practitioners. I was unhappy with the treatment I'd previously received at the obstetrician office, and I longed for the medical care of a single person who would get to know me well throughout the course of my pregnancy, instead of being rotated among four physicians. I had such a great experience with a certified nurse midwife (CNM) during my first pregnancy that I was determined to find another. Much to my delight, I found one at a hospital nearby.

My first prenatal visit was a comfortable one, in spite of my fears of another miscarriage. But I still found myself worrying almost constantly that something was going to go awry a second time. I even rented one of those home Dopplers so I could hopefully find the heartbeat myself instead of waiting for my ten-week checkup. I tried for several days, hearing nothing but placental noise (which was to be expected at eight weeks, five days), and realized that it was making me feel worse. I sent the Doppler back for a refund. I fretted and worried and agonized until a week before my checkup, when an afternoon thunderstorm passed through and I saw a rainbow.

It sounds silly to say that seeing a rainbow took away my anxieties, but there were times in the past, during particularly worrisome moments, when I'd seen rainbows and felt more at ease. Whatever happened, I would be OK; what mattered was being able to stay with my husband and take care of the wonderful little boy we already had. If I had another miscarriage, it would be very difficult and painful, but I could handle it. I'd handled it before, after all.

Blessedly, at my ten-week checkup, the CNM was able to find the heartbeat, strong at 160 bpm, after chasing the baby around with the Doppler. It was a relief to know that we'd at least made it that far, although that fact didn't fool us into thinking that we were off the hook—we'd heard the heartbeat last time, too.

About six weeks ago, we passed the point that we lost our last pregnancy and we've recently started to feel like we're really expecting a baby, especially now that we can feel regular movements. It's hard to connect with this baby just yet, but as we see more proof positive that he or she will be ours this time, I think it'll get easier. As most things in our lives are, it's in God's hands.

Kim, 27

Kim had been through two pregnancies without complications. When she conceived for the third time, she had no idea just how much this pregnancy would change the course of her life.

Although I already had three children (a set of twins and a singleton), I was so naive then. I thought pregnancy meant getting up sick every morning, getting fat, and forty weeks later having a baby in your arms. That fairy tale, that innocence, was stolen from me during my third pregnancy when, at a routine doctor's appointment in my twentieth week, they could not find a heartbeat. An emergency ultrasound revealed that my child was in fact gone, and my body had not naturally miscarried. I was scheduled to go to the hospital one week later for a D&C. I felt betrayed by my body. I felt alone. I felt like no one understood the pain I was going through or even cared. Sure, I had my mom trying to comfort me, but she didn't understand what I was feeling inside. I kept thinking that I was supposed to die before my children. Why was this happening to me? What did I do wrong that God chose to punish me?

At the hospital, they put me under and took my beloved child from my body. I was never allowed to see him, or hold him. I wasn't even sure it was a boy until the testing on him was completed. Because it was such a late-term loss, they sent my child to a medical facility in another state to have a pathologist determine the cause of death. She determined that he was in fact a boy, and had multiple congenital anomalies. He was also missing the sixth chromosome.

Given the severity of his problems they didn't know how I carried him as long as I did.

The doctors told me to wait three cycles before trying again. I wasn't sure I wanted to wait that long; on the other hand I was afraid of suffering the same fate once more. The innocence was now gone. Pregnancy was not as simple as I once thought, and I would now always face it with a certain amount of fear. My marriage, which was already almost nonexistent, ended with the loss of this child, who I named Lynyrd. My husband didn't even share in the grief and was completely unsupportive. I had to make all the calls to arrange for the gravesite funeral I wanted him to have, and to notify our friends and family. I had to do it all when all I really wanted to do was cry and lock myself away from the world.

The time that followed was a roller coaster of emotions. I lost my grandfather only weeks after I lost my son, which only compounded my feelings of hopelessness. I would cry at the drop of a hat, and people couldn't keep up with my volatile emotional state. I had my good days and my bad, and had to deal with all of those feelings alone. My ex-husband didn't take any of the burden off my shoulders. I felt like I was living in a nightmare that I just couldn't wake from. What made things even harder on me was trying to explain to my three daughters why God had taken Lynyrd from us. They were very upset and confused by the news, and to help them grieve and heal, I suggested that they come up with a middle name for their little brother. This would be a wonderful gift that they could give him, and it would let them know that their feelings about the loss were not going unnoticed. They chose the name Andrew.

On the anniversary of my son's death I went to the cemetery with a cake and sang happy birthday to him, all the while wondering what my little boy looked like, and thinking how much I wanted to hold him. I just felt so empty.

Two years later I met a man who was to become my second husband. He was wonderfully sweet, caring, and understanding. He allowed me to be who I was, and accepted everything I had to tell him about myself. He even accompanied me to the cemetery to "meet" my son Lynyrd. Although he didn't like the idea of me dwelling on the past, he understood it, and accepted it as part of who I was. Shortly after that, we found out we were pregnant.

Something told me that this child was bound for heaven as well. I couldn't put my finger on it, but I knew something was wrong. I was having all kinds of pains and cramps, and when I next went to the doctor, during my eighth week, it was confirmed that I had suffered another loss. They wanted my body to miscarry naturally, but I told them this approach did not work the last time. They set me up for a D&C that afternoon. This time I was seeing different doctors and they did the procedure in their office. I was given no anesthetic and was completely awake while they took my beloved child away. It was one of the most difficult things I have ever endured. I went home, devastated. My fiancé and I shared many tears.

After the procedure, I only bled for twenty-four hours, which is abnormal, and I began to feel very ill. I was cramping and could barely sit up. When I called the doctor's office they told me this was the result of my uterus shrinking back down and that it would pass. After three days of pain, which was only becoming more intense, I was asked to come in for another ultrasound. It revealed that my uterus was hemorrhaging and they needed to perform the procedure again. This time it was more painful than before and it served as yet another reminder of how my body had betrayed me. Once more, I went home heartbroken. My husband kept reassuring me that we would try again and that the next time we would have the baby we wanted so much.

After eight months of trying to conceive, with no success, I set up an appointment to see an infertility specialist. All the phone calls I had made prior to taking this step told me that I was more than likely suffering from secondary infertility. This term refers to a body that was once fertile but no longer seems to be and requires assistance to get pregnant. So, in our ninth month of trying I met with an infertility doctor. She suggested that I take (and record) my temperature daily, and at the end of the month she would review my chart and do a blood test to see if I was ovulating like I was supposed to. She also wanted to get a sperm sample from my fiancé to make sure that everything was OK in that department. Little did I know that I was actually pregnant at that appointment.

I began charting my temperature the day my period (or what I thought was my period) started and they were too high for pre-ovulation temps. My period also wasn't normal. So, on the fifth day of charting, with my temps still over 99.1, I called the doctor. I felt fine, although I was experiencing some flu-like symptoms. I wasn't showing signs of morning sickness, nor did I have the other usual pregnancy indicators, and, of course, I had my period, or so I thought. When they asked me to come in for a blood pregnancy test, I told them they were crazy. They insisted I come in anyway, and sure enough, two days later I got a call telling me that I was pregnant. I was so happy that I cried, and I ran in to wake my husband. His first words were "Are you sure?" Then I called my mom to tell her the good news. The euphoria lasted a few minutes, and then, suddenly, reality set in. I'm pregnant. What am I going to do? How am I going to be able to handle this? What if I lose this one too? And why am I bleeding if I'm pregnant? Now my tears of joy were tears of panic, worry, and fear.

When I went in for my first checkup, they ran the usual tests and did an internal exam. The doctor tried to reassure me that my bleeding was from implantation, but I was still very nervous. To ease my mind, and because I was considered high risk, she ordered an ultrasound for the following week to check viability and for dating purposes. When I left, I was a wreck. I couldn't stop thinking about what that ultrasound would show. I had nightmare after nightmare.

After a very long week of waiting, the ultrasound was performed and sure enough it revealed a little heart beating away, albeit slowly. They told me this was not unusual so early in the pregnancy and I was told to come back in a week when things would probably look much better. I did not find those words encouraging at all. My past experiences did a great deal of damage to my psyche, and I felt sure that I would return in a week to find no heartbeat. I was wrong. When I returned, the baby's heart rate was wonderfully strong. Things were looking great, until I began having one complication after another.

I was now six weeks into the pregnancy and was still having intermittent bleeding. Each time this happened, I would end up going in for an ultrasound where I would be reassured that everything was progressing fine. I was twenty weeks along before the bleeding finally stopped completely. For the next six weeks, I was able to fully enjoy the pregnancy. A level two ultrasound revealed that I was having a boy, and that he was very healthy. He had all his fingers and toes and he looked just like his daddy, who now was my husband. This ultrasound ruled out any abnormalities, including the ones that resulted in my first loss. It felt great to know that my son was OK, but I also knew that I wasn't out of the woods yet.

At twenty-six weeks, the next complication hit—preterm labor. Contractions began, and off to the hospital I went to be hooked up to a machine. They couldn't find the baby's heartbeat at first, but after a while they got it. They decided, however, that he wasn't moving around as much as he should, so they ordered an emergency ultrasound. It was clear that he wanted into the world, and I was given a shot of terbutaline to stop labor, and then sent home. I was told that I needed to see my doctor on a weekly basis.

In the twenty-ninth week of my pregnancy preterm labor struck again and they discovered that I was one centimeter dilated and 60 percent effaced. Back to the hospital I went. The doctor who was on call the night I arrived was very rude and condescending. We even got into an argument about how my condition should be treated. My husband and I felt that she was playing Russian roulette with our child's life and not doing everything she could to ensure his safe arrival. We decided to talk to the doctor in the practice who we had been seeing regularly and, after a difficult and unsatisfying round of exchanges in which they expressed their discomfort with our questions, the practice decided to discharge me as a patient.

Luckily, I was able to find a good doctor who was willing to take me on late in my pregnancy. I was first seen by a nurse practitioner who ordered an ultrasound to check on the progress of the pregnancy and to get a baseline. At the time, I was convinced that my water was leaking and, sure enough, they found a small tear in the sac, which was the cause. I was told to stay in bed and it would heal. They also found a second layer of placental tissue, which would need to be monitored very carefully, and a lot of scar tissue, which was the result of the D&C procedures. My previous doctor had overlooked these things and they could have cost me and/or my son our lives. I was told that I would need to be closely monitored and that, for the safety of us both, my son would be born via a cesarean.

The preterm labor started again only a couple of days after I switched doctors and I was given a prescription for terbutaline to take at home every four hours. I was told that it was absolutely vital that I not miss a dose (even during the night and even if I wasn't feeling contractions). I took the medication as instructed, but the contractions kept coming. Thankfully, they were not coming at regular intervals so I was told not to worry. At thirty-one weeks, however, they did become regular and I again felt like my water was leaking. It was time for the hospital once more, where my contractions were monitored at three-minute intervals and after two shots of terbutaline, were stopped.

One week later, at home, with no warning, I started vomiting. I felt a small leak of fluid but assumed this was no big deal because it had happened before and I was not having contractions at the time. Things only got worse as the night progressed and before long I was feeling gushes. I still wasn't feeling any contractions. I was admitted to the hospital, yet again, where it was confirmed that my water had broken. They didn't want to take the baby, however, until it was absolutely necessary. This meant that they would wait until he either showed signs of distress, the contractions became unstoppable, or an infection set in. The longer they could keep him inside, the better.

Seven days later, a blood test showed an alarming increase in my white blood cell count signaling infection, and at thirty-two weeks and four days my son was brought into this world. Despite the many complications, he scored 9/9 on his Apgars, he needed no oxygen, and he weighed a very respectable five pounds, one ounce. He was in excellent shape for being seven weeks premature and the doctors were impressed. Of course, he did have to go to the neonatal intensive care unit (NICU) for monitoring, but the outlook was very positive.

I was able to hold my little miracle immediately after his birth (although it wasn't for very long as they wanted to get him to the NICU and me into recovery as soon as possible—I had experienced some hemorrhaging during the cesarean) and my nightmares finally came to an end. He was able to come home rather quickly and, although he has experienced some problems, including a very dangerous virus (RSV) that premature children are especially susceptible to, and a condition (craniosynostosis) that required him to have major skull surgery, he is doing great. With all that my son has been through, not to mention my family and I, he is truly a miracle and I cherish him. I thank God for giving us such a precious gift and I feel certain that my two angels (who are in my heart and thoughts daily) also played a part in bringing him into the world safe and sound.

※ ※ ※

The grief we experience after losing a baby is deep and unending. As time goes on, this grief, and the loss itself, become an integral part of who we are. As devastating as the experience may have been, the bond we have with the baby we've lost has, almost certainly, enriched our lives.

Chapter Eight

Happy Birthday! When Babies Make Their Entrance

Many of us spend a lot of time studying up on the birthing process. There are a vast number of options available and decisions to be made: Midwife or obstetrician? Home, hospital, or birthing center? Medication-free or "Where can I sign up for the epidural?" Lamaze or Bradley? Photographs, video, or just the power of memory? Bach, Enya, or Aretha? By the time our labor begins, we'll likely have a sharp mental image of our ideal birth experience and some strong ideas about what we would like to avoid. This insight will serve us well as we try to make our baby's birthday as special and fulfilling as it can be.

We live in a time and place that allow us to plan and manage our lives in ways previously unthinkable. Technology makes it possible for us to conveniently gather massive amounts of information in much less time than it would take to walk through a library and pluck a book off its shelves. We can even examine the four chambers of our baby's heart while she or he is still squirming around inside us. There are still some situations that defy this kind of control, however, and childbirth is one of them.

We can certainly contribute to creating our most desirable birthing conditions and, obviously, there are numerous ways assistance can be provided if we run into rough patches. But there are many details about this wondrous experience we can't know in advance. When and how will our labor begin? How will it progress? Will it last several hours? A few days? How will we experience the pain? Will we be excited, scared, or just plain exhausted? Will we push for fifteen minutes or three hours? How will we feel when we get our first glimpse of our newly born child? Because of this, it is wise to approach childbirth not only with a birth plan but also with a nod to forces that are bigger and more powerful than we can ever be.

✻　✻　✻

Sara Michelle, 33 Years Old

Even though we fully realize that labor can begin weeks before a "due date" or weeks after, we still rely on that predetermined day in ways that can make us crazy. Sara Michelle, eagerly expecting her first child, was ten days past her due date and, as she says, "Ready to take the pain head on."

My labor began in bed around midnight with a gush of wetness followed by contractions that felt like menstrual cramps. They seemed to alternate between two and ten minutes apart, which was confusing. I'd learned that two-minute intervals meant I should be on my way to the hospital, but ten-minute intervals meant I should try to relax at home.

I decided that the irregularity and moderateness of my contractions meant that I had a long way to go. I calmly told my husband that I was in labor and he should try to sleep, then I got out of bed, and went into the living room. I put two pillows on the floor—one to cushion my knees and the other to support my lower arms—and curled into the kneeling position I had practiced in birthing class. I rocked slowly as the contractions, getting stronger, surged through my body. Like waves, one would come on the back of another, and then several minutes later, the next would follow.

I was ten days past my due date, and I felt ready to take the pain head on. Maybe I could deliver without drugs after all, I thought. I mused that my baby would have the same birthday as my best friend from childhood. Surely he would arrive by midnight.

By 4 A.M., my husband, Youssef, was up with me. We called our doula, Michelle, and arranged for her to come over midmorning. Our doctor told us to call again when the contractions came at regular, five-minute intervals. Michelle arrived around 10:30 A.M. and we offered her tea, showed her our apartment, and I acted cool, kneeling down to contract between wedding photo explanations.

By noon we decided to go to the doctor's office to check on my progress. That's when reality hit. The pain had become so intense and my body so contorted that I couldn't gather the courage to change my clothes. Michelle had to help me figure out what to wear and help me dress. The car ride was awful. We were stuck in heavy traffic and I was coiled up in the back seat, half sitting, half lying down, trying to take deep breaths. I wanted to crawl out of my skin. I resented Youssef and Michelle for carrying on a pleasant conversation up front. I began to moan.

By the time we reached the hospital—I had directed Youssef to skip the doctor's office—I was falling apart. I started crying in the elevator, and could not stop while I waited to be admitted. Once I got settled into a room, I calmed down. In between being monitored I would pace the halls with Youssef and Michelle, stopping to lean on counters or on my husband as I rocked and groaned through contractions. I kept asking Michelle why no one else was making any noise. I think the answer was that they were all hooked up to epidurals quite early in their labors, which she tried to tell me discreetly. In my pain, I could not understand her euphemisms, and kept asking, with more and more frustration, "Why am I the only one making so much noise?"

When I arrived at the hospital I was six centimeters dilated, and all the walking and swaying did not change that. My doctor suggested breaking my water (which might have only partially broken the night before) and trying some Pitocin to increase the intensity of my contractions. I wanted to continue trying to labor without medication, and I knew that I could not bear the higher level of pain that these interventions would create. We tried a few more hours of showering and various other pain-management techniques until I was at my wit's end. I felt that if I had one more contraction I was going to throw myself off a cliff. That's when I did it. I had gone twenty-four hours without medication. "Get me the epidural," I said.

For me, the epidural was an awesome experience. It delivered me from my pain. It allowed me to rest before a three-hour pushing session. I told the anesthesiologist that he was an angel from heaven, and I meant it. He smiled. It probably wasn't the first time he'd been told.

When the epidural had completely numbed my lower half, my doctor broke my sac, gave me a double dose of Pitocin, as well as penicillin in case of infection, and I relaxed, chatted with Youssef and Michelle, and worried only about becoming too sleepy as my contractions got stronger. By around 2 P.M., I reached ten centimeters.

Then I started to push, even though my baby still seemed to be nestled right below my rib cage. I could sense serious doubt in the room that I would be able to make the baby descend. I was told by my doula afterward that any other doctor she knew would have "sectioned" me. One of my doctors told me the next day that she and her partners hadn't believed I would be able to deliver vaginally.

But they let me give it a shot, and that's all I wanted. I think all my years of stretching and dance really helped. I imagined the baby at my core and tried to use my deepest muscles and breath to squeeze him downward. I could not feel any pressure from his body. The doctor stopped the epidural, so I could sense more. I felt increasing pressure as the baby bore down harder and harder on my colon. My doctor leaned over to the nurse and said, "She's a good pusher." The words seemed to be a code for "Maybe she can do this after all." At that point, my husband was the only one getting excited about seeing the top of the baby's head. I think the others were starting to worry about his size. The doctor called for a pediatrician in case the baby would be deprived of oxygen on a difficult exit.

I kept pushing with slow, outward breaths while Youssef and Michelle lifted my knees. I felt I was outside my body, watching myself do these impossible sit-ups with my feet up against the squatting bar, roaring. I had an episiotomy, and then tore some more, and didn't even know it. I could not tell when the baby's head or body left my body. There was no ceremonial cutting of the cord.

Suddenly this warm, sticky baby rose over my knees like a float in the Thanksgiving Day parade, and then landed with a thud on my stomach. The next moment he was whisked to the side of the room to be checked by the pediatrician. Youssef seemed stunned from witnessing the whole ordeal, especially that final twist two doctors gave the baby in order to extricate his shoulders. But I had missed that part, and suddenly felt serene. "Honey, why don't you go check the baby," I said.

Zakaria was born. And he was fine. It took me thirty hours to deliver him, all nine pounds, three ounces. A big, healthy boy.

Shannon, 25

As they prepared for the birth of their first child, Shannon and her husband attended childbirth classes and learned many techniques for enduring the long hours of labor. It never occurred to her that she wouldn't have time to test any of them.

On Monday, the last day of August, when I was in my thirty-eighth week, my routine obstetrician appointment revealed that I was already dilated to three centimeters and 80 percent effaced—what a shock! By Thursday's visit, dilation had reached four centimeters and effacement was 100 percent . . . but there still was no labor. My practitioner stripped my membranes on Friday morning, but after an hour of cramping and nothing else, labor seemed to be no closer than before. Frustrated, I decided that the baby was never really coming, so I might as well go home, eat Kentucky Fried Chicken, and watch *Casablanca*.

At 4 A.M. on Saturday, back pain chased me out of bed and to the couch—nothing terribly unusual for my pregnancy—and a couple of hours later, I wearily rejoined my husband in bed. At 7:30 A.M., our entire town was jolted awake by a solitary clap of thunder; Rob and I each woke up with a yelp as we were startled out of sleep. Almost immediately thereafter, I felt a hard contraction move from my back to my abdomen, and I curled up on the bed, groaning. As Rob sat down in the kitchen and prepared a bowl of cereal, I staggered over: "There's not time for breakfast. Let's go."

Because we had learned in our prenatal class that labor can take a long time and that there's often more time to do things at home than one imagines, he replied, "But, honey, don't you want to take a shower or something?" "Let's go. Now!" We hurried to the car, our bag packed with sugar-free mints and layette sets. Thank goodness the hospital was only five minutes away. When we reached the labor and delivery area, the attending nurse assessed my situation (between contractions, I was very calm) and slowly went about preparing the delivery room, thinking that I must not be very far along. When she got me up on the table and checked my progress, she scared us by exclaiming, "Oh my gosh! You're really having this baby!" Of course, we knew this, but we were shocked to hear that not only was I at eight centimeters already, but there was no time for breathing techniques or drugs: It was almost time to push. I couldn't believe it.

In our prenatal classes, we had learned different breathing techniques to use during the many hours of labor that we would all, of course, endure; to be told that I was basically bypassing the first two phases of labor and jumping right to the third was both exhilarating and terrifying. I had planned on having as natural a birth as possible—realizing that medication and intervention can sometimes be medically necessary—but it scared me somewhat to know that pain medication was no longer an option if I wanted it.

My son, Andrew, was facing the wrong way—faceup in the birth canal instead of facedown. When my midwife arrived, she had to reach in and try to turn him facedown while the contractions hit—excruciating pain! Rob was a fantastic coach and was extremely supportive, holding my head and counting as I pulled my feet up to my mouth (unusual position!) and pushed through the contractions. At one point I screamed so loudly that he instinctively put his hand over my mouth, much to my chagrin—but only once. At 10:30 A.M., after an hour and a half of pushing, Andrew Robert sailed into our life with a yell.

It was the most awe-inspiring experience of my life, to see and hold the little person who had been inside me for nine long months. I had torn quite a bit, since Andrew had emerged with one hand alongside his head, and it required twenty minutes of stitching to put me back together. Nonetheless, it was such a great feeling to be able to get out of bed almost immediately thereafter and take a shower, unassisted—one of the benefits of not having an epidural, I suppose.

I stayed in the hospital for a little over a day, eager to make the rest of my recovery at home and begin the adjustment to having a baby in the house. We were as prepared as we could be, and only experience itself could teach us what we didn't know.

Martha, 38

Martha endured the emotional and physical difficulties of four in-vitro fertilizations before she became pregnant. Then she experienced a complicated and frightening pregnancy. By her thirty-seventh week, when labor was induced, she still had a hard time believing she was going to be a mother.

In the thirty-seventh week of my pregnancy I was admitted to the hospital to have my labor induced. The doctor was concerned about my baby's very low weight, which was a result of his umbilical cord having only one artery (a normal cord has two). Something inside me kept telling me that I was going to have a cesarean, so I prepared mentally by convincing myself that I preferred a nonvaginal delivery. What I didn't want was twenty-four hours of labor and then a cesarean. I had no idea just how prophetic I was.

We had left our house at 9:30 A.M. for a 10:30 A.M. doctor appointment—we weren't admitted to labor and delivery until 3 P.M. I ate a piece of cheese (which would be the last solid food I would have for two and a half days) and labor was induced at 5 P.M. I responded fairly well to the prostaglandin, a labor-inducing gel, and began to go into labor. The contractions were fairly mild and we were pretty upbeat.

As for the facilities, it was like I was giving birth in 1957. The room was probably only three times the size of the bed and the only walking I did was to and from the bathroom. Let me dispel a myth: There is nothing natural about childbirth. I had a fetal monitor on me the entire time, and once I had the epidural, in went the catheter. The stories about walking around, getting into different positions, massage, showers, and rocking chairs are for the lucky few who have no complications. I walked around for one hour, and I had to go to the postpartum ward because there was no room on the labor and delivery floor to move.

At about midnight, the contractions were fairly regular, somewhat intense, and I was worn out. The nurses were proselytizing Demerol so that "I could get some sleep." We made the mistake of not reviewing our birthing class notes and forgot that under no circumstances did we want to take Demerol. I was exhausted, so we relented. What a mistake. It made me hallucinate and, although I slept in between contractions (anywhere from thirty seconds to two minutes), when the contractions began I was so out of it and unprepared that I could not handle the pain. I was that woman screaming her head off that everyone talks about. On the other hand, the epidural was great. It allowed us to sleep for three hours. At 5 A.M. I was ten centimeters dilated. They had to lower the epidural so that I could feel the contractions as the pushing began. It took over three hours for the epidural to wear off to the point where I could tell when I was having a contraction.

Around 9 A.M. I began to push. I spent the next three and a half hours in what I now term virtual labor. I could hardly feel the contractions and no matter how hard I pushed, the baby wouldn't descend, so I never felt him in the birth canal. By this time, I had an internal monitor, and although my pushes moved the monitor, the baby was not budging. Exhausted and upset, I announced that I could push no more. So after twenty-two hours of labor and three and a half hours of pushing, I was headed for a cesarean. I began to bawl. I never realized how important a vaginal delivery was to me.

Once the decision was made to have the cesarean everything changed: I was having surgery, I had to be shaved, and it no longer felt like a joyful event. The medications made me nauseous and gave me the shivers. I thought I was going to throw up and the anesthesiologist was about as comforting as Patton. It seemed to take forever and then I heard the obstetrician say, "No wonder he didn't move, that's the shortest umbilical cord I've ever seen." And then, "It's a boy." My husband got to hold him first (one of the most unfair rites of a cesarean). I did get to hold my son for about two minutes before they whisked him away, with my husband following, leaving me all alone.

During the delivery, my blood pressure had begun to rise and I was put on magnesium sulfate, an awful drug with terrible side effects. I was on the magnesium for twenty-four hours and could not breastfeed for a full twenty-four hours after that. I did not see my son until the next morning and was not moved to the postpartum ward until thirty-six hours after delivering. I still could not nurse my son; I spent the first few days pumping and throwing out the teaspoons of colostrum.

We were discharged five days later. I had been home less than two hours when a severe headache and my home blood-pressure machine, registering 205 over 190, indicated the need to return to the hospital. Because my son had been exposed to the germs of the outside world, my husband had to take him home without me.

My son's first night "home" was at a friend's house; I was alone in the hospital with an IV in one arm and a blood pressure cuff on the other. I was tethered to the bed, could not get up to go to the bathroom, and my milk came in. After forty-eight hours alone in the hospital I was discharged. For my husband and me, nothing about getting pregnant or having children was easy or natural. Yet, it is the best thing we have ever done.

Cynthia, 36

Cynthia is the kind of person who really likes to be in control, but she was careful to approach labor and birth with an understanding that she could not determine their course. She did, however, have a few minor expectations about how things would progress. As her labor began, even these simple notions were abandoned.

It was a very hot, humid night, two weeks before my due date. I'd seen the midwives that day and was feeling crampy, but thought nothing of it because it was the same feeling I'd experienced after the other internal exams I'd had. My husband decided to go out for a bike ride and when he got home we ordered Chinese food and settled in to watch a New York Knicks playoff game. Toward the end of the game and our meal, I heard a weird popping sound. I stood up, reported the pop to my husband, felt something trickling down my leg and said, "Do you think my water's breaking?" My husband seemed to remember hearing just how much "water" is involved in this phenomenon, and he hurried me away from our new Crate &

Barrel sofa and into the bathroom. There wasn't much water at this point, but there definitely was a kind of slow steady stream.

We called the midwife immediately, as we were instructed to do if labor began this way, and she wanted to know if I was having any contractions and if I could feel the baby moving at all. My answer to both questions was no. She instructed me to get in a warm bathtub, relax, concentrate on trying to feel any movements from the baby, and call back with a report in twenty minutes. At some point during this time, my body decided to purge itself to prepare for labor. I'd heard about women vomiting during labor so I wasn't completely surprised, but I had no idea how thorough this purging could be. Let's just say that I was sitting on the toilet with my head in the sink (feeling very lucky for the layout of our small bathroom at that moment) and the Chinese food I had just eaten was no longer welcome. Then the contractions started.

Nothing prepared me for contractions that were three to four minutes apart from the outset and that were so painful that I felt as though I were being knocked off my feet. Even more upsetting was the fact that I felt a pressure so intense that my body wanted to push. My husband watched the ugly scene taking place in the bathroom with a look of complete confusion as he called back the midwife to give her our twenty minute report. We were both dumbfounded when she said we should come to the hospital right away.

On this particular Tuesday evening our bags were mostly, but not completely packed (we'd counted on having at least a few hours of home-laboring time to add the final items) and our car was in the shop because the muffler had fallen off two days earlier. From my post in the bathroom, where the purge continued as furiously as the contractions, I remember hearing my husband racing through the apartment, collecting various necessities for our bags. Simultaneously, he was calling local car service companies trying to relate the gravity of our situation and get an immediate pickup and an air-conditioned car. In the city in which we live, this is no easy matter.

I have no idea how I got dressed or got out of the apartment, but I do remember another major contraction hitting just as I approached the waiting car. Not knowing what to do, I hurried over to the first flat surface I saw—the trunk—and leaned over it to wait out the pain. The driver thought I was trying to put something in, and he kindly and cluelessly, hit the button that popped open the trunk just as I was leaning over. This kind of chaos ensued and the ride to the hospital could have been written for a sitcom.

Once settled into the birthing center, it was determined that I was four centimeters dilated. My niece, a massage therapist, met us there and the five of us (me, my husband, my niece, the midwife, and a nurse) began what was to be a very long night.

I shed my clothes as soon as I arrived (I was to remain buck naked through the entire labor) and headed for the Jacuzzi, where I spent a great deal of time over the next several hours. During my pregnancy, we'd viewed more than our share of birth videos and whenever we encountered one in which the laboring woman was completely unclothed, I'd tell my husband that this au naturel approach wasn't for me. It's not that I'm timid about nudity, but I'm the kind of person who often gets cold and, even during the most intimate moments, likes to be wearing certain articles of clothing.

While battling intense contractions as well as dealing with back labor because my little girl was posterior (her spine lying against mine), I barely even knew I was naked until I later saw a few photos that were taken during that night. In fact, many things that I thought I wanted during my labor were completely abandoned in light of the intensity of the situation, but because of that same intensity, I was hardly even aware that they were missing.

My contractions remained steady and intense throughout the night. I was having a very "internal" labor experience, meaning I didn't want to talk to anyone else and I didn't really want them talking to me. I'm generally a very vocal person so this is not how I had pictured myself in labor. I wanted to focus inward as much as I could during and between contractions and try to breathe as steadily as I could to manage the pain.

I'm sure my contractions were no more intense than anyone else's but because they started out with the same intensity as they finished, giving me no steady progression to help prepare, I was already exhausted only a few hours into my labor. The one very weird symptom I'll report (because I have never heard anyone else describe this sensation) is that frequently at the end of a contraction, I would feel an incredibly uncomfortable burning sensation in my upper thighs that would hurt almost as much as the contraction itself. I still have no idea what that was all about. My niece massaged me the whole time and provided some amazing counter-pressure techniques to relieve the back labor. My husband sweetly and earnestly tried to give me something to eat or drink (which I always refused) and talk me through contractions (also which I refused). Although there wasn't a hell of a lot that he could really do for me, I remember feeling panicky if he even left my side for a moment, and he didn't.

When my midwife examined me about six hours later, I was eagerly awaiting news of progress. When she reported that I was still four centimeters dilated, it sounded as though her voice was coming from very, very far away. The news was so devastating that I remember consciously trying to distance myself from it. I felt completely broken.

She then suggested that she give me some Stadol through an IV to take the edge off the contractions so I could get some rest, which she thought I really needed. Although I'd envisioned a completely natural birth, I trusted her judgment completely and was willing to do what she advised. The Stadol began, the lights were dimmed, and my husband and I settled onto the bed. I was looking forward to a respite from the pain. The Stadol did allow me to rest, even fall asleep. The problem was, however, that it let me sleep for the two to four minutes in between contractions, and then I'd wake up yelling out and writhing in pain as a contraction hit (which I had no time to prepare for), and then fall asleep again.

A couple of hours later, a new midwife came on duty, I was examined, and it looked like I was making some progress. In the period that followed, every time I had a contraction, she would reach inside me and help the dilation process along manually. Through sheer will and physical strength she helped me dilate fully, all along cheering me on. When she told me that I could now push, I was thrilled (as were my husband and niece, who at that point were looking as emotionally wrought as I was). I was instantaneously able to find new energy for this next step as I gladly put the long night behind me. It was now morning, I had no idea exactly what time, and I started to feel confident that my baby was actually on her way.

The pushing began, and it continued, and it continued, and it continued. I think the baby was still posterior and we later figured out that she had quite a noggin. Whatever the reason, however, no matter how hard I pushed, I could not get her out. I pushed in every position possible and I pushed while the midwife tried to push the baby down and out from the outside. After the whole thing was over, the broken blood vessels all over my face and neck confirmed for me that the pushing was as arduous as I thought it had been. I remember everyone telling me that I was doing a great job to which I meekly replied, "No, I'm not." In my mind, at that moment, I was a complete failure.

After three and a half hours of pushing, with some tense moments involving the baby's heart rate and oxygen being administered to me between every contraction, my husband and my midwife conferred (I was really too out of it at that point to participate in the conversation) and it was decided that other measures were necessary. Once again, from very far away, I heard someone telling me that they were going to consult with the obstetrician who was on-call in the labor and delivery ward.

When the doctor arrived, he took a look and thought the baby had room to get through and that a vacuum extraction might be the best approach. It was clear that if this didn't work, a cesarean was in my very near future. I didn't care how the baby got out of me at that point. I'd failed to do the job and it was now out of my hands. I've heard people say that when their labor took a turn for the worse, they knew the most important thing was getting the baby out healthy. In my head, I knew this, but, in my heart, I was extremely disappointed that I needed help.

I was put into a hospital gown, ending the naked period of my labor, and brought into an operating room where I would have a cesarean if the vacuum extraction didn't work. My midwife, of course, stayed by my side, but I was now in a very white room with lots of lights and lots of people. Doctors, nurses, residents, you name it. After the serene birthing center, this was quite a shock. During an earlier conversation with the doctor, my husband was told about the possible risks (to the baby) of vacuum extraction so he was carrying quite a bit of fear with him into that room. I had conveniently skipped those parts in the many pregnancy books I'd read and was in no shape to ask any questions now.

The vacuum was attached to the baby's head and I was told that when another contraction hit, I was to push, while the doctor pulled. "Push? I still had to push?" I thought this device was just going to suck the baby out of me while I lay on my back, my feet in stirrups, in a highly sterile medical environment, as though I were asleep and having my worst childbirth nightmare. But I still had to push.

As "the team" all stood around me waiting for my uterus to contract, I felt intense performance anxiety. As I pushed, the doctor pulled with all his might, and someone else pushed down on my belly from the outside. Once the baby crowned, the vacuum was removed and I did the rest of the pushing unassisted. My contractions were petering out by then, and my body was totally exhausted, so these last several pushes were intensely difficult. I remember feeling the baby as she slowly, slowly, slowly descended those final inches through the birth canal and into the world. I also remember being given an episiotomy by my midwife, which I dreaded all through my pregnancy, and was amazed not to feel at all (until the next day).

And then, there she was: Zoe Elizabeth came into the world at 1:46 P.M. (about sixteen hours from the moment my water broke) weighing seven pounds, four ounces. Despite all the pushing, her Apgars were 9/9 and, of course, she was perfect. Unfortunately, because we were no longer in the birthing center (where births are handled differently), Zoe was put on my chest (but not my bare chest) for a minute or two and then whisked over to a table in the corner of the room to be checked out, cleaned, weighed, etc.

The moments that I'd most anticipated—touching her head as it came out of me, feeling her skin against mine, nursing her immediately after birth, and just generally having an intimate post-birth experience with my husband and daughter—were, unfortunately, not a part of my birth. But I had my baby, I'd avoided a cesarean, and I was very pleased with the care I'd received. Even though the experience was nothing like I expected (or wanted) it to be, it was wondrous, and it made me into a stronger, wiser, and more fulfilled woman than the one I'd been before.

Lauren, 32

Lauren's pregnancy had gone very smoothly so she was completely caught off guard when a routine ultrasound two days after her due date revealed that her baby was much smaller than he should be.

It was two days after my due date. I was down to one pair of shoes that fit, I hadn't worn my wedding ring in months, and I was feeling generally blob-like and ready to get this kid out of me. Or at least, that's what I thought I was feeling—until I went in for a routine amniotic fluid check and was told I *had* to get this kid out of me, pronto.

I had waited what seemed like hours (no, wait—it actually *was* hours) at the hospital, while ectopic pregnancies and problem cases got taken in to the ultrasound room first. I wasn't the least bit worried—I'd had two ultrasounds before, and an easy and healthy pregnancy (in spite of nagging fears about two-headed babies inspired by a *Time* magazine article in my fifth month). After a few minutes, however, I realized that the technician seemed to be repeating one measurement over and over: click, move the wand, click again. Repeat. She didn't say anything. After a while, she got up and left the room, only to return with another technician. Click, move, click. Silence. Finally, the second technician spoke up. "When was your last ultrasound?" "Three weeks ago." "And everything was *normal*?!" The incredulity in her voice was unmistakable. I looked at my husband, and all I could think was, "Oh, my God, they found the second head!"

After what seemed like hours (but this time it was only minutes), a doctor came in and told us that the baby seemed small—much smaller than he should be. Or, to be more precise, skinny—he was long and skinny. I was whisked out of there and sent over to my doctor's office; she told me that I probably had intrauterine growth retardation (IUGR). For some mysterious reason (often an infection, but in my case never determined), the placenta had simply shut down during the last few weeks of the pregnancy. The baby had continued to get taller, but he gained no weight (and this is the period when all they're supposed to do is add fat). This meant that he wasn't being nourished, and we had to get him out—sooner rather than later.

I scheduled an induction for the next morning and went home in shock. I'm five foot ten and certainly ate more than enough for two during my pregnancy—how on earth could I end up with a tiny baby? Would the baby be OK? And what about all those notions I'd had about a natural childbirth?

We slept very little, got up at 6 A.M., and caught a cab to the hospital. I gave my history to the nurse, waited around, fretted, and finally at 9 A.M. started a Pitocin drip. The first two hours were completely uneventful—a few mild contractions, an amusing episode with a terrified medical student, a lot of ice chips. I made my husband read out loud to me (when he wasn't pacing frantically). Around 11 A.M. the contractions started to feel a bit stronger, though still no worse than bad menstrual cramps, and at 1 P.M. the doctor suggested breaking my bag of waters. I'd initially been opposed to this sort of intervention, but I figured what the hell, I'm on the Pitocin, might as well go all the way.

As soon as the membranes ruptured, labor began in earnest, and I really mean in earnest. In the space of about ten minutes, I went from having a few desultory contractions now and then to having savage contractions every two minutes (that's contract for a minute, rest for a minute, start again). It's hard to describe the kind of pain—like menstrual cramps, but menstrual cramps that bowled me over and paralyzed me, all made worse by the fact that I was basically immobile. (Most women can walk around during labor, but those of us with risky conditions must be hooked up to all sorts of monitors and gadgets.) For two and a half hours this continued. My husband tells me I looked like one of those alien creatures on *Star Trek*, the ones that have had all the blood sucked out of them by some mysterious creature with tentacles. At around 3:30 P.M., the idea of an epidural seemed like heaven, and that huge horse needle looked no bigger than a pin. By 4:15 P.M. the drugs were coursing through my body, and shortly thereafter I'd gone from four to ten centimeters and was ready to start pushing.

OK, now here's the confessional part: I *liked* pushing, I really did! It was incredibly hard work, pushing down with all my might, but it no longer felt like meaningless pain. With each push I could tell that I was making progress, that the baby was inching its way down. Of course, it helped that I had a fairly short and easy pushing phase. My son was born at 5:43 P.M. The doctor eased out my poor skinny baby and deposited the bloody squirming bundle on my chest. Benjamin looked up at me, with the same soft, deep blue eyes he has now, and his little red mouth began to mew, rooting around for my nipple. And that did it—I was in love.

Nell, 33

Like Lauren, Nell's pregnancy had been free of complications until the end. When she developed symptoms three weeks before her due date, she was sure she had a stomach bug. By the next evening, not only would she be admitted to the hospital to give birth to her daughter, she would also be diagnosed with preeclampsia (see Nell's story in chapter five).

After we were so unexpectedly admitted to the hospital, there was little to do but wait and watch monitors. I was transferred from the triage room to a labor room where my husband, Bryan, and I chatted and called family and friends to let them know I was not only in labor, but had preeclampsia. I was strangely proud. Our baby Nibblet's heartbeat was going strong.

The contractions were five, then four minutes apart. My obstetrician arrived. She pointed to the squiggles on the monitor at the peak of the contractions. The baby is kicking, she said. She's moving into position. The staff hooked up magnesium sulfate to an IV to prevent seizures, as well as Pitocin to quicken the contractions. I started deep breathing. I wanted to move to a child's pose, or to walk. I'd taken months of prenatal yoga; this was the big time; I wanted to use my stuff. "You're not allowed," I was told. "I'm not allowed?" I was told the condition I had required that I lie on my left side (for hours, unceasing). I'd be more relaxed were I able to get into a more comfortable position, I said. The medical personnel were not swayed.

Everyone watched the monitor. Time passed, quickly. I breathed into my stomach, exhaled, and counted to twenty, again and again. The magnesium made me feel flushed, hot. I sucked an occasional ice chip and dreamt of a cup of water. The contractions were now four minutes, then three minutes apart. My obstetrician checked back in. She murmured to Bryan. The intern approached. They wanted to put in an epidural catheter. "I'm doing fine," I said. "I don't think I'll need one." The intern looked away from me, toward my doctor, who then approached. Her eyes looked intense, but her voice was calm. "You have a variation of preeclampsia called H.E.L.L.P. [Hemolysis, Elevated Liver enzymes, Low Platelets] syndrome. Your platelet levels are dropping. Your liver enzyme levels are askew. On the chance that you'll need a cesarean, an epidural is the preferred anesthetic. We should put in the catheter now, while the platelet levels are still high enough." Oh. Bryan nodded to me, silently, with a tension edge, "Do it." I shrugged. I sloughed off the plan of natural childbirth. "Sure," I said, "OK. Do what you have to." I felt strangely calm. I knew everything would be OK. I didn't deal well with needles, however. I wondered if it would hurt to put it in. I didn't want to look at it.

It took the intern two attempts to get in the catheter. He was not, as they say, a whiz with a needle. For minutes, I felt him search for the proper passage through my spine. It didn't really hurt, but felt a bit like a prolonged nauseating pinch, kind of like novocaine going in at the dentist—slowly. When they delivered the sample dose of the epidural to test for proper placement, I didn't feel the tingling I was supposed to. The resident then took the needle from her student and inserted the catheter with agility to spare. I asked if she needed to administer another sample dose. She laughed, "It's not necessary, it's in correctly." I wondered at the drawbacks of teaching hospitals.

The contractions continued. They were between one and two minutes apart. I continued to breathe. My obstetrician returned; I was only four centimeters dilated. She looked tense. She tried to further the dilation manually. I squirmed with sudden pain. The contractions had been OK; her forearms were a different story. I was four and a half centimeters dilated. She focused her gaze on me again. She would have liked for me to deliver vaginally, but she was concerned that if we waited too long my platelets would drop even further. She paused. If they dropped too low, clotting would become an issue, and they wouldn't be able to do a cesarean. I filled in the rest—the seizures and coma that might come with a vaginal delivery. It seemed that there was little choice. I glanced at the monitor for the baby's heartbeat; it was still regular and strong. My obstetrician told me we could wait a bit longer; then, as an afterthought, she asked if I wanted an epidural.

At this point, I knew I was going to end up with a cesarean. Why make it through the contractions now, only to be faced with surgery? "Sure," I said. "Bring it on." She looked vaguely surprised; perhaps she'd thought I'd hold on longer to the dream. An anesthesiologist administered the epidural (no more fooling around). I felt some tightness as it went in.

Suddenly, magically, I wasn't sure I was still having contractions. I looked at the monitor, and they were still registering. Powerful stuff, that epidural. Maybe twenty minutes passed. Bryan and the obstetrician left the room. I stared at the monitor, wondering how the contractions could be occurring so painlessly. My obstetrician reentered the room, looked me over, and sat at my bedside. I knew what she was going to say. I agreed to the cesarean, feeling almost surprised that I needed to OK it.

The room erupted into purposeful energy. The anesthesiologist administered additional epidural and I was prepped for surgery. They called for plasma in case I needed a transfusion—my platelets were low. A scant fifteen or twenty minutes later I was wheeled to the operating room, holding Bryan's hand, chatting with the residents as I went, shocked that I was still conscious; I'd never expected to be awake through surgery.

Once in the operating room, they drew a curtain across my midsection and talked as they performed each part of the procedure. The atmosphere was focused but pleasant, far more jovial than I'd imagined it would be. As they made the incision, I smelled burning flesh—an unexpected odor, to say the least. I commented. From across the curtain came the explanation: to minimize bleeding, they were cauterizing the incision.

Then came the exclamations: "There's so little blood!" A pause. "There she is!" Then a sudden, joyous declaration of life; Rachel wailed. I heard my doctor laugh, "She's crying and only her shoulders are out!" Then a gasp, "Oh my gosh, she's a peanut!" (Rachel weighed four pounds, eleven ounces.) Bryan was called to the other side of the curtain. I saw a flash of a snowy bundle with flailing limbs and an irate, bawling mouth. It was my daughter and she was very much alive. I felt like crying.

Bryan was much more active from here on out than I was. He had cut the umbilical cord, and was then summoned to hold her. After I was sewed up, he carried her over to where I could see her, and giggled, giggled, and gasped with the wonder of her. The love, for Bryan, was instantaneous: "She's holding my finger! What a grip!" She stopped crying for a moment and seemed to look at him.

It was Bryan's theory, formed in this moment, and still strongly held, that Rachel was aware of the circumstances surrounding her birth, and was intent on facilitating delivery. Hence her position, her kicking, her strong heartbeat. As Bryan reports it, when she gripped his finger, she was silent awaiting word. After he told her that Mommy was OK, Rachel then resumed crying (cries of triumph if Bryan is to be believed) and the nurses hustled her away for cleaning.

The downside of the cesarean is that I had to hang out in recovery for hours before they'd let me hold my daughter, though she was eventually brought to me and I was able to nurse her. They also kept us off the regular maternity ward and I was supervised for a day and a half because I was still being administered magnesium. It seems that the symptoms of preeclampsia often linger after delivery, though my levels normalized virtually immediately afterward.

In the end, I know we were extraordinarily lucky. I was lucky to be full term before contracting the preeclampsia, and lucky to be riding it out in the hospital. I was lucky to have my doctor, who allowed me some sense of control, even though I ended up doing everything she advised. Despite having nine needles in me by the time it was over, my doctor helped me to feel unexpectedly calm through the delivery. As it turns out, Bryan had been far more nervous than I. Perhaps because he knew more than I did about what was going on. He foolishly asked for assurances that everything would be OK from an intern who felt it would be disingenuous to assure him of anything. I hadn't even thought to look for assurances—I was just dealing with what I felt like, and I felt strong throughout. I think we were luckiest that there were no complications with Rachel. It's one thing to deal with your own body and mind, and quite another to be worried about your baby. I guess an easy labor is essentially a selfish one, and Rachel's strength enabled me to focus on myself.

Ginette, 31

Ginette's first son was delivered by cesarean and she was really hoping for a vaginal birth the second time around. She was, however, carrying twins and she knew that this opened the door to numerous possibilities.

Murphy's Law: You go into labor when your husband is not sleeping next to you. My husband was working at a nearby youth camp when my water broke at 4:30 A.M. during the thirty-fifth week of my pregnancy. My mother had insisted on staying over that night since I was on my own and I'd had a twinge earlier that evening. I was happy she was there now because it meant I wouldn't have to wake up my three-year-old son, Joshua, in the middle of the night. I called my husband and he arrived home shortly. We took our time packing our things, leaving instructions for Joshua, setting out the breakfast dishes, and cleaning up a bit.

We got in the car just as the sun was rising. It was really nice. I could already tell that this labor was different than my first. It just felt better, like things were going the way they were supposed to even though this time I was carrying twins. When we arrived at the hospital around 6 A.M., my contractions were coming every three to five minutes, but they weren't too painful. I was examined and told that I was only one centimeter dilated and that the baby that would come out first was still high. I had been hoping that I would be further along than that so I was a little disappointed.

I had several ultrasounds during my labor, which revealed that both babies (boy twins that we'd already named Jonah and Jackson) were vertex (head down). This was great news because through most of my pregnancy Jackson was transverse (lying sideways in my belly) or breech (feet down, instead of head down). I wanted to deliver these babies vaginally (I had a cesarean the first time around) and my doctor would not have entertained this possibility at all if the first twin had not been positioned head down.

At 9 A.M. I asked for a shot of Demerol for the pain. It made me woozy, but I found that it didn't help that much. Around 10:30 A.M., my doctor encouraged me to get an epidural. I was three centimeters dilated and the first baby was coming down. I wanted to wait a little longer because so far I was tolerating the pain well and I wanted to see how much I could accomplish on my own. They were treating me as a repeat cesarean, just in case of an emergency, so I was hooked up to monitors and an IV. I was fine with that since I knew complications were not uncommon with twin deliveries, especially with the second baby. Better safe than sorry! At 11 A.M., after being convinced by the nurses, my husband, and my doctor, I agreed to the epidural. Shortly after it was administered, while they were inserting a urine catheter, they discovered that I was now nine centimeters dilated. When I heard this I was unhappy that I'd had the epidural. I was so far along I probably didn't need it after all, and now I would have to wait a while for it to wear off before I could push.

The nurses told me that as soon as it wore off and I felt the urge to push, these babies would be born. They said this could happen by noon. At 2 P.M. the epidural was finally starting to wear off, but I still didn't have the urge to push. Considering that I'd been fully dilated for two and a half hours already, I was starting to become frustrated. For the next three hours we labored and continued waiting for the infamous urge to push.

At around 5 P.M., I was so upset and tired that I told my husband to tell the doctor that I wanted another cesarean. The nurse could see how unhappy I was and she suggested that I start pushing even though I didn't have the urge. Finally, I could start doing something. I had now been fully dilated for six and a half hours. I pushed against painful contractions and it was awful. People tell me that it would have been different if I'd felt like bearing down but that never happened. Also, no one told me what it would feel like to try and push one baby out while there was still another baby up near my rib cage.

At 6 P.M. my doctor came in to see how I was doing. I was tired and frustrated and had been pushing for over an hour. Finally, my husband said he could see the first baby's hair, and that became my motivator. When my doctor came back about thirty minutes later, he said, "Let's get this show on the road!" The room was filled with people, but I didn't care. There were two neonatal intensive care unit (NICU) nurses for each baby, because they were preemies, my obstetrician, his resident, and about three other nurses. It was a full house.

My doctor decided to perform a vacuum extraction to help me along. By then he could have taken out the Hoover and I wouldn't have cared. I pushed a few more times and Jonah Alexander was born at 6:59 P.M. I turned to my husband and said, "I did it." I think these must be the first words out of every woman's mouth when she's given birth vaginally after a cesarean. It is a great feeling of accomplishment. No matter how much one justifies a previous cesarean, even though they would have done anything necessary to have a healthy child, it's easy to feel as though you've failed if you didn't deliver vaginally.

They held Jonah up and he was beautiful. He looked just like his older brother, Joshua, and that made me very happy. They put him on me for a minute and that was a thrill because I didn't get to do that with Joshua. Then a nurse whisked him away because he was having minor problems with his breathing. I was getting upset and my husband, of course, was torn between staying with me or going with Jonah to the NICU, but I told him to go with Jonah. I remember crying and saying, "Go, go, go, just go!"

My doctor looked at me calmly and said, "He's OK, but you're not done here!" I had confidence in him so I relaxed as my husband went to check on Jonah. They gave me Pitocin to be sure that my contractions continued, just in case my body thought that its work was done and was ready to quit, and they did another ultrasound. Jackson had floated up after the delivery of Jonah and when they broke my water to move things along, Jackson assumed the transverse position he'd favored through most of the pregnancy. My husband returned and reported that everything was OK with Jonah. Then the doctor said they were going to manually turn Jackson around.

As he examined me internally with one of his arms inside me up to his elbow, another doctor (a resident) was pushing on my belly externally to try to move Jackson into position. Believe it or not, this was the worst part of delivery—very painful! They finally turned him, but now he was in a footling breech position (feet poised to come out first). I still had no urge to bear down, but I was instructed to push again. This time, however, I felt better because I knew I could do it and I also knew that Jonah was OK. So I pushed and pushed. First I pushed out some toes, then an ankle, then a shin. One leg was out, as were the toes and ankle of the other, when the baby's heart rate dropped dramatically.

I remember my obstetrician quickly pushing the resident out of the way (I can still hear the sound of the chair wheels squeak across the hospital floor) so he could perform an episiotomy that helped Jackson out up to his chest. Then, using special breech forceps, the doctor delivered the rest of him. At 7:45 P.M. Jackson William was born. He was healthy (with the exception of a black/purple foot from circulation being cut off), and they took him to the NICU to check him over and to join his brother.

It was determined that the twins were six weeks early. Jonah weighed five pounds, seven ounces and was eighteen inches long. Jackson measured six pounds even and was eighteen and a half inches long. Not bad for preemies. My first son, Joshua, was also a big baby—ten pounds, eleven ounces at full-term birth. Considering that I'm five feet tall and, when not pregnant, about 100 pounds, people are always very surprised at the size of my babies.

We were told that the twins would probably stay in the hospital for two to three weeks, but that they were doing great. As I was getting stitched up, I asked how many stitches I needed. The doctor said I didn't need any from Jonah's birth, but after Jackson's I needed about forty. But I still felt so much better than I did after my cesarean. I was able to get myself out of the delivery bed on my own, and to stand up to see my babies in their incubators. My husband brought Joshua in to see me and then took him to meet his new brothers. I felt so very proud of my new family and myself. When my husband brought Joshua to the neonatal nursery he didn't want to hold his new brothers at first, but a little while later he did. When Jackson was put into his big brother's arms, Joshua, in his tiny little three-year-old voice, said, "Hi, I'm your big brother and I'm gonna love you forever." Even the nurses were crying.

I went to see the boys at five the next morning (who can sleep after such a thing?) and was told they were doing great and were expected to be released in a couple of weeks. I slowly walked the quiet halls back to my room feeling like I was on top of the world, my greatest moment! At 10 A.M. the same morning, a nurse came in with some wonderful news. She said the babies had been discharged from the NICU, that they were perfectly healthy, and that I could bring them down to my room. We were able to take them home two days later and now I have three active, beautiful, and smart boys.

Audra, 24

Audra gave birth to her first son in a hospital. The experience was fine, but this time she felt strongly about birthing at home with a midwife. She wanted more support for her drug-free approach to childbirth than the hospital provided. She also desired an immediate postpartum experience that would allow her to curl up on a big bed with her husband, son, and new baby, without having nurses "barging in every once in a while to check my bottom."

Although my first son, Clark, was born in a hospital, when I became pregnant with my second child I felt strongly about giving birth at home. Midwifery and home birth recently became legal in my Canadian province, but I was fully willing to break the law had this not happened.

My midwife was scheduled to be out of town for ten days very close to my due date. I'd hoped that I would give birth before she left, but that didn't happen. My backup midwife, Lorna, lived three hours away and, for obvious reasons, this made me a bit nervous. Of course, after going to bed one Saturday night, while my midwife was away, I woke up gradually to the sensation of increasing pain. As it peaked, I checked the time—2 A.M. on the dot. I fell asleep again only to be aroused by the same sensation. I checked the clock—2:07 A.M. Hmmm. Could this be it? I got up to pee. No bloody show, no leaking water. I had another contraction on my way back to the bed—2:13 A.M. I figured that three contractions pretty evenly spaced apart must be a good sign. I tried to wake my dear husband with not much luck. Another contraction. I said, "Phil, I'm calling Lorna" to which he replied by leaping out of bed, exclaiming, "I'm up, I'm up."

Lorna started the trek to our place and I phoned the assistant midwife and doula who arrived shortly thereafter. The mood was that of a slumber party, nice dim lighting, good music on the stereo, Phil and me in our jammies, and everyone staying up late and chatting. Phil moved our son Clark upstairs to go sleep with his grandpa so we wouldn't wake him with the noise, but alas, the move itself was disruptive and I could hear the pattering of his little feet during my entire labor.

Phil and my doula, Christie, filled the large inflatable pool, and Eileen (the assistant midwife) checked me and found me to be four centimeters dilated with my bag of waters still intact. This would end up being my only vaginal exam. Nice! It was now 3:30 A.M. Up until this point I could talk and relax through the contractions. I was confident and excited, although some pain in my back made me nervous because I had back labor with my first son that was so unbearable I opted for an epidural. Lucky for me, Christie is a massage therapist so she worked on my back and it felt lovely.

When I first entered the pool, there was a welcome pause in my labor that lasted about ten minutes. I took the time to horse around with Eileen and told her I'd been constipated lately and was worried I might have a bowel movement during delivery.

When the break ended it was no-nonsense for the rest of the labor. I moaned a lot this time (with my first child, in the hospital, I felt like I had to be quiet) and it felt great. As the intensity of the contractions increased—each one was peaking two or three times—I was not really able to talk between them any longer. I kept reminding myself to relax my bottom, and that panic and fear were not going to help. Everyone commented afterward that I didn't seem to need any help and that they were all standing around watching my body take charge.

For the next few hours I had my eyes closed, only opening them when someone would ask me to take a sip of juice, which I did not want to do. I had terrible heartburn and hiccups and this, combined with the multiple peaks of each contraction and the fact that they were right on top of one another, made me know that I was in transition. It was then that Lorna arrived (I didn't even open my eyes but breathed a silent thank-you that she had made it).

Suddenly I called out, "Push! Push!" as my body writhed in a totally unfamiliar pushing reflex (the epidural I had last time did not allow me to feel this at all) and something burst inside me. I was certain it was my water, although it seemed to break again later in a big splash as I pushed the baby out. Lorna had a peek inside and asked me to get out of the pool and on to the bed. I didn't want to leave the pool but remembered the desire I expressed in my birth plan to give birth on my hands and knees to maximize the chances of my perineum remaining intact and to prevent opening an anal fissure that had torn during my last birth. I was met with nice warm towels and led to my bed. I had no energy to get on my hands and knees so I just lay on my side (as I had during my three hours in the tub).

There was another brief "rest and be thankful period" after which I gave one push on my side and then flipped over to my hands and knees. My pushing urge did not begin with the onset of a contraction. The contraction would start, I'd moan, and then after the peak I would have an irresistible urge/reflex to push. It was so powerful and so out of control that it reminded me of vomiting. I remember thinking that with my first birth the epidural prevented me from feeling this urge and I was instructed to push at the start of each contraction. Perhaps I tore because I wasn't pushing at the right time?

Two more pushes and the head was out along with some of the dreaded poop. I remember apologizing profusely as it was paper toweled away. Lorna instructed me to stop pushing and pant. It took all the strength I had to hold back the push. I let out a mighty trumpet sound reminiscent of an elephant and then felt enormous relief as the baby slipped out into Lorna's hands. There was a terrific splash, then a pause. It was as though nothing had happened. No more pain.

I turned around to see the baby lying on the bed under me. Phil and I looked and saw that it was a boy. How nice not to be told by someone else. The midwives began suctioning him. That great splash I heard had meconium in it, and the suctioning was done to ensure he didn't breathe it into his lungs. He was so alert, eyes wide open and looking around. He was breathing fine, just not crying. My labor, from first contraction to baby on bed had lasted exactly five hours and six minutes. And it only took three pushes for him to come out.

I felt terrific. Lorna took a peek and there was no perineal tearing. I let out a "whoop." I was too tired to push anymore so I was helped to a standing position on the bed and the placenta fell out on its own. We later buried it in our yard.

We were left alone for a while, and Phil and I marveled over our beautiful new boy. They then came back in to weigh him, a whopping eight pounds, thirteen ounces, twenty-one and three-quarters inches long. He had some blisters on his hands from sucking in utero. He started doing the "birdie mouth" and I put him to my breast. What a nice latch (although in the days that followed we ended up having some major latch battles). Christie stripped the bed and after I had a shower she brought me muffins and juice and tucked us in. The midwives did the dishes and laundry while Phil and Christie drained the tub. At 9:30 A.M. my son, Clark, came downstairs and we all sat at the breakfast table, me nursing little Paul. It was as though his arrival had not disrupted a thing.

The midwives checked up on us daily for about a week, provided all the paperwork, and arranged for the PKU test (given to all newborns to screen for the disease phenylketonuria) to be performed in our home. How nice not to have to venture out into the prairie winter, or trek to the hospital nursery, or worry about the baby being given a pacifier or formula by a nurse. Just push out the baby and snuggle in bed together. And the food is much better at home, too.

Caroline, 33

Sometimes births do go according to plan and this was the case for Caroline. With no major surprises and a reasonable amount of time from start to finish (especially for a first pregnancy), her birth experience was, in her eyes, "textbook."

Looking back on it, I knew I was going into labor shortly before I actually did. I heard that your system shuts down right beforehand. I couldn't eat and didn't go to the bathroom. I also had a nesting attack. I ironed all of the shirts in both my husband's closet and mine, and I hate to iron.

At 3 A.M., my water broke. It felt like a balloon breaking between my legs. Then there was another pop. I was six days early. I woke my husband up and ran into the bathroom and immediately started panicking and shaking. My husband reminded me that my contractions might not start for a while and we should go back to bed. I put towels down on the bed and lay down but was back in the bathroom fifteen minutes later as my contractions started. I kept going from bed to bathroom and realized that at least my husband should get some sleep. So, I moved onto the couch between trips.

I showered and then called the doctor at 6 A.M. She kept me on the phone for a while, probably to see if I would have a contraction while talking to her. I described the contractions as alternating between OK or completely unbearable. Then she informed me, "You still have some work to do. Call me when they are all unbearable."

The return call woke my husband up and he showered and began getting ready. I called the doctor again at 8 A.M. to let her know I couldn't stand it anymore. I never really timed my contractions but knew they were two to five minutes apart. Because I had been three centimeters dilated at my last appointment, my doctor told me we could go to the hospital.

We both called our parents to let them know. My husband's father told him not to waste time on the phone and we better get there soon, thus sending my husband into panic mode. It took me an hour and a half to get dressed and put the items I had put aside to bring to the hospital into a bag. In between, I was lying on the floor and running to the bathroom.

We had planned to walk to the hospital since it's only seven blocks away, but I could barely make it down the stairs. We hailed a cab and made it in two minutes. I had another contraction outside the hospital.

When we got to the labor and delivery ward at 9:30 A.M., we handed over our forms to the registration desk. We were directed to the waiting room where we sat for fifteen minutes, which seemed like an hour, before we were admitted. As we waited for our doctor to arrive, two interns examined me and told me I was at four centimeters.

I informed anyone who came in that I was ready for an epidural. The nurse started me on an IV drip, attached a fetal monitor, and told me I had to wait until my doctor arrived before I could receive the epidural. I was still hopping in and out of bed to run to the bathroom. The labor nurse tried to stop me, telling me that I didn't have to go to the bathroom, it was the baby's head moving down. I couldn't stay in bed, so I took the IV drip and ran into the bathroom hitting my head on the wall in the process. I remember it all vaguely, but I was in a completely different zone. I do remember my husband's voice telling me to breathe and his hand rubbing my back. That really helped calm me down.

The doctor arrived at 11 A.M. and determined that I was five centimeters dilated. I received an epidural and had to be held still so I didn't move when the needle went in. The epidural did eliminate a lot of pain, transforming it into what felt like very strong pressure in my lower back. An hour later the doctor told me I was ready to push.

It all seemed so quick. I couldn't believe I had just been sleeping at home and was now ready to push. I pushed for forty-five minutes. When I pushed correctly, I really felt like I was being ripped apart. Then the head came and I felt it move. The doctor said, "The baby's turning its head. It knows just what to do." Then it started sucking the doctor's thumb. I pushed a few more times and the shoulders came out. The doctor held the baby up and my husband announced it was a boy.

Sara, 36

When they decided to try for a second child, Sara and Terry were already the mothers of a daughter that Terry had given birth to three years earlier. Using the same sperm donor they'd used for Terry's pregnancy, this time Sara would be the one to carry the baby. The pregnancy was about twenty-six weeks old when the unthinkable happened.

Fourteen weeks before my due date, I woke up on a Monday morning around 7:30 A.M. with a splitting headache. We had been out with friends for dinner the night before, and I went to bed feeling tired but fine. Part way through the night I had gotten up to take a couple of ibuprofen for a budding headache. My first thought was, "Oh, this must be the kind of sinus headache that Terry, my partner, always gets and says hurts so much; if I take a shower, maybe it will dissipate." It didn't. I soon started throwing up constantly. Then, my vision got blurry. I didn't know it, but I was having a stroke.

Terry started calling the obstetrician's office around 8:30 A.M. The answering service never paged a doctor who responded. At 9 A.M., when the office opened, she talked to the people at the front desk, and said that we needed to speak to a doctor. She told them that her partner was throwing up and had a headache so bad she couldn't see straight. No call back. At 9:30 A.M. she called again and repeated the message more insistently. She called again thirty minutes later. About a half hour after that one of the doctors finally called us back, one we'd never met. She casually said, "Maybe you should get her to the hospital," and then tried to convince Terry to bring me to a hospital that was thirty minutes away as opposed to one ten minutes away because the one nearest our house was farther from their practice.

Terry got me dressed as best she could. I stumbled down the stairs and out to the car but couldn't get in beyond sitting sideways with my feet out the door. At that point, Terry decided to strap our daughter, Hannah, into her car seat and call an ambulance, which took ten minutes to arrive.

From that point on, I remember very little.

When I arrived at the hospital, I suffered a seizure. It became clear that I was experiencing a sudden onset of eclampsia and that my only chance of survival was dependent on delivering the baby right away. My blood pressure was up to 240 over 120. Being the overachiever that I am, I skipped the preeclampsia phase of eclampsia, so prior to that day, there had been no warning signs at all that we were headed in a dangerous direction. Due to the seriousness of my condition, I was treated that day by the head of our practice, who, in his thirty years of experience, has only seen five cases like mine. Terry was appalled that they were going to deliver our child while we were only twenty-six weeks along.

That afternoon, at 3:33 P.M., our son, Toby, was delivered via an emergency cesarean. He weighed 1 pound, 11.2 ounces and was about thirteen and a half inches long. Terry was not in the delivery room and I was not conscious so neither of us saw him at that moment. Terry did go to the NICU not long after his birth, and couldn't believe that such a small and early baby might have a chance of survival. Clearly, the doctors thought that Toby did have a chance, and they did not give Terry the "we've done everything possible and he's not doing well" talk.

I spent three days in the intensive care unit (ICU). The day after our baby was born, it looked like I was having another stroke. My speech was pretty unintelligible, my left leg was more or less immobile, and part of the functioning in my right leg as well as my left arm was gone. Several CAT scans were done and luckily they didn't find evidence of a second stroke. They also performed an MRI, after which a neurosurgeon came into my room to report that they'd found evidence of an "incidental" aneurysm, totally unrelated to the eclampsia. I later found out this term meant that it was not harmful at the moment. He wanted to see me again in about six weeks for a cerebral angiogram and to evaluate the treatment options. At that moment, I started having intense and very weird visual and auditory hallucinations. Whether they were due to drugs that I was on, or to the news of the aneurysm, I don't know. (When the angiogram was finally done we found out that the MRI had been inaccurate and that I do not, in fact, have a cerebral aneurysm. Great, but stunning news.)

I spent seven more days on the maternity floor. I was supposed to go to the rehabilitation section, but they had no beds and my doctors argued for me to be kept close to the NICU where Toby was. I was not a typical maternity patient, but the nurses were all troopers and provided astounding care.

My leg, arm, and speech functioning started resolving themselves without rehabilitation for the most part. At one point, I felt the feeling from my left hip to my left knee simply trickle down and reappear, like a glass of milk filling up. As I write this, six weeks later, the front of my left foot still feels like pins and needles much of the time, but that's the only residual sign of the stroke.

I first saw Toby on Thursday—day four of this trauma. It felt very surreal to no longer be pregnant, to be the parent of a son, to have a preemie child in the NICU. It still feels surreal to some extent and, in a way, it's hard to remember how it felt to be pregnant.

By day nine, I started to have inklings of feeling like myself, and I went home on day ten. I was weak, but I was alive. Terry and I both had a new perspective on life, and a new appreciation for being alive, having each other, and having our strong relationship. For days, all I could say when folks asked, "How are you doing?" was "I'm alive!"

Rather than constantly wondering "Why us?" Terry and I actually feel rather lucky and thankful. Terry thought fairly realistically that she might lose me and she certainly didn't think that Toby would survive. In fact, the doctors were more confident about Toby's chances than they were about mine.

In the end, I survived the eclampsia and all of its complications, which was not a sure thing, and Toby is doing well in the NICU. He's growing, albeit slowly, and has been a basically boring preemie patient for the last two weeks or so. Just today he passed the 2 pound, .9 ounce mark. He's been drinking breast milk on an increasing basis and tolerating it well. He looks bigger than he did a month ago and more filled out. We call him our feisty little "Toby Tiger." We expect to bring him home some time in the next six to eight weeks, not too far from his original due date. (See Sara's postpartum story in chapter nine.)

In the end, there is a lot to be thankful for.

Jenny, 36

Jenny approached the birth of her first child with the standard amount of anxiety. The whole experience went so smoothly that soon after she used the word "easy" to describe it. Two years later, when expecting her second child, she was confident about the birth ahead. After all, it's even easier the second time, isn't it?

When I was single and twenty-seven years old, I watched my older sister give birth to my niece, without the aid of modern painkillers. That event had the single biggest effect on the planning of my own birth experiences. After witnessing my sister's uncontrollable howls, I decided that when it was my turn to sit on a labor and delivery bed, I would make sure my shrieks were pacified with drugs.

Every woman has her own specific level of tolerance for pain. For instance, my sister hates to have hairs tweezed from her brow. Doesn't bother me at all. But the thought of seven pounds emerging from between my legs frightens me. When I was pregnant with my first baby, I prepared well for the experience. I did prenatal yoga three times a week, hoping my naturally open hips would come in handy when I gave birth. I practiced breathing exercises and I also read the book *Easing Labor Pain* (Lieberman 1992) to mentally prepare for what was to take place. I found that the more I knew about what was going to happen to my body, the less afraid I was.

Since I knew I wanted an epidural, I paid attention in my childbirth class when they discussed the procedure. I figured out that it wasn't a good idea to have one too early in your labor, because certain schools of thought believe that it can slow down the birthing process. I decided with my husband that I would try and wait until I was close to five centimeters dilated before asking for an epidural.

As it turned out, dilating five centimeters took a lot longer than I imagined. First of all, I was eleven days past my due date when I finally went into labor. When my labor started it was very, very slow, with painless regular contractions. Because I was so many days late, however, my doctor wanted me to come to the hospital. We went in at 1 A.M. and I was only one centimeter dilated. Real labor didn't start until 6 A.M., at which point I woke my husband and he started massaging me through my contractions. I had a male nurse whose very maleness terrified me at first. But he turned out to be a New–Age guru type who was in awe of the birthing experience, and he was a great masseur. With sage-like wisdom he convinced me to wait to get an epidural, and I held off from drugs until I was nearly five centimeters, as planned.

I got the epidural around noon, at which point, exhausted from being up all night, I fell asleep, woke up, and had enough feeling back to push the baby out one hour later, at 6 P.M. A girl.

The whole experience was so seemingly easy that the first thing I said when the baby popped out was: "Was that it? It was so easy." To which both my doctor and nurse said, "Don't tell that to other women."

I expected my second birth, two and a half years later, to be just as easy. Weren't second births supposed to be? Unfortunately, during my second pregnancy I'd moved to a new city and the new hospital wasn't quite as "patient friendly" as the first.

The night I went into labor, it took us four and a half hours to convince the triage nurse that I was actually in labor so that she would give us a room. The hospital apparently had a policy that you had to be four centimeters dilated before they'd admit you to a labor room. Nobody told us that ahead of time. My husband and I went on several one hour walks in an herb garden in the hospital's court-yard waiting for my contractions to become stronger. Hospital staff kept trying to send us home in between the walks. They would ask, "Don't you want to go home and take some Seconal and get a good night's sleep?" "If I go home I'll just turn around and come back, " I said. "I'm in labor."

We figured out that the women who were screaming the loud-est in the triage area were being admitted to the hospital rooms faster, so I started making noise, with encouragement from my husband.

By the time we were admitted and approved for an epidural I was at six centimeters—and it was a lot more painful than my first experience. At one point, perhaps the apex of my pain, I turned to my husband and said, "Where's the fucking epidural?"

One of the hardest things to endure, and this goes for both of my birth experiences, was holding still for the epidural shot during contractions. Looking into my husband's face while he helped me breathe made this more tolerable both times.

What I didn't expect was that the pushing would be so much harder the second time. I had such an easy time with my first. I think the baby was at a more difficult angle and I just had a much harder time bearing down. We tried all kinds of positions, including squat-ting and using a bar. Finally what worked was playing tug of war with a sheet with the doctor. When the baby did start to emerge, the pain was excruciating.

In the end, I bore another beautiful girl. It was my second labor, but it felt like it was the first time I really experienced the pain of giving birth.

Katherine, 32

Unlike Jenny's, Katherine's first birth was, according to her, "a night-mare." As she neared the end of her second pregnancy, she hoped for the best, while preparing for something much less ideal than that.

Toward the end of my first pregnancy my husband, Niko, and I eagerly attended a childbirth class given by a woman in our neighborhood. We practiced breathing and massage and we tried out a number of positions, all intended to make it possible for us to have the natural labor and delivery we were told every woman can (and should) have.

As my due date came and went, I was feeling good, though certainly unwieldy. My pregnancy, except for minor spotting in the beginning, had been an easy one. The only concern at this point was the baby's size. Both Niko and I had been big babies and it seemed that our baby would be large, too. From feeling around the outside of my spectacularly bulging belly, the doctor guessed that the baby was probably more, maybe much more, than eight pounds, and she suggested we do an ultrasound to get a better idea. At the end of a pregnancy, ultrasounds can be off by a pound or more when determining weight, so the technician's pronouncement of nine pounds could have meant I was carrying an eight-pounder. Then again, it could have meant that my now very ripe child was going to hit double digits in the weight department. My doctor recommended we head to the hospital that night so that I could be induced.

Somewhat surprised to find ourselves in this situation, we dutifully went to the hospital where a prostaglandin gel was applied to my cervix to help soften it up. The next morning, if necessary, I would be given Pitocin to get labor started. Niko went home to get some sleep and, despite earplugs, I spent a largely sleepless night listening to the sounds of other women giving birth.

I went into labor without the Pitocin, starting with crampy contractions in the very early morning, progressing to real, regular contractions by mid-morning, and, by early afternoon, it looked like it wouldn't be too long before we were holding our baby. Then all hell broke loose. As the baby came down, I started having back labor. I had been handling the contractions well up to this point, but the unrelenting pain caused by the baby's spine pushing up against mine made me truly miserable. I had no desire to push, but they told me to and, as I did, it actually seemed like the baby was going back up the birth canal. After three and a half hours and virtually no progress, I took a break from my then guttural howling and asked the doctor attending my birth (of course, my least favorite in a practice of six!) if he really thought this baby was going to come out vaginally. He said he thought there was a chance and suggested I try pushing for another half an hour. I told him that I couldn't push anymore and that I wanted a cesarean and I wanted it now.

He acquiesced and, moments later, I was getting an epidural and being prepped for surgery. The epidural made me shiver uncontrollably, so I was strapped to the table, and it also made me nauseated, so I was given something intravenously to keep me from throwing up. Niko, who had been so encouraging and sweet as I'd labored away, was visibly shaken to see me in this state when he came into the operating room, but he sat by my head, holding my hand, telling me how brave I'd been and how everything would be fine. I just couldn't believe what was happening, nor could I believe it when they finally yanked Julia out of me and showed her to us. She was enormous and had a truly gigantic, and rather strangely molded, head. I said to Niko, "She looks ready for kindergarten!" and the doctor said, "She would never have fit out."

One of the worst parts of a cesarean is not being able to get your hands on the baby. After they finally got me sewn up—a rather dramatic process, since I seemed to be bleeding a lot—I had to go to the recovery room so I could be monitored as the epidural wore off. Julia was whisked off to the nursery and there she stayed until I was finally taken to my room several hours later and they brought her to me. The other really hard part of having a cesarean is, of course, the pain and discomfort that follow, which can make the simplest tasks—changing a diaper, lifting the baby to the breast—really awkward and difficult. Luckily, Niko was with us in the hospital and at home pretty much all day every day for the first week and a half, and together we managed pretty well. Then my mom came and helped out for another week. By the time she left I was able to do most things by myself.

My second pregnancy and birth were dramatically different. I was miserable for the first trimester—thoroughly exhausted and often queasy. Just when the morning (or, in my case, all day) sickness was on its way out, my alpha-fetoprotein (AFP) results came back indicating that I might have a Down's syndrome baby (see Katherine's story in chapter four) and the rest of my pregnancy was fraught with nagging worry. I fully expected to grow another gigantic baby and figured we'd simply schedule a cesarean appointment to have it. I did not want to go through the same sort of agonizing labor and pushing again, and my husband was very anxious to avoid seeing me suffer, too. In addition, with a three-year-old at home, we liked the scheduling aspects of a planned delivery. We could arrange to have grandparents in place to help take care of Julia, me, and the baby.

As my due date grew nearer, though, I started to reconsider. The idea of recovering from another cesarean, this time with a baby and another child to care for, was giving me pause. I figured Julia would be upset enough with our suddenly larger family without the added frustration she would experience if I was unable to lift her for a month. Frankly, looking back on it and dreading going through it again, I relived just how scary my first cesarean had been. Surgery is no picnic and there are more risks involved in a cesarean than a natural birth. I talked to my doctor and she suggested that another option might be to induce me a little early so that there would be a better chance that the baby would be small enough to fit out. I really liked this idea for a couple of days and then I started thinking about it and a few things bothered me. I always had the sneaking suspicion that being induced, instead of just waiting until Julia was ready to come out, might have been part of the reason for my needing a cesarean. (Considering her size, this might not be realistic, but that was a feeling I had and still have.) Also, I didn't like the idea of having the baby come out before she was ready; I wanted her "fully cooked" and ready to face the world.

Another feeling I had was that this baby was nowhere near as big as Julia had been. Though my weight gain was almost the same, my belly didn't seem as enormous as it had during my first pregnancy. I decided to do nothing but wait for nature to take its course.

Nine days before my due date, I woke up very early in the morning having crampy contractions. I didn't get too excited about it because the same thing had happened the night before and they'd petered out after a few hours. These just kept coming, though, every fifteen minutes, and then a little closer together and still closer after that. The contractions weren't letting up even when I got up and started moving around, so I decided to call the doctor. She said it sounded like I was either experiencing false labor or early labor and to keep her posted. I knew it was real labor when I went to the bathroom and was startled to find the infamous "bloody show" I'd read about in so many books.

I figured things were still in the very early stages and encouraged my husband to go to the park to play basketball as he often does on weekend mornings, though I asked him to take Julia along so I could take a shower and pack a bag. Once I'd done this, I headed down to the park to meet them. It was a beastly hot day and my contractions were starting to feel a bit more painful as I walked the quarter mile or so to the park. As I was pushing Julia on the swing, the contractions started to feel even more intense. I asked one of our friends to get my husband off the court and we headed home with Julia. Much to her bewilderment, I now had to stop and grip telephone poles every few minutes. We sent Julia to her best friend's house and then went to the hospital. On the way, I kept pestering Niko to stop and get himself something to eat because I figured we'd be at the hospital for a long time, but he said he thought we really ought to get there and see what was going on. It's a good thing we didn't stop.

By the time we got to the hospital I was already six centimeters dilated. I got rushed from the triage area into the labor/delivery room, where they started an IV. I was much more uncomfortable now that I had to sit and also because I was then right in the midst of transition. I was requesting an epidural loudly. They needed an attending physician to approve the procedure, though, and couldn't find any of the doctors from my practice. One of the doctors lives nearby, so they paged her. Since she's an Orthodox Jew, she doesn't drive a car on Saturday (the Sabbath). She started walking quickly to the hospital. The nurse-midwife checked me again and was surprised to see that I was now fully dilated. They paged the doctor again saying "Complete—ASAP." She hitched up her skirts and ran the rest of the way.

In the meantime, I was feeling the urge to push like I never did with Julia. The nurse and nurse-midwife told me to push if I had to, so I did. The doctor, who was sweating even more than I, arrived after a couple of pushes and got ready to deliver the baby. There was some drama when the monitor showed that the baby's heart rate was dropping every time I pushed, so the doctor decided to hurry the process even more by using the vacuum extractor. She quickly gave me an episiotomy and applied the vacuum to the baby's head and, two or three pushes later, Eleanor arrived, red and screaming and weighing a full three pounds, one ounce less than her big sister. She was in great shape, despite the cord having been wrapped once around her neck. As they were cleaning and examining her, Niko and I just kept looking at each other and then over at her in disbelief. Ellie had been born a mere forty-five minutes after our arrival at the hospital and I don't think either of us could quite comprehend that she was actually here. The doctor delivered the placenta, which hurt a lot, and sewed up the episiotomy.

Giving birth vaginally hurts like mad, but the discomfort afterward, though not inconsiderable, is localized. Ice packs and Tylenol made it manageable. I was able to nurse comfortably and to move around, though very carefully. I felt such a tremendous sense of relief that the birth had gone so well that I was on a natural high for a couple of days. After we'd been home for a few days and I'd had very little sleep for about a week, the euphoria wore off and the reality of how hard it can sometimes be to have two young children set in. But even now, a couple of months later, when Ellie is having a hard day or being particularly fussy, I can call up the deep sense of gratitude I felt toward her for her amazingly swift arrival.

Whatever the details of our particular experience, we definitely walk away from childbirth feeling as though something amazing was accomplished. Whether circumstances were pretty much as we'd hoped or whether they seemed reminiscent of an episode of *Twilight Zone*, once our babies are in our arms, we soon come to terms with even the most difficult births. This doesn't mean that the days, weeks, and months that follow a less than ideal experience will be completely free of disappointment, anger, or even regret. However, it is likely that when, and if, these emotions make an appearance, they'll be somewhat tempered by the presence of our amazing little babies and by a new appreciation for the strength and wonder of our female bodies.

Chapter Nine

Is There Really a Fourth Trimester? The Harsh Realities of Postpartum Life

We often are so focused on pregnancy, labor, and birth that we're caught off guard by the monumental challenges of the early postpartum weeks. After months of studying every condition and product related to pregnancy, we find ourselves having to learn a whole new vocabulary shortly after our babies are born. Squirt bottles, witch hazel pads, sitz baths, and inflatable donut-shaped pillows become new friends we hope to abandon soon. If a cesarean was performed, we're becoming acquainted with afterpains, incision care, and finding ways to hold and feed our little ones that don't make us wince.

Additionally, as we're coming to terms with yet another version of a body that we're not sure is really our own, we're also learning to feed and care for our precious newborns. If we're breastfeeding, we may be facing some of the many obstacles that can accompany this wondrous process: sore nipples, engorgement, trouble latching on, worries about whether we have enough milk, and more.

Then there is the baby. We may have carried around this mini-person for forty weeks, but now that the little being is on the outside, it's a whole new ball game. Constant feeding, the counting of wet and dirty diapers, figuring out how to clip fingernails and give sponge baths, and trying as hard as we can to stay away from that frightening-looking belly-button clamp, all seem to interfere with what we'd like to be doing most: staring in awe and amazement at our beautiful baby.

Just as pregnancy is a unique experience so are the early months of motherhood. Some women may find the physical recovery from childbirth nothing more than a minor nuisance. For others it may take months to start feeling normal again. Emotionally, there can be major highs and major lows, and it is impossible to know how much of each your own experience will include. We might feel stronger than we've ever felt before or we might feel more vulnerable than we ever thought possible. Perhaps we'll feel both depending on the day. Some women will have an immediate and strong bond with their child while, for others, it can take a little while to come to terms with this profound new relationship.

Whatever our particular situation, the early weeks and months of our baby's life will leave an indelible impression as they teach us some important lessons about exactly what it means to be a mother.

❊ ❊ ❊

Nicki, 30 Years Old

Nicki did not enjoy being pregnant at all. She couldn't wait to give birth and she was eager to have her body back. From the moment her son made his first appearance, it became clear that her body and her life would never be her own in quite the same way again.

For nine months, I focused—no, obsessed—almost exclusively on my pregnancy, each symptom and fetal development, and later on, the birth process. In some ways, I regarded the birth of my baby as the end of the pregnancy, as opposed to the beginning of our new family. This is not to say that I didn't think about it at all, but it wasn't until my son was born that I gained the perspective that the pregnancy was just a blip on the screen and the real work and reward were yet to come.

Toward the end of my pregnancy, I counted down the days until I'd "have my body back." It didn't have to be my old slim, healthy body, just a body that wouldn't be inhabited by an extra person. Foolishly, I thought that the birth of my son would free my body from his control and return it to its rightful owner (me!). I was completely wrong, but I didn't mind a bit. From the second the doctor placed that tiny, slippery, helpless angel on my breast, I couldn't bear the thought that we would be apart for more than a moment. And for months after that, we weren't.

I chose to keep my baby with me in my hospital room, even sleeping with me in my bed. It felt right. I was also eager to breast-feed and wanted to do all I could to ensure its success. Breastfeeding wasn't what I had expected in the beginning. It really hurt, even though everyone told me I was doing it right. My nipples were sore and raw, one to the point of slight bleeding, and, after a few days, I was painfully engorged. My son was literally attached to me for most of his waking hours. When he wasn't nursing, I was often holding him as he slept, as I changed him, or just to admire him. The seemingly constant nursing combined with the throbbing pain in my vaginal area made me realize that my body was still not my own. It was several months before the nursing slowed down enough that I could be without my son for more than three hours without my breasts engorging.

Even though I didn't have my body back, I can say without hesitation that nursing my son has been one of the most beautiful and rewarding experiences of my life. Slowly, reluctantly, I have come to realize how utilitarian my female body is, and that, in truth, it doesn't belong to me, but to my son. My breasts are for nourishing him, my arms for holding him, my hips for carrying him, my face for amusing and kissing him, my womb for growing him, and my vagina for delivering him to the world. This discovery has put some of my vanities and petty concerns into perspective and I am thankful for it.

In many ways, I never experienced the problems I was expecting in those first days and months after the birth; challenges that I had never considered presented themselves instead. For example, I was worried I'd be nervous with the baby and wouldn't know what to do or how to care for him, but this wasn't the case. From the moment I held him it felt very natural, and though I asked a lot of questions and read all the books, I never felt nervous or as though I didn't know what I was doing. I sought advice but trusted my instincts. Also, I thought I would be deadly tired all the time as new moms are characterized to be, but this wasn't the case for me either.

Although I had no help other than my husband for the first week, I never felt exhausted, thank heaven. That's not to say I wasn't tired, but I wasn't a zombie. I think this is because the baby slept a lot during the day, and our nursing sessions at night, even diaper changes, were quick and in dim light. Also, we were fortunate to have a calm baby who didn't cry very much.

What I wasn't prepared for was the pain. Childbirth hurt and the wounds and discomfort in my vaginal area lingered for about three weeks before I could sit, walk, and generally move without throbbing pain. Also, I immediately dropped to second billing in the family. People (namely my husband, parents, and friends) who were concerned with my slightest symptoms, activities, and moods just days before barely acknowledged my existence now as I hobbled and leaked around the house. It was hardest losing that attention from my husband, but there is a different kind of satisfaction from watching him dote on our son.

Finally, one of the most subtle but remarkable things that happened in the months after my son's birth was the way the world suddenly changed. OK, maybe not the world but my perception of it. I'm a mama now. Everything I read, see, hear, touch, and think is skewed through my "mama lens." It has made me both more empathetic in some ways, and more closed off and protective in others.

I never got the so-called "baby blues" often associated with the immediate postpartum period, but I am a little more sentimental, if not outright weepy, about sad news stories and TV melodramas. I can't help but envision my son in the tragic circumstances of the story and feel intensely for each victim and his mother. But this may have more to do with my just being a freak than my being a new mom.

Sara Michelle, 33

Giving birth to her first child, a son, made Sara Michelle feel stronger than she'd ever felt before. At the same time, however, taking care of this vulnerable little being sometimes filled her with fear.

When my son was just a few days old, I had a terrible nightmare. I dreamt I was on a small boat holding Zakaria, who was dressed in a delicate nightgown, when suddenly the boat lurched to one side and he slipped out of my arms. I could see his small, white form slowly disappearing into the dark sea below but could do nothing. His weight carried him downward much faster than I could swim. He was already out of my reach.

Nothing epitomizes the beginning of my "fourth trimester" better than this horrible dream. Zeki seemed so vulnerable. I felt so unable to care for him. I thought he was going to die.

It's true that the first three months after birth are difficult because of sleep deprivation, around-the-clock breastfeeding, and possibly even larger health issues that can come up for babies or their mothers. What I remember most about that time, however, is the emotional intensity.

I would spend hours with Zeki while he nursed or slept on my lap, just watching him and touching him. His skin was softer than I could have ever imagined possible; his hands and feet so small and so perfectly formed. I used to call him a "bundle of nerves" because any little jarring movement would send his arms flying up into the air, fingers outstretched. His nervous system seemed to be all scrambled up like the wires inside a TV set, setting off responses that were completely spontaneous and exposed.

Sometimes this made me laugh, but most of the time it made me feel distraught, because I knew that my baby could not control his movements enough to even lift his head or turn away from danger. Images of torture came into my head all the time. Zeki seemed like a human being at its most defenseless and primal. With him on my lap, I watched the TV coverage of atrocities in Kosovo and imagined the babies involved. I thought about how easy it must be for an over-tired parent to neglect or even hurt a crying newborn. I thought about how easily a baby or child could fall to its death.

But there were also many funny moments. Zeki used to stare off into the distance with this wistful, pensive look in his eyes, which was really just his response to seeing a far-off light. His expression would make me laugh and recite some made up Shakespearean line like: "Hark! Far yonder light doth shine ... " I talked aloud constantly.

My friends and I coined silly expressions for our newborns' post-breastfeeding bliss—one called it PNN, "post nipple nirvana," and another described her satiated daughter as a drunken sailor. I thought Zeki looked more like he was tripping on acid. When he was done drinking my milk he would latch off my breast and arch his back, bringing one hand to his forehead as if to say, "Man, this stuff is good."

The first few months, I was on an adrenaline high. I felt that my baby's birth had been a true miracle, and that in pushing him out of my body I had performed a Herculean feat. I remember feeling religious and my husband and I telling each other often, "We are so blessed." I also felt invincible, able to lift a car off a trapped driver, or walk a thousand miles. I couldn't stop fantasizing about having another baby.

Motherhood has settled down a lot since then. I now take Zeki to day care twice a week so that I can work at home. I stopped breastfeeding at six months and almost have my old body back. My days with him feel a bit more structured; our nighttime sleeps are almost normal. But I still look at him in wonder constantly, and remember that newborn, so stunningly beautiful and so utterly fragile. Part of me thinks that I'll always see him that way.

Nell, 33

After nine months of pregnancy, hour upon hour of physically exhausting labor, and who knows what kind of birth, it only seems right that we should be given a few weeks off to rest up before we begin the monumental task of mothering. In fact, the realities of postpartum life descend immediately. In Nell's case, the final stitch had barely been sewn into her cesarean incision when the next adventure began.

The disillusionment with postpartum life came early. It began, I think, as I lay in the delivery room, after they sewed up the cesarean, and they handed off my newborn to my husband. Bryan held our daughter, awed and laughing, as I strained from my supine position to catch a good look at her. Then, remembering me, Bryan walked her over to my head for a hello, and just as he was leaning her down so I could hold her, the nurses swooped in and carried her away to the nursery for cleaning.

Uh, wait a minute! What's up with hustling her away from *me*? What about bonding? What about nursing? What about justice? Was I not the person who'd just been through the perils of labor and cesarean delivery to bring this young mewler into the world? Should I not be holding her as others struggled to peek?

I was assured that once she was cleaned and warmed up she would be brought to me immediately. Well, five hours later, after I'd insisted for the umpteenth time that I felt OK and really didn't need to lay in recovery any longer (they won't bring babies in to the recovery room), after it took a rather worrisome length of time to warm her, after the doctor's rounds, after my change of room and then the nurses' change of shift, I got to hold Rachel for the first time. She nestled in. It was delightful.

Delightful, yet slightly tense, too, for hovering over this first encounter was the specter of the first nursing. I knew virtually nothing about the postpartum experience, but I was familiar with certain facts about nursing. I knew you were supposed to do it immediately. I knew that some women had difficulty with it. I knew that "latching on" was important. So, here I was, five hours after "immediately" with no idea of what constituted a good "latching on." While I felt somewhat self-conscious about asking someone to observe my nipples in action (something only lovers had been privy to up to this time in my life) I thought it best to seek some assistance. Fortunately,

I knew from my hospital tour that lactation consultants were available for the asking, and so I asked if one might come in.

Two and a half days later, I did get a visit from a lactation consultant. Needless to say, by that point, Rachel and I had already mastered the rudiments. Once it had become clear that lactation consultations were not the ubiquitous offering I thought they'd be, I sought out suggestions from the nurses. I'll admit, they were taken aback at first by my eagerness to display the latch, but, once recovered, they were quite helpful with matter-of-fact suggestions such as, "Stuff in the whole nipple, including the areola." By the time Rachel completed her first couple of meals, I was well on my way past my decades-long breast modesty. It had also begun to occur to me that while I'd received wonderful treatment as a pregnant woman, now that the baby was no longer inside, I was getting much less attention.

Meanwhile, I was being introduced to many other grisly aspects of postpartum life. Things like engorged breasts, profuse bleeding, and uterine cramps were not only unwelcome but also "udderly" (forgive me) unexpected. Somehow, I'd been under the illusion that the hard part was the delivery. Well, maybe it was the surprise aspect that gave it undue significance, but for me postpartum discomforts rivaled what had come before.

I suppose I should start with the blood; I experienced it first. After months of enjoying a menstrual-free existence, the bleeding was back—with a vengeance. Certainly it was naive of me not to have expected some bleeding, but I came to the hospital unprepared, and so I was introduced to that once cutting-edge tool, the "sanitary belt." While not horrendously uncomfortable once they are fastened, the fastening itself was something my surgery-depleted body seemed unable to manage. Here, my husband came to my rescue and we established bonds more intimate than even the delivery room had brought. It wasn't worth it, really. Bring "modern" sanitary pads with you to the hospital. Books say the bleeding can last for as little as two or as many as six weeks. I bled for six and a half.

If memory serves, the next phenomenon I was unexpectedly subjected to was the postpartum uterine cramp. I discovered through my delivery that I have a rather high pain tolerance: I found contractions painful, but bearable, and I felt little discomfort from the cesarean. In fact, while all cesarean deliverers are hooked up to a morphine drip, I (thankfully) never felt even an iota of an urge for it. The nurse kept coming in to check the levels, saying with disbelief, "It looks like you haven't taken any of the morphine!" and I'd nod back, wondering what pain it was that I was supposed to be experiencing. Well, the second night in the hospital, after my morphine drip was discontinued, I was introduced to uterine cramping and the delivery of my milk simultaneously. The levels of my pain tolerance had been breached. My breasts felt as though they'd been attacked by two enormous rock-bearing aliens determined to stretch my breast tissue to breaking, and then my abdomen was concomitantly seized with cramps as bad as any I'd experienced in labor. Meanwhile, because of the incision, it was difficult to move in any fashion but gingerly. My body had been possessed by sadistic beings, and I was too weak to run away.

I felt more miserable than I had at any point in labor, I thought it monstrously unfair that no one in any Lamaze or other pregnancy class had thought to mention this misery, and I wondered how I'd gone from five or so attendants at my delivery to only my sleep-deprived husband to witness this current horror. After I rang for the nurse and she brought me two painkillers of the Percoset variety, I slept. The pain was nowhere near that bad at any subsequent point.

It is my theory that pregnancy serves as a lead-in to child care. The increased attention to food intake prepares for nursing; the lack of sleep from frequent runs to the bathroom prepares (at least nominally) for the nighttime feedings; the discomfort of sitting in a movie theater prepares for the utter lack of films you will see as a new parent. I figure the way my body changed during pregnancy was meant to serve as a reminder that everything in my life would be upended by the coming of my daughter. The sudden discomforts post-delivery are, perhaps, a reminder that it can all be more demanding than what you've prepared for. It's important, however, to remember that these discomforts are short-lived. The baby—the delightful part—has arrived for a much longer stay.

Trudi, 32

Trudi, too, felt a bit stunned by the harshness of the postpartum period. In the weeks and months after her son was born, she had more physical woes than she'd had through her entire pregnancy.

There is no doubt in my mind that pregnancy includes a fourth trimester. For me, this was the most difficult part of my initiation into parenthood, which began when my husband's sperm met my egg, and ended, in my mind, the moment I was able to stop drooling on myself after my child was born, which was around his third month of existence. OK, that's a small exaggeration, but from the minute I took him home, I was fraught with more physical symptoms than at any other time during my pregnancy.

Aside from the pain of a hemorrhoid the size of Texas, my healing episiotomy, and all the various stuff that was flowing from my body for at least six weeks, a bevy of unexpected afflictions and affectations also popped up. First off, although I was hormonally challenged throughout my pregnancy, nothing could have prepared me for the flood of emotion I experienced after giving birth. I am horrified to see myself, on videotape, stomping around the apartment one minute, demanding a pillow because it was time to breast-feed, and weeping the next. Just about anything could set me off—I just had to look at my beautiful baby boy and I would start to cry (tears of joy, of course). Considering I was around him 24/7, there were a lot of weepy moments. That's normal I guess, but I also got in the habit of putting on old Cat Stevens tapes just to make myself cry. Now, that was a little extreme. When it came to breastfeeding, which is not necessarily the simplest skill to master, I shed many tears. Horrifyingly enough, I found myself so overdetermined to make it work that I was willing to let my son go hungry rather than give him supplemental formula from a bottle. That was the pinnacle of evil hormones at work.

The other condition, which was certainly hormonally related, was an unnerving case of night sweats. Like morning sickness, beginning about a week after I gave birth, this misnamed state came over me at any time of the day or night. At first I was somewhat unaware that my excessive sweating wasn't actually normal. It was the middle of July, after all. But finally I realized that it wasn't just the 90-degree heat that was getting to me—my damp brow and need to change my shirt every few hours were directly related to having a baby. When I called my doctor about it, she cheerfully explained that "it's just as if you're going through menopause—it should only last a couple of weeks." She was right, but it didn't mitigate waking up in a puddle, or having my son slide off my nipple because I was pro-fusely dripping on him.

Another major part of my fourth trimester was sleeplessness. Throughout my pregnancy, I often experienced sleeping difficulties, from insomnia to plain old discomfort. That was barely an adequate primer for the sleep deprivation that comes with a newborn. People told me that I wouldn't sleep, but I really didn't get what they meant until nighttime became a time of day that I began to dread. Sleep as I knew it was a thing of the past. My clearest memory of the conse-quences of sleep deprivation was when a good friend of mine trav-eled several hundred miles to meet my son, and I literally couldn't stand up to greet her. I mumbled a few unintelligible words, and then began to weep.

The good news is that like the first, second, and third trimesters, the fourth, too, really does pass in about three months. By the end of that blur of a time, my beautiful son could smile and coo at me (yes, they really do coo), I was catching sufficient shut-eye, and the hormones had subsided enough to stop my drooling, sweating, and weeping.

Cynthia, 36

Three days after Cynthia's little girl came home from the hospital, she had to go back. After forty weeks of occupying the same body and five postpartum days of nursing, cuddling, and sleeping together, the separation anxiety she felt when her baby was put into an isolette, where only very limited contact was possible, was intense.

My fourth trimester began rather traumatically. After only three days at home, a slight case of jaundice turned much more severe, and we had to bring our little girl back to the hospital for treatment. When our pediatrician told us this, after taking one look at Zoe, we were devastated. She was just getting used to the world, to us, and to her new home—the hospital was the last place we wanted her to be.

When we arrived at the emergency room to have her blood tested that day, we were in a state of shock. The shock turned to fear as the day wore on. After watching a resident try to take blood from the tiny little veins in her arms while she screamed and squirmed, and then waiting several long hours for the results of the test, I was asked to sit in a wheelchair with my daughter in my arms, and we were whisked upstairs to the neonatal intensive care unit (NICU). When we got there, she was taken from me immediately and put into an adjoining room. Through the wall, I could hear her screaming like she'd never screamed before in the five days since she was born. The NICU nurse started to take a history from me and began to explain what was going on. Her bilirubin level was dangerously high and they had to get it down immediately to avoid complications. The usual methods (phototherapy lights) would not be enough on their own and the doctors wanted us to give them permission to do a blood exchange as soon as possible.

I was totally numb and could barely hear anything beyond the sound of my baby screaming next door. I couldn't hold her, I couldn't comfort her, I couldn't nurse her, and I couldn't deal with having her so far away from me. The idea of a blood exchange terrified me, especially because they needed to do it so quickly that we couldn't donate blood ourselves, or have family and friends do it. But it seemed that we had no choice.

After waiting in the emergency room all afternoon, everything was suddenly moving very, very fast. Before we knew it, we were sitting in a little waiting room, waiting for the procedure to be finished. I couldn't believe what was happening and had no idea what to expect. The thought of losing her was unbearable, as was the thought that the jaundice might have already caused some serious problems.

The procedure went smoothly but it was awful to think of our five-day-old having to endure it. They did the exchange through her umbilicus, without any anesthetic, and it was reported to us that she was fighting them so much that her arms and legs needed to be restrained. This was relayed to make us feel good about what a "fighter" she was. Instead, it made us cringe.

After the procedure, we were allowed to see her as she lay in an incubator under phototherapy lights (with blindfolds over her eyes). She was hooked up to various monitors and an IV since this is how she would be fed for, at least, the next twenty-four hours. She was, again, screaming louder than she ever had in her short life. She'd grown accustomed to seeing light, to nursing, to being held and all of this had been taken away from her. All we could do to comfort her was to stick our hand through a hole in the incubator and touch her. At times I found myself unable to stay in the room and watch her in this state of misery. This made me feel as though I was failing my first big test of motherhood. My husband stayed with her, talked to her, and touched her until he was able to calm her down (and he did this repeatedly over the next few days). After the first eighteen hours or so, I was allowed to take her out and nurse her, and once I could hold her, things started to improve. One of us, or one of my husband's parents, was at the hospital at all times, and Zoe was never left alone.

We were finally able to take her home four days later, but we brought much more baggage to this second homecoming than we did to the first. Our baby was fine, but we were definitely more on edge, and her hospital stay had really taken a toll on me. I was on my feet way more than I should have been and was hardly able to eat. My episiotomy opened a bit leaving me extremely uncomfortable and more reliant on my little squirt bottle and witch hazel pads than I wanted to be, for a much longer period of time. We all had a lot of healing to do.

We'll never know how much of an effect that traumatic experience had on the months that followed. Were we more nervous as a result? Was our daughter less secure? Did we have a much harder time than usual hearing her cry?

Looking back, there are definitely some things that stand out about those early months. The first is how unprepared I was for just how much time we spent nursing. I'd heard people talk about two-hour intervals between feedings. In my case, on that rare occasion when I had the luxury of two whole "unattached" hours, I felt like I'd just returned from a weekend in Paris. I learned to nurse while I ate, while I responded to e-mails, and while I wrote thank-you cards. I spent more time than not, sitting in a very comfortable glider in the corner of our living room, baby in one arm, book, phone or remote control in the other. There were times when I'd arrive at "nursing central" without some crucial supply (glasses, water, etc.) and I'd just sit there waiting for a little break so I could go and get it. Yes, of course, it was also wonderful just to sit and watch her nurse, but, believe me, we nursed so much that there was no lack of precious moments.

I also remember being shocked that I could barely find time for things like showers or bowel movements. When I'm not caring for a squawking two-month-old, I'm an incredibly efficient and organized person. Being unable to carve out little spaces for very necessary activities made me feel like a complete loser. I craved a little order in my life and observed my daughter microscopically to find any hint of even a tiny little pattern or routine that might be emerging (and which I could nurture and support until it grew into a beautiful schedule). Never happened.

Most intensely I remember how day after day and night after night, she amazed me. I never knew I could take so much interest and find so much enjoyment in such tiny gestures and subtle features but there was no end to my fascination. I was also in awe of the fact that, even as a newborn, she had a distinct personality and a way of expressing herself that was all her own. I had to get to know her just as I did anyone who I'd only met a few weeks ago. Similarly, the longer I knew her and the more she revealed of herself, the more comfortable I became in my new role. I was intrigued by what I was learning about myself as I responded to her every need and desire. Although I sometimes feared that the "me" I used to be was disappearing, I was really eager to see who I was about to become.

Jennifer, 26

It is quite common to experience varying degrees of depression following the birth of a baby. Usually caused by a combination of hormone changes and the overwhelming challenge of caring for a newborn, this depression may last for several days or several months. In its milder forms it's referred to as "baby blues," when more severe, it's called postpartum depression (PPD).

Writer Sarah Bird (1997) describes a moment in her difficult postpartum life this way: "There is something that feels so incurably hormonal about my mood that I've looked up depression in all my pregnancy and baby books. They talk about the 'baby blues,' about feeling weepy in the third or fourth day after the delivery as hormones settle out. They suggested going out for a special dinner. 'Weepy' and 'special dinners' sound so pastel in contrast to the violent colors of my own emotional palette that I can only assume my problems are something else entirely. Something caused by a diabolical combination of health misfortunes and bad character."

Jennifer's life changed drastically when she developed preeclampsia and was forced to deliver her daughter prematurely. The excitement and happiness she'd felt were replaced with exhaustion and depression as she struggled with the demands of new motherhood.

After the drama of preeclampsia and induced labor, and my daughter arriving in the world safe and sound, I thought I would feel relief. Instead, I felt terror. I had just come face-to-face with my own mortality, and now I was responsible for a baby who was smaller than my forearm. I looked at her tiny face and wondered how I was ever going to take care of her. I had no idea how to change her diaper, let alone be her mother.

My husband wanted our daughter to stay in the room with us at the hospital, which I had agreed to eight weeks earlier in a glowing state of pregnancy. Now all I wanted to do was sleep. I felt like I had done my job: I had carried the baby, I had given birth. Let the nurses take care of her. I had no idea how demanding babies were after they arrived in the world, and I was overwhelmed with the pain and the emotion of childbirth combined with a constantly crying baby. I should have overruled my husband's request, but the idea of doing so made me feel selfish and instead I chose to suffer.

I tried to breastfeed in the hospital, but I had no milk to give. The nurse claimed my daughter's suck to be too weak to breastfeed anyway, having been born so early, but I took my inability to breast-feed my baby as my own personal failure. I cursed my body for not being able to nourish a baby like a normal female. Physically, I had already failed as a woman. Now I was failing as a mother, too.

On the day my labor was suddenly induced, I was supposed to have enjoyed a surprise baby shower. When they heard the news of my imminent delivery, my friends decided to go ahead and have the shower without me. They knew I needed the baby gear sooner rather than later and they videotaped the party and each guest opening up the gift they had brought, for me to watch later. As a result, when I was released from the hospital, I came home to a living room littered with stacks of baby gifts and equipment that I'd never seen before and had no idea how to use.

I appreciated the nice gesture but walking into such a cluttered room when the only thing I wanted was a calm and peaceful environment, definitely added to the tension I was already feeling. I wanted to hand the baby to my husband and go back to the hospital. I felt so unprepared for motherhood. I spied an unopened box of nursing pads that I would never be able to use, and I started to cry. My daughter was barely four days old, and I already began wondering if I should have died in childbirth after all.

My daughter was very "high-maintenance," as should be expected with a premature baby. However, her constant crying, her constant hunger, and her constant needing overwhelmed me. I thought babies slept all the time. My daughter slept for about twenty minutes every four hours. I became a zombie after the first week. I thought babies only cried when they were hungry or wet. My daughter cried all the time unless I held her. She was basically attached to my elbow as I cradled her every minute of the day.

My body and my life were no longer my own, and I felt an intense jealousy watching my husband escape to work. Because he travels for business anywhere from two to three weeks each month, and my family didn't live close enough to help me, I was mostly taking care of the baby by myself. It felt intrusive to ask my friends to watch her; after all, she was my daughter and my responsibility. So I was alone. The baby didn't care that I was still having pain while sitting down, or that I had slept a total of five hours in one week, or that I hadn't taken a shower for four days. She was hungry, and I was the only one around to feed her. I felt like a married single mother, and I was drowning.

When my daughter turned five weeks old and finally reached her due date, I thought she would start acting like my friends' full-term babies. Instead she developed colic, and an inhumane schedule of walking the hallway emerged. My daughter has never been a sleeper. Up through her first six months of life, she slept an average of three hours a night, which meant I did too. We slept on the couch, with me on my side and the baby nestled in the crook of my arm. (She still doesn't sleep through the night, and she's almost three years old.) I returned to work after seven weeks of maternity leave, and I was more than happy to leave the baby with someone else during the day. I was crying all the time and the sleep deprivation had robbed me of my memory. I felt I was losing my mind. Outside of work, I isolated myself in fear that my friends would see what an incapable mother I had turned out to be.

I hated myself and resented my husband, but I never felt negatively toward the baby. My daughter was a miracle who had not asked to be born five weeks early. It was my body that forced her into the world before she was ready. It was my inadequacy that left her so fussy and unsatisfied. It was my fault that I wasn't a good mother. I blamed myself for developing preeclampsia, for being unable to breastfeed, and for feeling overwhelmed by tasks I thought a good mother should instinctively know how to do. In my soul, I knew my daughter deserved a better mother, and I slid into a deep depression that didn't dissipate for nearly a year.

Overcast with a sleepless haze and excruciating sadness, my daughter's first year of life will always be distorted in my memory. I realize that my circumstances were rather extreme, and that I allowed my frustrations to pile up on top of each other to the point of suffocation. It took a long time for me to accept that I didn't have to do everything myself, that I didn't have to know all the answers, and that I didn't develop preeclampsia because I was a bad person who was being punished for doing something wrong. If I had one wish, it would be for women to understand there is no "right" way to be pregnant or to be a mother, that all of us experience insanity as well as joy. As difficult as it was, I would never trade my experience for a life without my daughter. Not for a second. Not even for more sleep.

Lauren, 32

The early months of Lauren's motherhood were affected by colic. Although Benjamin was not screaming through these "fussy periods," he was quite miserable for about five hours every night. During that time, the only activity that seemed to soothe him at all was marathon nursing, which Lauren selflessly provided, with a few twenty-minute breaks thrown in for the sake of her sanity.

Our time in the hospital passed in a haze. My son was born with extremely low blood sugar, and had spent most of our three days in the hospital on a glucose IV in the neonatal intensive care unit. I was so pleased to get him back and out of there that I hadn't really focused on the fact that I was bringing this baby home to live with me.

When we first came home, I felt supremely confident. I had birthed this baby, yes I had, and now I was going to nurse him and nurture him and watch him grow. Within an hour my confidence had been completely shattered. Benjamin was very small, and because of that and his glucose problem we were under strict orders to make sure he ate. So, shortly after we arrived home, I picked up my skinny child and attempted to latch him on. No doing—he was asleep and would not be wakened. We tried everything—tickling his feet, rubbing his cheek, patting him with a cold wet washcloth—and he continued to sleep almost nonstop for twenty-four hours. I was frantic, and of course put in a phone call to the pediatrician at 9 P.M. on a Saturday. (By the time we showed up at his office the next morning, of course Benjamin was awake and eating with gusto.)

For the next three weeks, life settled into a blurry sleepy routine of nursing, cuddling, forgetting to shower, and spending two hours trying to get the boy into the Baby Bjorn to go out for a walk. (How, you wonder, can that take two hours? Well, first you have trouble with the straps. Then the baby spits up all over you and you decide you need to change your shirt. Then as soon as he's back in the carrier he poops, and you have to change his diaper and clothes, and maybe your shirt again, too. Then you get him strapped in again and he starts screaming for milk, and you unstrap him and sit down to nurse him. Then—well, you get the idea.)

In week three, wrestling with the Baby Bjorn started to seem like child's play. In retrospect, I suppose you might say that Benjamin had colic, though we were never quite willing to label it so. But from three weeks until about twelve weeks, he had a "fussy period" every night from 9 P.M. to 2 A.M. Never flat-out wailing, mind you—but a period of whining and fussing and clenching his little fists and turning red. For five hours. Every night.

At first, my husband and I took turns walking him around the living room in the dark, listening to lullabies and trying to soothe him. Sometimes the sound of the shower worked. I knew we'd hit a new low when I walked out of the bedroom one night to find my husband sitting in the steamy bathroom in the dark, singing "Oh, What a Beautiful Morning!" After a while, though, we realized that pretty much the only thing that worked was nursing. So I nursed for forty-five minutes, took a break and let my husband deal with the crying boy for twenty minutes, and then started all over again. During the day, mind you, the child was a perfect angel—slept a lot and rarely cried. (Except for that one day when he cried for five hours straight and I got hysterical and made my husband come home from work, only to have Benjamin fall asleep in Robert's arms as soon as he walked in the door. . . .)

People kept telling us that everything would change at three months—that it would feel as though a switch had gone off, and the child would suddenly stop fretting and start sleeping. We did not believe them. But one evening, Benjamin seemed unusually calm after the first nursing session of his "fussy period." My husband looked at me and said, "What do you think would happen if we just put him into the bassinet?" I looked skeptical. "Well, he'd scream, just the way he always does," I replied. "Let's just give it a try." Ever the indulgent wife, I agreed—and wouldn't you know it, he squirmed around a bit, squeaked and burbled, then calmed right down and went to sleep—for *seven* hours.

The next morning, the world looked bright and clear. I leapt up to get Benjamin at the first peep, bounding with energy after so much sleep. He cooed and smiled at me. I nursed him, popped him into the Baby Bjorn and was out to the park within half an hour. And it seemed like the easiest, most natural thing in the world.

Tass, 29

Trying to cope with the demands of an infant, as well as the physical and emotional aftereffects of childbirth, can be overwhelming under any circumstances. For single moms, like Tass, who are bearing this burden on their own, this period presents even greater challenges.

Aliah Daché is now eleven weeks old and she is a beautiful, healthy, and happy baby. She is also very alert for her age and an extremely content little soul. Aliah's father, who had not been supportive of my decision to have this baby throughout most of my pregnancy, turned up at the hospital during my labor and to the surprise of everyone, including me, said yes when asked if he would like to witness the birth. He even cut the umbilical cord. I will never forget the love in his eyes when he held our baby for the first time.

It has been an extremely unsettling and difficult time for me since Aliah's birth. Single motherhood is a lot harder than I had imagined. The sudden turnaround of Aliah's father and his parents, as well as my own (both of whom did not support me during my pregnancy and are now very proud grandparents), has made it even more confounding.

My feelings when I first came home from the hospital were of intense isolation. I have no family around me and, although I have quite a bit of experience with babies, I've found it exhausting to look after a newborn by myself. The first several weeks were hard physically, as I was breastfeeding and Aliah loves to feed (and is well above average for her weight to show for it!), and I felt very "immobile." Days went by where I quickly ate toast for dinner and had two-minute showers. Although the feeding routine is now a bit more regular and she sleeps very well at night waking only once or twice, she still doesn't sleep much during the day. This is very taxing since she needs my constant attention, but I am told quite often that I should count myself lucky because I get my sleep at night. However, I often find myself feeling very lonely as the end of the day approaches and, as Aliah sleeps, I am left to ponder the realities of single motherhood.

Aliah's father has been very supportive. During my "immobile" times he came over and cooked dinner, accompanied us to doctor's appointments, and shopped, amongst other things. A few weeks ago he helped me buy a car so that I would feel less isolated and dependent on others. Long ago I resolved to forgive him for all the pain and hurt he caused me and I am very grateful for all the contributions he has made since Aliah's birth. I've been told that there is no revenge as complete as forgiveness, and this is very true.

My feelings for my daughter's father are still very strong and although shortly after her birth there seemed to be an indication that he was starting to feel something, it now appears that although he cares for me, he does not want us to be together just for the sake of the baby. I, too, don't want to live together in a loveless relationship since, in the end, that would not be a positive environment for my daughter. Yet it saddens me that I cannot move past the love I have for him, all the more apparent as I am reminded of him constantly through Aliah.

As for his feelings for his daughter—it goes without saying that he is completely besotted and who can blame him? She is absolutely beautiful. I know that he will always love her. We still encounter hurdles every few weeks in relation to visitation issues, but we are working on these and ultimately we will do what is best for Aliah.

Getting through pregnancy, childbirth, and the early months of motherhood alone has certainly been the most challenging feat I have ever faced. I'm sure there is more to come, both in terms of the actual care of Aliah and the overwhelming feelings of loneliness I experience every day. Everything I've endured, however, has been worth it just to see that beautiful cherub smile on my daughter's face when she sees me. She will always have my unconditional love.

Corinna, 32

Political commentator Mary Matalin (1998) describes a moment that many new moms can relate to: "I remember sitting on the front porch with my new infant in my arms, crying hideously, while singing to her: 'You are my sunshine, my only sunshine.' What was that about?"

By the time we've given birth we've probably already had at least a few emotional roller coaster rides, and during the postpartum period there are likely to be many more. This was certainly the case for Corinna who found herself bouncing back and forth between joy and sadness.

When I was rolled into the recovery room after giving birth to my daughter, I was physically no longer pregnant. The baby who had spent the last thirty-eight weeks growing inside me was now a total separate person. And yet she wasn't.

Although my daughter was no longer inside me, her dependence on me was no less than when she was. I was her sole source of nourishment, and my husband and I, together, shared the rest of the duties involved with her care. When she cried, we responded right away. We knew that as a newborn, this was her only means of communicating with us. We had no idea what she needed, so we would go through "the checklist." Was she hungry (always on top of the list)? Was she cold? Was she hot? Did she need to be burped? Was her diaper dirty? An important point that we learned very early on is that newborns do not have wants—only needs. By the time that she cried, whatever it was that she needed was now urgent (from her point of view).

Just as my body had dedicated most of its resources and energies to developing and nurturing the baby when I was pregnant, my husband and I were now living our lives for the sake of our daughter—dedicating ourselves completely to caring for her. This was a huge adjustment for my husband. I was shocked to discover just how challenging it was for me, too. I never dreamed that breastfeeding would be a learned skill (for both of us!). On the other hand, I never imagined just how rewarding nursing my daughter could be. As she enjoyed my milk, I savored the closeness and the fact that she was being nourished with the best food that I could give her.

Between the almost constant demands on my body to satisfy this new little person and the lack of sleep, I was also finding that I was sad. The postpregnancy hormones definitely affected me. One of the sources of my sadness was that my pregnancy, which I'd really enjoyed, was over. I've talked with other women who had similar feelings following the birth of a child. Despite the elation they felt about their baby and about being a mother, they also felt empty. Although I would never want my daughter to be "put back," I missed having her inside me, kicking and rolling. That feeling was addicting. I also became upset about any news item that involved children. I obsessed over them, horrified that something could happen to my baby. It got to the point where I refused to watch or read the news.

In addition to the sadness, I found myself completely overwhelmed with love and joy. In the late evenings or very early mornings when I was nursing my daughter, enjoying the silence of the apartment, I would just watch her, thinking about how lucky I was and how beautiful she was. This intense love for my daughter, mixed with amazement that I had actually created her, and spiced with postpartum hormones, brought me to tears on many occasions.

In spite of the challenges, those early weeks were incredibly special and will hold a very dear place in my heart forever. They went by entirely too fast.

Sara, 36

When circumstances make it necessary for you to be separated from your child after birth, the days and weeks that follow can be almost surreal. Sara's son Toby, born prematurely, spent three and a half months in the hospital before he was able to come home. For Sara, this meant that the usual events of postpartum life were quite delayed. In their place were daily visits to the neonatal intensive care unit (NICU), very limited physical contact with her son, and fears about his future.

Since Toby was delivered fourteen weeks early, my third and fourth trimesters collided in a rather unexpected manner. After his birth, Toby spent twelve and a half weeks in the NICU, so we essentially watched the last trimester of fetal development as we concurrently began to experience postpartum life. That postpartum life continued once Toby was finally able to come home.

Toby was well cared for in the NICU at a hospital about ten minutes from our home. We had full access to visit whenever we liked and we visited once or twice a day without fail. During the NICU time, it felt like our lives settled into a pattern of taking care of ourselves and doing whatever small things we could to take some care of Toby. At the beginning, there was not much we could do—he was hooked up to a ventilator, we could not hold him, and I had a lot of recovery to do myself. Toby's untimely birth was the result of a severe case of eclampsia (without the warning signs of preeclampsia), which led to extremely high blood pressure, a stroke, and an emergency cesarean to save both of our lives. (See Sara's birth story in chapter eight.)

Visiting the NICU so often was made easier by a team of fabulous nurses and doctors. They were sensitive, caring, and knowledgeable, and were extremely patient with our questions as well as our emotions. Clearly, they have a healthy sense of how tenuous life is, and they were able to give us realistic amounts of hope without deluding us in any way.

When Toby was about three weeks old, we were able to hold him—skin to skin on our chest—usually once a day. Holding Toby was both calming and stressful. Finally, I had my baby in my arms and the twenty minutes or so that we'd stare into each other's eyes was blissful, but it was also quite surreal to be holding such a tiny baby. Before that, we were only able to compress his extremities (hold his legs and arms close to his body) while he was in his isolette. He had little muscle tone because he was so young, and containing him helped to calm him down. We continued to do this "squishing" even after we began holding him.

Before we could hold our little boy on any given day, it was necessary for us to ask permission and we soon learned that there was always a very real possibility that the answer might be "no." Medically speaking, it was not always in Toby's best interest to be held, and a few times the staff made sure that he stayed in his isolette. Emotionally, that was incredibly difficult. Once Toby's weight hit four pounds (a few weeks before he came home), things got much easier as we started to take over more of his care (diapers, baths, swaddling, feeding) and we could hold him more frequently.

Holding him made a world of difference for many reasons, not the least being that it helped increase my milk flow. Because of my condition, I wasn't able to start pumping milk until nine days after delivering Toby. It was difficult to establish a milk supply but I succeeded despite the fact that more than a few nurses and doctors told me that it was unlikely. Fortunately, there was an excellent lactation consultant who helped me tremendously. I pumped every three hours during the day, and with the addition of some hormone supplements, I got a good supply going.

The next challenge was to get Toby to nurse. We put him to the breast for the first time when he was thirty two and a half weeks along gestationally, or six and a half weeks old. He latched on and suckled—much to our surprise as well as the nurses'. Preemies are often not strong enough to nurse for quite some time. At the time of writing we still don't know if he'll succeed with a full-time nursing schedule, but he's been doing wonderfully and his bottle-feeds are down to about two a day.

While he was in the NICU, Toby was usually nursing once a day, occasionally he nursed twice. Additionally, he continued to have some IV feeding (fat and nutrition supplements) and he was also given breast milk through a tube that ran from either his nose or throat to his stomach. The IV feedings stopped when he was getting enough calories through the tube feedings, and the tube feedings stopped once he was strong enough to bottle or nurse all of his feeds. Now that he's home, he nurses much more, but he's pretty pokey about it, so we bottle-feed him several times a day. He would be perfectly happy to be at the breast all day long. It takes him over an hour to nurse, then he rests for forty-five minutes and then he's ready to start all over again. With bottles, he feeds in twenty minutes, and then sleeps for three and a half hours.

Holding and nursing Toby has really helped me to bond more fully with him. The utter calm that I feel while he's in my arms is inexplicable, although it is similar to the feeling I get when I look at our three-year-old, Hannah, as she sleeps. A sense of deep serenity and wonder about the perfection of these little beings takes over.

During much of the experience so far, neither my partner, Terry, or I have felt particularly depressed. Mostly, we continue to feel lucky in our wealth—emotionally and in terms of friends who surround us. However, we've certainly had our "meltdown" moments including one that involved trying to get the NICU nurses to remember to do a teeny foot imprint of Toby when he was one month old (they did not do one at his birth). It was really a simple request, but I had to expend a great deal of energy and effort to get it done. In light of what we were going through this was incredibly frustrating and it really pushed me over the edge.

I also have some leftover feelings about how abruptly my pregnancy ended. I continue to regret that I never had a chance to experience my third trimester, and I have emotional attachments to some of the clothes that I was looking forward to wearing during those last few months. I had a few visits with a psychologist who specializes in helping women resolve issues surrounding difficult births, which helped quite a bit in this regard. I now accept and understand what a traumatic experience I lived through and am more able to cut myself a little slack when I start feeling badly about not getting to wear a favorite pair of maternity overalls.

Toby came home about a week and a half before his due date. The first few days were nothing short of strenuously difficult. He came home with oxygen support (which means he has an oxygen tank connected to a nasal canula taped onto his face), an apnea/bradycardia monitor (which alarms if Toby's heart or breath rates slow down too much), and a pulse oximeter—which tracks how well he is oxygenating his bloodstream. The pulse oximeter is a model that sounds false alarms whenever there is movement, even a toe wiggle. Since the discharge doctor wanted us to use it twenty-four hours a day, its alarm went off anywhere from six to twenty times an hour. We used it that way for four days, but we could not continue sleeping in five to ten minute chunks. Another of Toby's neonatologists told us that he didn't think we needed to use it at all, and his pediatrician thought that it would be fine to use it several times a day to spot-check his oxygen saturation levels. With three vastly different medical opinions on the use of the pulse oximeter, we decided to take the middle road and use it to spot-check. Once we did that, life got considerably less stressful. The four days we used this monitor nonstop, I was pretty depressed and overwrought. Life with this baby in our care seemed insurmountably difficult.

I also had a very hard time the first few days that I had to watch Toby and Hannah (our three-year-old) without another adult around. If Toby had been more portable, it would have been easier, but it's difficult to entertain a three-year-old while tethered to a baby's side when the baby is not terribly mobile. (His monitors and oxygen tank make it cumbersome to move him around much.) For a few days, I was quite depressed. It felt absolutely impossible to get through the six weeks or so that we expected Toby to be on the monitors. We regrouped, and did some brainstorming, which resulted in more adult help on the days when Terry is at work. That has helped immensely.

Toby is now one week older than his original due date, and he is eight pounds, four ounces. He's as plump as any other newborn, and he has head control and some motor skills of a two-month-old. His development in some areas will be delayed until he is about a year old, and his respiratory system is compromised so we need to be very careful about shielding him from colds and the like. But he is rapidly starting to feel like a regular baby. Once he's off the oxygen support and monitors, life will proceed much like it did when we first brought Hannah home.

In all, life is settling down, although we still have a long way to go. While I don't wish this experience on anyone, I also don't feel, in retrospect, that the NICU stay, itself, was horrendously difficult. Certainly, the delivery and the conditions that led to it were shattering, but having a premature baby in the NICU was more stressful for me than traumatic. Perhaps that is because Toby did quite well medically. He was very sick for the first half of his stay, but he really pulled through without many complications. He did give us a few scares, including the possibility of surgery to correct for a condition called "retinopathy of prematurity," but the condition corrected itself and surgery was avoided. Even with all we've been through, we've had our share of joyful moments these past few months and we definitely treasure our lives together more than ever.

Anne, 31

When in the midst of postpartum tumult, many of us console ourselves with the thought that, before too long, life will return to normal. Once we've had our babies in our homes and our arms for a while, it becomes clearer and clearer that the "normal" to which we've become so accustomed is gone for good.

As Anne waited for the symptoms of her fourth trimester to subside, she realized that one of them would never go away . . . motherhood!

I have experienced two very different pregnancies, births, and newborns. My first daughter was a very easy pregnancy, but a long labor (thirty hours), and a difficult delivery. Because she was a "face-presentation" (she came out nose first), she was very swollen and needed to be kept in the NICU for the first day. I wasn't doing so well myself and wasn't able to nurse her for nearly twenty-four hours. She had trouble latching on for weeks and I was engorged to the point of needing to pump before every nursing session. I have vivid memories of hobbling around the house with my donut pillow (a handy device that allows one to sit, more comfortably or at all, after an episiotomy), dripping milk from my huge throbbing breasts, with my daughter crying every two hours for her next meal (which of course was only about an hour after I last finished feeding her). I was delirious with exhaustion—at one point, having been awakened by her cries in the night, I ripped all the buttons off my nightgown in a frantic, sleepy haze, a true Superwoman gesture, as I prepared to nurse her. I could have sworn I had gone to bed wearing the nightshirt with snaps.

My second daughter, now four months old, has provided a completely different experience. It was a much more uncomfortable pregnancy. She was breech and I had a cesarean. While it was major surgery, the immediate recovery was much easier than my first, vaginal delivery. I was able to nurse my daughter just a couple of hours after she was born and she latched on easily and ate well from the first day. She rarely cried in the first weeks and always had a four or five hour stretch of sleep at night. While it was difficult not to be able to lift my older daughter (just eighteen months old—still a baby herself) or hold her on my lap, I felt better physically and mentally and could "deal" with life much easier. I knew what to expect from this new little person and was more relaxed and confident in my skills as a mother.

What did they have in common? Both were overwhelming experiences that were thrilling, frustrating, and sometimes lonely. My husband was wonderful during the births, but I felt somewhat separated from him in the early weeks of caring for both babies and was often jealous and resentful as he headed out the door to "normal" life at the office. The first six weeks were the most difficult in both cases. Physically I was still healing, but I wasn't pregnant anymore. Now my complaints and tears were chalked up to the intangibles of exhaustion and hormones. It seemed that now that I no longer had a bulging belly, the sympathy from family and friends (and my husband) was just not there.

The physical "fourth trimester" did end—my body healed, my hormones quieted, my newborns gradually adopted a schedule, and nursing became an enjoyable routine. The emotional effects are a different story. Being a mother is not something I had to learn as it came very naturally for me, but the staggering intensity of my love for my children is something that I am still getting used to. My life is no longer my own. As much as it is shared with my husband, it is even more intrinsically entwined with my children. I know that part of me can no longer survive without them. After nine months of worrying about whether my babies would be born healthy, I was faced with the crashing realization that the worrying had just begun. This time it is never going to end. I am a mother.

❈ ❈ ❈

There's no denying that when a baby enters our lives, so does a healthy portion of chaos. Now that we are officially mothers, chaos is a thread that will be woven into our very existence. But for that we should be grateful. In the words of Ariel Gore (1998), "Chaos comes anyway. It comes whether we want it or not. It comes even if we pretend we don't see it coming. And here's the other thing: Chaos is good news. It's movement. It's change. It's revolution. It's scary. But like intuition, I think we can trust it."

Chapter Ten

Views from the Other Side: The Perspective of Partners

As we navigate our way through the twists and turns of our pregnancies, those closest to us are likely to be affected. Perhaps they're beside us helping us through. They might be ahead of us trying to clear a path, but only getting in the way. They could even be far behind us, still wondering what hit them.

Chances are our partners will play all of these roles at one point or another. Even the most devoted, compassionate, and empathetic among them will never be able to truly understand, never mind predict, exactly what it is we're going through from day to day, month to month, contraction to contraction.

Whether you have the kind of partner who says "we're pregnant," or the kind who turns a bit green during the video portion of your childbirth class, you'll have very clear ideas about what it is you expect this person to do to help you through the various stages of gestation. As the carriers, the actual bearers of life, the ones who must wrestle with the pregnancy goddess for nine whole months, pregnant women, quite rightly, will occupy center stage. But it certainly can be interesting, even illuminating, to find out what this looks like from the other side.

❋　❋　❋

Charles, 33 Years Old

Charles watched Cynthia's magnificent transformation with wonder, realizing in the process that he was a bit jealous that his role in this part of their baby's development was, at best, secondary. (See chapters one, two, three, six, eight, and nine for Cynthia's stories.)

Watching Cynthia's body grow and change and mold itself to bear and nurture our child was one of the most awe-inspiring things I've ever witnessed. That said, there was also some jealousy involved, as I felt concretely my gaping distance from the actual process of "growing our child." Once I sent my genetic letter on its way, hoping for the proper address and enough postage to make the trip, I felt often as though I had little to do but wait for a response some nine months later, with only a couple brief shimmery ultrasound images to hold me over.

But there Cynthia was, transforming. Perhaps it's hard for a woman—accustomed to dramatic life cycle events, including puberty, menstruation, and menopause—to appreciate how her changing body appears to a man. A man who inhabits, essentially the same body, give or take some hair and muscle tone, for his entire life. Cynthia's evolution into a modern day fertility goddess, albeit one in black tights and chic tunics, was a phenomenon to behold.

First trimester changes are subtle, and more behavioral than physical, at least from an outside perspective. I quickly learned that my predominant emotional posture throughout the pregnancy would be steady and stolid, unflappable in the face of Cynthia's suddenly mercurial moods. I didn't always thrill to this role—one that would continue in the difficult week after our child was born—as it didn't allow me my own full range of feelings, but I accepted it as what she needed, and what we needed at the time.

With her breasts suddenly heavy and full and her skin taut and shiny, she was the picture of maternal glow in her second trimester. Selfishly, it was a magical three months, as I found that glow sexually irresistible, and it was apparently working the same aphrodisiacal magic in her. Sex itself was spectacular, her body alive and receptive and exquisitely sensitive, the whole of her flushed and coursing with the stuff from which life is made.

The third trimester saw that sexual glow shift to the more serious business of finishing our child and preparing for birth. Her soft curves became tightly covered globes, the glow sometimes breaking into a sweat, and her posture became that of some other heavier person, one with wider hips and a burden to bear. As her body solidified, so did her moods, her confidence, and her determination.

Her metamorphosis became a vehicle for understanding the development of our child, imagining how the fetus's growth was creating the changes in Cynthia. I felt our daughter move, sang to her in utero, and listened in vain for a heartbeat with my naked ear; I rejoiced in the spectacular strength and capaciousness of Cynthia's body, of all women's bodies.

I recognize in retrospect, however, that I was perhaps also a little impatient during this time, growing more so as she came closer to term. It was Cynthia's time for solitude with our daughter, but I so wanted to meet her, to hold her, to smell her, and to feel her hands on my face. I wanted to hear the mystical noises that she would make once she was born. Now that she's here and I can do all of these things, I can't believe I was ever without her, even during those nine months when she was becoming herself. As much as I wouldn't want to go through the physical hardship of pregnancy, it is a spectacular gift that women have been given, and that they, in turn, choose to give back.

Pat, 34

When Amanda experienced preterm labor, the role Pat played in her pregnancy became indispensable. (See chapters two and five for Amanda's stories.) As she endured bed rest, he became primary caregiver, doing everything he could to ensure that both she and their unborn son were being given everything they needed.

We had just named him Finn. The pregnancy was at twenty-three weeks and the ultrasound showed that it was a boy. Once we had a name, the whole experience became much more real for me. Our little boy was growing and that's why Amanda was working so hard every day, trying to eat well and fight her way through fatigue and general queasiness.

Only a few days later, Amanda began to feel something strange. She didn't think it was anything serious, but once our doctor heard that the sensation was occurring in waves we were told to head for the emergency room. It was the first of many trips. Amanda was experiencing preterm labor.

Suddenly, the excitement and anticipation of pregnancy were replaced by terror. Those first twenty-four hours were a blur of tears, then hope, and then tears again as one drug worked and then didn't.

I remember calling my brother and saying just one or two words between sobs. He quickly appeared at our bedside with a heap of diner food and much needed support. Amanda was released from the hospital a few days later, but complete bed rest was advised and our lives changed dramatically.

Looking back now, with Finn as a healthy and joyful two-year-old, I am still affected by how amazing our family and friends were during that time. Food was dropped off and friends stopped by to keep Amanda company. Still, it was a time when Amanda and I were alone much more often than usual.

One memory that sticks out is Thanksgiving. Bed rest made it necessary for us to stay home and for me to be in charge of the meal. I talked to both Amanda's and my mother as I planned the preparation. We went with a small chicken instead of a turkey. I still remember that the sweet potatoes were excellent. (I always like my own cooking.) Anyway, at the time it was hard to see exactly what we had to give thanks for, but I did—for Amanda, for friends and family, and, finally, for a little boy who had, at least for the moment, decided to remain in utero.

Amanda was on varying degrees of bed rest for the remainder of our pregnancy. I was her caretaker. It was hard work and I was exhausted. I don't know how I managed to teach my five classes of high school history and then come home to care for her. My colleagues and students were wonderful. I remember going back to school after the first preterm labor episode and just trying not to cry. Friends and students alike just reached out to express their concern and offer help. They made me realize how lucky I was to work in such a caring environment.

Looking back, I have mixed feelings about my role as caregiver. The time that Amanda was in bed was my chance to care for her and Finn. Each day when I got home, I needed to make sure there were enough provisions for the patient as well as healthy doses of love and emotional support. I also had to try and keep a positive tone, which became easier as we made it through one week and then another and another. I remember hearing all about what the characters on *Law and Order* and *Northern Exposure* had been up to that day. I remember trying to coax Amanda into eating a little more. I remember worrying. And, I remember really engaging in the role of primary caregiver in a way I didn't even know I could. It was simultaneously arduous and invigorating, and I'm sure it served as a way to avoid contemplating the all too real negative possibilities as well.

I still very clearly remember the moment when Finn arrived. The labor had been hard and, in the end, our doctor needed to use a vacuum extractor to help Finn out. When the doctor placed Finn on Amanda's chest, the mixture of joy and relief was overwhelming. The long months of worry and effort were over. I will always hold onto the incredible warmth and glow that I felt at that moment. I remember looking at Amanda and knowing how lucky we were.

After Finn's joyous birth, with Amanda back on her feet and breastfeeding our son, I no longer occupied the central caregiving role that I had during the pregnancy. This sometimes left me feeling helpless. It seemed as though I was less capable of caring for our son at that point than I was before he was born. To this day, I wish I had been as focused during the first few months of Finn's life as I had been during the time I was helping Amanda bring him to term. In retrospect, I probably could have done more to comfort and entertain our newborn.

Over time, I've realized that my role might have changed, but, in many ways, my responsibilities had not. Although Finn still sometimes prefers his mom, I am much better at pitching in and playing the role of daddy-distracter whenever possible. And, although it might sound like a cliché, I know that our experience with preterm labor makes me appreciate even more every single day with our little man.

Terry, 37

When Sara became pregnant she couldn't accuse her partner Terry of not understanding what she was going through. These two women were already the mothers of a daughter, whom Terry had carried and birthed three years earlier. During Sara's pregnancy, however, Terry would be dealt one of the most frightening experiences a partner could have. (See chapters one, two, eight, and nine for Sara's stories.)

I was a little worried about Sara's pregnancy, but no more than usual. My own pregnancy had been uneventful until delivery when a strep-B infection flared up shortly after I went into labor, leaving me very weak and with a high fever. The circumstances resulted in a cesarean and a week in the hospital during which my daughter, Hannah, and I were treated with five different kinds of antibiotics. Hannah was fine after a few days in the neonatal intensive care unit (NICU), but it took me at least a month to feel OK again. After that, we thought we had used up any "bad luck" and, as a result, believed that Sara's pregnancy would be trouble free. Who knew we had such a high "bad luck" quotient?

Sara's pregnancy, after seven attempts at artificial insemination, was a big relief. Now we could get on with growing a baby and put the getting pregnant part behind us. It wasn't that simple. I love my partner dearly, but she can be just a tiny bit irritable and the hormones were making this inclination much worse. Sara was sure that everyone she knew (especially me!) had suddenly turned into a moron and that we were all conspiring to make her life more difficult. Nothing I did made her happy and she was full of complaints. At some point, her grumpy state of mind made me stop listening to her very well. That was probably a bad idea.

One morning, just twenty-six weeks into her pregnancy, Sara woke up complaining of a headache. She took some ibuprofen and a shower, thinking she had a sinus infection. She started feeling nauseous and vomiting. I thought she had the flu. I called her doctor's office and, after describing Sara's symptoms to a nurse, I was told a doctor would call us back. An hour later no one had called and Sara was telling me that she was having a hard time seeing and that her head was really hurting. I thought, "Well, you're not wearing your glasses and of course you feel bad, you have the flu." Still, I was starting to get more concerned. We found out later that she had already had a stroke at that point.

I continued to try to get in touch with the doctor, getting more and more worried as Sara started to feel worse and worse. When I finally spoke to a doctor she suggested that I take Sara to the hospital. I was furious. I couldn't believe someone hadn't told me that two hours ago. I became really frightened when I realized that Sara couldn't even make it into the car on her own. While she was sitting sideways on the front seat, unable to move her legs enough to get them in, I called 911. An ambulance came and with lights and sirens, she was taken to the hospital. I followed, with our three-year-old daughter, Hannah, in our car.

Sara had a seizure very shortly after arriving at the emergency room. This was terrifying because it was only minutes after we'd left home. I couldn't help thinking about what would have happened if she hadn't been in the hospital when the seizure began. I called a friend to take Hannah. Sara and I were going to be a while.

An emergency room doctor spoke to me and said that Sara had eclampsia and that the baby would need to be delivered immediately if either of them had any chance of living through this. At just twenty-six weeks, I was sure we would lose our son. Sara was in no shape to make decisions and because I had power of attorney for her, it was up to me to decide what to do. I didn't hesitate at all. I knew she would be terribly sad about losing this baby, but I was terrified I would lose her. I couldn't even imagine my life without her.

They took Sara to labor and delivery to prepare her for the surgery. The practice we were using for her obstetrical care had midwives and doctors, but the midwife we had been seeing was punted immediately for the senior physician. I was still seething at the delay in reaching someone earlier. The poor man walked in the room to me yelling, "Why the hell didn't you call me back?!"

They delivered Toby by an emergency cesarean at 3:33 P.M. He immediately went to the NICU and Sara was sent to the intensive care unit (ICU). Because these units were on opposite ends of the hospital, I'd walk miles getting from one to the other.

The first time I saw Toby there must have been five doctors and nurses working on him. He was one pound, eleven ounces, on a warming tray with tubes and wires everywhere. I couldn't understand why they were doing all this stuff to him, I didn't think it possible that he could live through this. I tried to ask the doctor in charge why they were hurting him, but he just told me what they were doing and how it would help. Much later, he explained that tiny babies like Toby very quickly show signs indicating whether they are likely to survive. They already knew he had a decent chance at the point I first saw him, but there was no time to explain everything to me then, and I was confused by what was going on.

It didn't even feel like we had a baby. He wasn't yet a person to me. In fact, I was a little ambivalent about him, even blaming him for Sara's illness. I know this might seem irrational, but my whole life had just been completely turned upside down.

Sara was in the ICU having had a stroke and a seizure. She was unable to see, her speech was impaired, and her left side was paralyzed. No one could tell me if any of these things would improve or get worse. I had visions of being left with a three-year-old, a preemie, and my partner paralyzed and blind. Prior to this, if you had asked me my worst nightmare I could not have even thought this up.

Slowly at first, then more quickly, the situation started to improve. Sara had a brief downturn the day after delivery. It looked like she'd had another stroke and they did an emergency MRI. Luckily the MRI showed no signs of a second stroke. She improved steadily after that. Currently, her only residual problem is a little tingling in her left foot. If we get away from this trauma with just that one problem, I'll feel incredibly lucky.

Toby has improved remarkably. At three and a half months he weighs more than eight pounds and he looks like a real baby—

pudgy and happy. So many things could have gone wrong, but they didn't, or at least haven't so far.

In some ways Sara and I are more patient with each other and the world these days, and in other ways we are less so. I feel like we smile more than we might have in the pre-Toby part of our lives and we show more compassion to one another. But we are less patient with people who are difficult to be around. They're just not worth our energy. On the other hand, we have a new respect and a major debt of gratitude for all of those people who cared, listened, and showed up during our time of need. We couldn't have gotten through this situation alone and their constant support and generosity served to remind us just how healing the power of friendship can be.

That first week in the hospital, I told Sara, over and over, "Whatever happens, we'll get through it together just like we always do." And we have.

Niko, 35

Niko has now been "the partner" twice, and the two experiences were vastly different. Perhaps this was due to the fact that he felt more prepared, even wiser, the second time around. More likely though, it was because Katherine's first birth experience was dreadful, and watching someone you love deal with that kind of pain and fear can be excruciating. (See chapters four and eight for Katherine's stories.)

The births of our two children were studies in contrast. Julia, our first, was induced and born via emergency cesarean after three and a half hours of hard pushing that left my wife Katherine completely spent. Eleanor, born three years later, came into this world nine days early, a scant hour after we crossed the threshold of the hospital, after three and a half hard pushes, leaving Katherine and me gaping at each other with surprise

The pregnancies, too, were quite different, but in some ways similar, at least for me. Pregnancy is a time of endless questioning, even for the reasonably self-assured, and when you are biologically involved only at the onset, these questions often reflect a kind of helplessness, perhaps even inadequacy, about just what your role really is: What can I do to help? Am I doing enough? Am I too reactive? Other questions touch on fears and anxieties that seem of great import except when you consider sharing them with your very pregnant partner: How will this affect our sex life? Will I faint if she has an episiotomy? How many glasses of water can the woman drink?

What was reassuring, however, was that the s[
around, everything came easier. Yes, that deeply thrill[
has worn off a bit, but you're no longer so insecure an[
enced, and you're much less anxious. So even while the[
Katherine's second pregnancy were much more probl[
stressful, I often felt more confident about the decisions[
make and this, in and of itself, was comforting.

For instance, when we received the worrying res[
alpha-fetoprotein (AFP) test and we decided not to have[
centesis to further investigate, I simply knew that aborting[
Down's syndrome fetus was not an option and was relieved at how
quickly we agreed on this. That, however, was not the end of the
introspection. Having reached that decision, we were both preoccupied by the question of whether we were simply unrealistic and idealistic about what the ramifications of having a child with Down's
syndrome would be for our first born and us.

I was—and remain—irritated at the way in which our doctors
hemmed and hawed in their interpretation of the AFP results, clearly
unwilling—for fear of a lawsuit down the road—to reassure us by
relaying that false-positive test results are common. Much, if not all,
of the stress was truly unnecessary. Reducing the complexity of
pregnancy to a universe of competing statistics and risks made me
feel at times as though I was being asked to wager on a pony instead
of making a potentially life-altering decision regarding my child.

It's been eight weeks since Ellie was born and I can still tap into
my palpable sense of relief—not so much about the fact that she isn't
a Down's baby, but about how quickly and relatively painlessly she
arrived. (In the last month of the pregnancy, I, for some reason,
became completely convinced, with a borderline mystical certainty,
that everything was fine. I was so confident of this that I wasn't even
thinking of the Down's possibility during the birth. Go figure.)

During the last weeks of Katherine's second pregnancy, my
daily outlook was influenced by two overriding emotions: a luxurious knowledge that anything I was doing at any given moment,
regardless of how seemingly important, would immediately recede
in significance as the result of one phone call, and, at the same time,
a creeping sense of dread at the thought of "going through that
again."

To be clear, the birth of my first daughter, Julia, was one of the
defining moments of my life, resulting in such a surge of emotions
that for three days afterward I felt weepy. But it was also genuinely
traumatic to watch Katherine suffer so. Much is made of the way in
which men respond to the physiological aspects of birth: the sight of

the vagina expanding to such proportions, the episiotomy, the blood, the placenta, etc. What really affected me, however, was Katherine's screaming, a deep-throated, ragged, desperate screaming that I had never, in the thirteen years we'd known each other, heard.

The moment during Julia's birth that we decided to go with the cesarean, with the doctor still hesitating and Katherine all but begging for it, she was whisked off to the surgery room and I was left pacing and overwrought outside the door. Once she had been prepped, which took an agonizing twenty minutes, I came in to find her strapped down like Jesus to the cross. Apparently the epidural can result in such bad shaking (chattering, actually) that she could potentially injure herself. Further, there was a screen separating her head from her body. So I was, in fact, met with the vision of my wife's disembodied head, adorned with a shower cap. Almost immediately, the epidural induced nausea and Katherine began to shudder, fearful that she was going to throw up.

After a surprisingly short time, Julia arrived, all 10-plus pounds of her, red-faced and bawling, a little of that weird, white "birth cheese" under her arm, but otherwise the picture of health. Because they still have to sew up Katherine's incision, Julia is placed in a little bin, with a warm bulb above her. Unfairly, the bin is located above the level of Katherine's head so she can't really see the baby. At this point, I'm shuttling back and forth between Katherine and Julia, just completely out of control and weeping for the first time in I can't remember how long. At one point I make a mistake that results in an image I'll bear with me for the rest of my life: I turn to the left instead of the right as I make my way from Katherine (well, Katherine's head) back to Julia, and I catch a fleeting glimpse of my wife's uterus lying on her stomach.

The birth of our second child was much less traumatic for everyone involved. At 11 A.M. on the day of Eleanor's arrival, we were all in the playground, when Katherine decided that the pangs she'd been having since the previous night maybe weren't false labor after all. We head into the hospital, arriving at noon, to learn that she's six centimeters dilated. It was too late for an epidural. (It was at this point that I saw for the first and only time that same look of utter desperation that had so often crossed Katherine's face during Julia's birth.) Katherine went straight into the delivery room, and was suddenly at the center of a flurry of activity.

Very soon after, she was fully dilated and the attending doctor was paged with an urgent message. Upon her arrival, the doctor quickly tugged on her scrubs, and, within five minutes, was urging Katherine to push. After only two sharp screams and barely four pushes, and an episiotomy that I barely saw, Eleanor was born, quieter, three pounds smaller, and without the cone-shaped head that Julia had sported.

We could scarcely believe that two hours after we'd been bouncing around the playground we suddenly had a second child. There had been no problems; Katherine, in fact, said, "I feel like walking down the hall and getting a cup of coffee." Perhaps because it was so unexpected and fast, perhaps because I was much less overwrought, and perhaps because it was the second time around, I was fairly calm throughout the entire process, even able to call up relatives within half an hour and conduct a conversation.

In sum, while in retrospect I relish the raw intensity of Julia's birth (or at least aspects thereof), I'm also very grateful that we got off a little easier the second time around.

Our partners assume a variety of responsibilities during pregnancy. These include fetching us crackers when we're nauseous, accompanying us to prenatal appointments to look on as tape measures are stretched over our growing bellies, taking on all cat-related tasks for the duration, and, finally, repeating over and over and over during labor, "You're doing a great job, honey, a really great job."

As our bodies grow and our needs multiply, our partners struggle to figure out exactly what their role is now that the "ball is out of their court" so to speak. Simultaneously, however, they are often in the midst of their very own transformation, coming to terms with all of the emotional baggage that impending parenthood carries with it.

Contributors

Amanda, 31, a former publicist, is currently a stay-at-home mom who works part-time from a home office. She describes her battle with preterm labor as disappointing and difficult but definitely filled with interestingly gratifying moments. The end result, her now two-year-old son, Finn, is incredible. Her husband, Pat *(who has a story in chapter ten)*, is a high school teacher. *Her stories appear in chapters two and five.*

Angela, 28, lives in Hope, Indiana with her husband and their four-month-old daughter, Samantha. After fourteen years of military life and work in the public sector, she is now a stay-at-home mom and loving it. *Her stories appear in chapters two and five.*

Anne, 31, a marketing manager in a publishing house until her second daughter was born, is now a stay-at-home mom. She lives in Connecticut with her husband and two daughters, ages two and six months. Her first daughter entered the world face first (not a common presentation) after a tough labor. Her second tried to come out feet first and was delivered by cesarean. *Her stories appear in chapters one, four, and nine.*

Audra, 24, lives with her husband, Phil, and two sons, Clark and Paul, in Saskatchewan, Canada. She gave birth to her first son in a hospital but opted for a home birth the second time around. She received her college degree shortly before her second son was born and is starting a career as a dietitian. *Her stories appear in chapters one and eight.*

Carol, 34, lives with her husband, son, and daughter in a rural area in the foothills of the Sierra Nevada mountains. A former employee of the California Department of Transportation, Carol is now a stay-at-home mom. *Her story appears in chapter five.*

Caroline, 33, is an internet project manager. She lives with her husband, Todd, their son, Samuel Jacob, and their three cats in Manhattan's East Village. Caroline didn't have much of an appetite throughout her entire pregnancy, but she was eating an Italian sub shortly after she gave birth. *Her stories appear in chapters two and eight.*

Corinna, 32, is a stay-at-home mom who lives with her husband and daughter, Catherine, in British Columbia, Canada. She developed gestational diabetes while pregnant and after the initial shock and worry, she found strength in her ability to live with and control the condition. *Her stories appear in chapters four, five, and nine.*

Cynthia, 36, lives with her husband, Charles, and their daughter, Zoe, in New York City. She currently works as a freelance writer and editor. *Her stories appear in chapters one, two, three, six, eight, and nine. Charles also has a story in the book in chapter ten.*

Dakota, 45, suffered through two miscarriages before she gave birth to her daughter. She had a wonderful pregnancy and could still touch her toes during her eighth month. She currently works as a managing editor at a publishing house. *Her stories appear in chapters one and four.*

Emily, 35, lives in North Carolina with her husband and five-year-old daughter, Davia. Emily is the director of marketing at a Durham-based publishing house. *Her stories appear in chapters one and four.*

Gina, 24, lives with her husband and three children in suburban New York. She battled preterm labor in all three of her pregnancies. She works as a paralegal in an intellectual property law firm. *Her stories appear in chapters one, two, three, and five.*

Ginette, 31, lives with her husband and three sons, Joshua, age seven, and twins Jonah and Jackson, age four, in New Brunswick, Canada. A part-time stay-at-home mom, she also works part-time for her local board of education. *Her stories appear in chapters one, two, three, and eight.*

Jeney, 29, lives in Columbus, Ohio with her husband and eight-month-old son, John Spencer. She is an accountant/office manager for a commercial real estate firm. *Her story appears in chapter five.*

Jennifer, 26, is an administrative assistant in the housing department of Southwest Missouri State University. She lives with her husband and their three-year-daughter, Nicole, who was born five weeks early due to complications arising from preeclampsia (pregnancy-induced high blood pressure). *Her stories appear in chapters one, two, four, five, six, and nine.*

Jenny, 36, lives in California with her husband and two daughters, Minna and Tilly, ages three and one. She works part-time as a freelance writer. *Her stories appear in chapters three, four, and eight.*

Katherine, 32, is an elementary school teacher who is currently taking some time off to be with her two daughters, Julia and Eleanor, ages three and four months. Her husband, Niko, who also has a story in this book *(see chapter ten)*, works in publishing. *Her stories appear in chapters four and eight.*

Karen, 36, a former dancer and current freelance writer, divides her time between rural New Jersey and New York City. She and her husband, Steve, are planning a home birth for the arrival of their first child who is due in about eleven weeks. *Her story appears in chapter four.*

Kim, 27, lives in New Hampshire with her husband and four children, who range in age from eight to eight months. She is currently a stay-at-home mom who moderates several Internet bulletin boards that focus on pregnancy-related topics. *Her story appears in chapter seven.*

Lauren, 32, her husband, and their four-year-old son, Benjamin, live in New York City where she works as an editor in a book publishing house. *Her stories appear in chapters one, eight, and nine.*

Liz, 26, lives in Cincinnati, Ohio with her husband. She has lived through two devastating first-trimester losses but is thrilled to have just entered the second trimester of a pregnancy that is going very well. *Her story appears in chapter seven.*

Lynn, 42, lives in bucolic Western Massachusetts with her partner and two-month-old daughter, Yelena, who was born absolutely perfect, despite Lynn's fears about her "advanced maternal age." She works as a writer, editor, and designer of educational materials. *Her stories appear in chapters two and four.*

Maggie, 31, works as an operations manager for a real estate firm. She lives with her husband and two children (seven-year-old LeRoy and five-year-old Emilia) in Southern California. She is currently expecting her third child. *Her story appears in chapter five.*

Marie, 41, is a part-time attorney who lives in suburban Southern California with her husband and two daughters. In the last few years she's endured a miscarriage as well as the extremely painful experience of terminating a pregnancy when learning that the fetus had a severe chromosomal abnormality. *Her story appears in chapter four.*

Martha, 38, is a former prosecutor who currently works part-time for a city agency that investigates fraud and corruption. After working very hard to get pregnant, she and her husband endured a difficult nine months but the outcome—their now eighteen-month-old son, Noah—was worth every minute of it. Martha and her family live in Brooklyn, New York. *Her stories appear in chapters one, two, three, and eight.*

Miriam, 34, a part-time university teacher and writer, lives in Atlanta with her husband and two-year-old daughter, Samira. *Her stories appear in chapters one, two, and three.*

Nell, 33, is currently taking some time off from teaching fifth grade to be with her one-year-old daughter, Rachel. Her pregnancy was a breeze until she found out she had preeclampsia just hours before her daughter's birth. She lives with her husband and daughter in Brooklyn, New York. *Her stories appear in chapters four, five, eight, and nine.*

Nicki, 30, a former management consultant, is a stay-at-home mom who lives with her husband and their eighteen-month-old son. Although she fell in love with her son the first time she saw him on an ultrasound screen at twelve weeks, she did not enjoy being pregnant, most of the time. *Her stories appear in chapters three and nine.*

Rachel, 30, is a high school English teacher. She lives in Brooklyn, New York with her husband, David, and their one-year-old daughter Amalia. *Her story appears in chapter five.*

Renee, 32, a social worker, lives in Southern California with her husband and their newborn son, Benjamin Gabriel. Now that her son has arrived, Renee is eager to get back up on her rollerblades and skis. *Her story appears in chapter six.*

Sandra, 36, is a freelance writer. She and her husband, Bill, live in San Francisco with their two children, three-year-old Sophia and one-month- old Jacob. *Her stories appear in chapters four and six.*

Sara, 36, lives in Norwalk, Connecticut with her same-sex partner, Terry, their three-year-old daughter, Hannah, and five-month-old son, Toby, who's doing wonderfully even though he was born fourteen weeks early. Sara is a professor in a teacher-training program, specializing in deaf education. *Her stories appear in chapters one, two, eight, and nine. Her partner, Terry, has a story in chapter ten.*

Sara Michelle, 33, is a freelance writer who lives in Brooklyn, New York with her husband and their son, Zakaria. While pregnant, she felt her son move for the first time while she was having gum surgery. She found much comfort in the fact that he was there helping her get through it. *Her stories appear in chapters three, eight, and nine.*

Shannon, 25, lives in the Chicago area with her husband, her two-year-old son, Andrew, and her newborn daughter, Samara Lee. A former teacher of English as a Second Language, she is now a stay-at-home mom. *Her stories appear in chapters one, seven, and eight.*

Sheila, 33, is an attorney at a nonprofit agency in New York City. She and her husband have a three-year-old daughter and a one-year-old son. *Her stories appear in chapters four and six.*

Tass, 29, lives on the Gold Cost of Australia with her newly arrived daughter, Aliah Daché. Physically, her pregnancy was ideal. Emotionally, it was quite rough since her expartner did not support her decision to have the baby. *Her stories appear in chapters one, two, three, and nine.*

Trudi, 32, is the vice president of marketing for a video distribution company. She and her husband live in Brooklyn, New York with their very redheaded one-year-old son, Jordan Matthew, who, they recently discovered, will have a little brother or sister in about four months. *Her stories appear in chapters two, three, and nine.*

Wendy, 31, lives in Sparta, Wisconsin with her husband and their eight-month-old daughter, Daria Kay. She is a service advisor for a car dealership. *Her story appears in chapter five.*

Whitney, 33, lives in Raleigh, North Carolina with her husband, two-year-old daughter, and one-year-old son. Now a stay-at-home mom who takes on consulting work from time to time, Whitney worked full-time in sales management and new business development before she had her children. *Her stories appear in chapters one, four, and six.*

Glossary

AFP (alpha-fetoprotein) test—A test, requiring only a blood sample, most commonly performed between the sixteenth and eighteenth week of pregnancy that assesses the risk of neural tube defects and Down's syndrome.

amniocentesis—A diagnostic test, most commonly performed between the sixteenth and eighteenth week of pregnancy, that involves having some amniotic fluid withdrawn from the uterus with a long hollow needle (inserted through your abdomen), which is then tested for a variety of genetic disorders.

Apgar score—A measurement of a newborn's condition taken at one and five minutes after birth. Ratings are based on **A**ppearance (color); **P**ulse (heartbeat); **G**rimace (reflex); **A**ctivity (muscle tone), and **R**espiration (breathing). 10 is the highest score, 1 the lowest.

beta number—Refers to the level of beta (one of two molecules that make up the pregnancy hormone hCG) in a pregnant woman's body.

bilirubin—The product of broken-down red blood cells, an excess of which can cause jaundice in newborns.

Braxton-Hicks contractions—Random, usually painless contractions (sometimes called practice contractions), experienced by some women beginning around the middle of pregnancy, sometimes earlier. They get their name from the English doctor (John Braxton Hicks) who first described them in 1872.

centimeters—The unit of measure used to describe the opening of the cervix during labor. Ten refers to a fully opened cervix, ready for delivery.

cervix—The entrance to the uterus that opens during labor so the baby can reach the birth canal.

Clomid—A drug that stimulates ovulation.

colostrum –The earliest form of breast milk, quite rich in proteins, that is secreted by the breasts in late pregnancy and right after child-birth. It will change to mature milk a few days after delivery.

craniosynostosis—A condition in which the edges of the skull bones grow together.

CVS (chorionic villus sampling)—A diagnostic test, performed between the ninth and twelfth week of pregnancy, that involves having chorionic villi (tiny fingerlike projections on the placenta) withdrawn to test for genetic abnormalities. Depending on the placement of the placenta, this sample will either be taken using a long thin tube inserted into the cervix through the vagina or with a thin needle inserted through the abdomen.

D&C—Dilation and curettage. A surgical procedure in which the cervix is opened and the uterus emptied.

dilation—The word used to describe the opening of the cervix during labor measured in centimeters. One is fully dilated and ready to push at ten centimeters.

Doppler—A device that uses ultrasound vibrations to listen to the fetal heartbeat.

echocardiogram—A noninvasive procedure that takes ultrasound images of the heart.

ectopic pregnancy—A pregnancy that occurs outside of the uterus, usually in the fallopian tube.

effacement—The thinning of the cervix in preparation for birth, described in percentages. 100 percent is fully effaced.

epidural—A common form of anesthesia used during labor, administered through a catheter into a space in the lower spine.

episiotomy—A surgical incision to the perineum (the muscle between the vagina and the rectum) to enlarge the vaginal opening for delivery.

hCG (human chorionic gonadotropin)—A pregnancy hormone secreted by the placenta that can be found in a pregnant woman's blood and urine.

H.E.L.L.P. syndrome—This abbreviation stands for Hemolysis, Elevated Liver enzymes, Low Platelets, and refers to a form of preeclampsia that doesn't necessarily increase blood pressure but causes abdominal pain, nausea, and sometimes vomiting.

hyperemesis gravidarum—A condition that causes severe nausea and vomiting in pregnant women and can result in dehydration, changes in body chemistry, and hospitalization. If not monitored carefully, this affliction can be harmful to both mother and baby.

in vitro fertilization (IVF)—A fertility treatment that attempts to achieve pregnancy by fertilizing the egg outside the body and then putting it into the uterus.

jaundice—A fairly common condition in newborns that is caused by the liver's inability to break down excess red blood cells (bilirubin). Babies with this condition will have a yellow tint to their skin.

Kegel—An exercise that involves tightening and relaxing the muscles in the vaginal and perineal area to tone the muscles in the pelvic floor. This can lead to fewer tears and episiotomies during birth and can prevent urine leakage.

La Leche League—An organization devoted to the promotion and support of breastfeeding.

magnesium sulfate—A strong medication used to treat preterm labor and preeclampsia. Unpleasant side effects include nausea, vomiting, heart palpitations, headaches, and muscle weakness.

meconium—A baby's first bowel movement, which is formed before birth and passed during the first few days after. Presence of meconium in the amniotic fluid can be a sign of fetal distress.

molar pregnancy or trophoblastic disease—An unviable pregnancy that occurs when the cells that line the gestational sac do not develop into a healthy placenta.

mucous plug—The mucus that seals off the cervix and protects against disease and infection. As the cervix opens before labor this pinkish mucus may discharge (referred to as "bloody show").

nonstress tests—A noninvasive test that monitors fetal movements in combination with changes in fetal heart rate.

ovulation–The ovary's release of a ripe egg.

perineum—The area between the vagina and the rectum.

Pitocin—A synthetic version of the hormone that stimulates labor (oxytocin) that is used to induce labor.

PKU (phenylketonuria)—An inherited disease that is checked for shortly after birth with a sample of the baby's blood.

polycystic ovarian syndrome—A hormonal disorder that results in enlarged ovaries that contain numerous cysts. Infertility and irregular or absent menstruation are two of its symptoms.

preeclampsia—Pregnancy-induced high blood pressure sometimes referred to as PIH (pregnancy-induced hypertension).

prostaglandins—Natural substances that can stimulate labor and are often applied to the cervix in gel form.

PUPPP (Pruritic Urticated Papules and Plaques of Pregnancy)—An itchy bumpy rash that can erupt in the last few months of pregnancy.

retinopathy of prematurity—The growth of abnormal blood vessels in the retina that can affect premature babies and result in blindness.

RSV (respiratory syncytial virus)—A virus that attacks the mucous membranes of the respiratory tract and can be very dangerous when occurring in newborns.

sickle cell anemia—An inherited disease that affects a protein in red blood cells called hemoglobin.

spina bifida—A neural tube defect which causes the spine to grow incorrectly.

Tay-Sachs disease—A fatal genetic disorder that causes the destruction of the central nervous system.

Trisomy 18—A chromosomal disorder characterized by an extra eighteenth chromosome.

vacuum extractor—An instrument used during difficult deliveries that attaches to the baby's head to help it through the birth canal.

Resources

Books on Pregnancy, Childbirth, and Early Motherhood

Active Birth: The New Approach to Giving Birth Naturally, Janet Balaskais, Harvard Common Press, 1992.

The Bed Rest Survival Guide, Barbara Edelston Peterson and Hallie Beachum, Avon Books, 1998.

The Birth Book: Everything You Need to Know to Have a Safe and Satisfying Birth, William and Martha Sears, Little Brown & Co., 1994.

Birthing from Within: An Extra-Ordinary Guide to Childbirth Preparation, Pam England and Rob Horowitz, Partera Press, 1998.

Breastfeeding Your Baby, Sheila Kitzinger, Alfred A. Knopf, 1998.

A Child Is Born, Lennart Nilsson, DTP, 1986.

Child of Mine: Writers Talk About the First Year of Motherhood, edited by Christina Baker Kline, Hyperion, 1997.

The Complete Book of Pregnancy and Childbirth, Sheila Kitzinger, Alfred A. Knopf, 1997.

Empty Cradle, Broken Heart: Surviving the Death of Your Baby, Deborah Davis, Fulcrum, 1999.

Everyday Blessings: The Inner Work of Mindful Parenting, Myla and Jon Kabat-Zinn, Hyperion, 1997.

The Girlfriends' Guide to Pregnancy, Vicki Iovine, Pocket Books, 1995.

The Hip Mama Survival Guide, Ariel Gore, Hyperion, 1998.

I Wish Someone Had Told Me: A Realistic Guide to Early Motherhood, Nina Barrett, Academy Chicago Publishers, 1997.

Laughter and Tears: The Emotional Life of New Mothers, Elisabeth Bing and Libby Colman, Henry Holt, 1997.

The Mother Dance: How Children Change Your Life, Harriet Lerner, HarperPerennial, 1998.

The Mother Trip: Hip Mama's Guide to Staying Sane in the Chaos of Motherhood, Ariel Gore, Seal Press, 2000.

Motherprayer: The Pregnant Woman's Spiritual Companion, Tikva Frymer-Kensky, Riverhead Books, 1995.

Mothers Who Think: Tales of Real-Life Parenthood, edited by Camille Peri and Kate Moses, Villard, 1999.

Operating Instructions: A Journal of My Son's First Year, Anne Lamott, Fawcett Columbine, 1993.

Pregnancy Day by Day, Sheila Kitzinger and Vicky Bailey, Alfred A. Knopf, 1997.

Real Birth: Women Share Their Stories, Robin Greene, Generation Books, 2000.

The Spirit of Pregnancy: An Interactive Anthology for Your Journey to Motherhood, Bonni Goldberg, Contemporary Books, 2000.

Spiritual Midwifery, Ina May Gaskin, Book Publishing Co., 1990

Surviving Pregnancy Loss: A Complete Sourcebook for Women and Their Families, Rochelle Friedman, Citadel Press, 1996.

Taking Charge of Your Fertility, Toni Weschler, HarperPerennial, 1995.

Two of Us Make a World: The Single Mother's Guide to Pregnancy, Childbirth, and the First Year, Prudence and Sherill Tippins, Henry Holt, 1996.

The Ultimate Guide to Pregnancy for Lesbians: Tips and Techniques from Conception to Birth, Cleis Press, 1999.

The VBAC Companion: The Expectant Mother's Guide to Vaginal Birth After Cesarean, Diana Korte, Harvard Common Press, 1998.

Wanting a Child: Twenty-Two Writers on Their Difficult but Mostly Successful Quests for Parenthood in a High-Tech Age, edited by Jill Bialosky and Helen Schulman, Farrar, Straus and Giroux, 1998.

What to Expect When You're Expecting, Arlene Eisenberg, Heidi Murkoff, and Sandee Hathaway, Workman Publishing, 1991.

The Womanly Art of Breastfeeding, La Leche League International, Plume, 1997.

Websites

About.com Pregnancy/Birth Pages
http://pregnancy.about.com/health/pregnancy

Baby Center
http://www.babycenter.com

Baby Zone
http://babyzone.com

Breastfeeding.com
http://www.breastfeeding.com

Childbirth.org
http://www.childbirth.org

ePregnancy
http://epregnancy.com

La Leche League International
http://www.lalecheleague.org

The Labor of Love
http://www.thelaboroflove.com

ParentsPlace
http://www.parentsplace.com

Pregnancy Today
http://www.pregnancytoday.com

References

All, Elisa Ast. 2000. Bouncing Back from Baby: An Interview with WNBA Star Sheryl Swoopes from *pregnancytoday.com*.

Beck, Martha. 2000. *Expecting Adam: A True Story of Birth, Rebirth, and Everyday Magic*. New York: Berkley Publishing Group.

Berube, Michael. 1998. *Life As We Know It: A Father, A Family, and an Exceptional Child*. New York: Vintage Books.

Bird, Sarah. 1997. Baby Blues: A Journal. In *Child of Mine: Writers Talk About the First Year of Motherhood*, edited by Christina Baker Kline. New York: Hyperion.

Eisenberg, Arlene, Heidi Murkoff and Sandee Hathaway. 1991. *What to Expect When You're Expecting*. New York: Workman.

Erdrich, Louise. 1995. *The Blue Jay's Dance: A Birth Year*. New York: HarperCollins.

Gawande, Atul. 1999. A Queasy Feeling: Why Can't We Cure Nausea? *The New Yorker*, July 5.

Goldberg, Bonni. 2000. *The Spirit of Pregnancy: An Interactive Anthology for Your Journey to Motherhood*. Chicago: Contemporary Books.

Gore, Ariel. 1998. *The Hip Mama Survival Guide*. New York: Hyperion.

Herrick, Amy. 1997. Mortal Terrors and Motherhood. In *Child of Mine: Writers Talk About the First Year of Motherhood*, edited by Christina Baker Kline. New York: Hyperion.

Iovine, Vicki. 1995. *A Girlfriends' Guide to Pregnancy*. New York: Pocket Books.

Kabat-Zinn, Myla and John. 1997. *Everyday Blessings: The Inner Work of Mindful Parenting*. New York: Hyperion.

Lamott, Anne. 1993. *Operating Instructions: A Journal of My Son's First Year*. New York: Fawcett Columbine.

Lerner, Harriet. 1998. *The Mother Dance: How Children Change Your Life*. New York: HarperCollins.

Lieberman, Adrienne B. 1992. *Easing Labor Pain: The Complete Guide to a More Comfortable and Rewarding Birth*. Boston: Harvard Common Press.

Matalin, Mary. 1998. Sidebar in the special issue of *The New York Times Magazine*, Mothers Can't Win. April 5.

Mavor, Anne H. 2000. A Performance Pregnancy Diary. In *The Spirit of Pregnancy: An Interactive Anthology for Your Journey to Motherhood*, edited by Bonni Goldberg. Chicago: Contemporary Books.

National Institute of Child Health and Human Development. 1999. First Trimester Biochemistry and Ultrasound Nuchal Membrane Assessment (BUN) Screening. A study.

Purves, Anna. 2000. Seen and Not Seen. In *The Spirit of Pregnancy: An Interactive Anthology for Your Journey to Motherhood*, edited by Bonni Goldberg. Chicago: Contemporary Books.

Schulman, Helen. 1998. The Habitual Aborter. In *Wanting A Child*, edited by Jill Bialosky and Helen Schulman. New York: Farrar, Straus and Giroux.

Schwartz, Judith. 1997. Waiting for Brendan. In *Child of Mine: Writers Talk About the First Year of Motherhood*, edited by Christina Baker Kline. New York: Hyperion.

Verrilli, George E., and Anne Marie Mueser. 1998. *While Waiting*. New York: St. Martin's Griffin.

Cecelia A. Cancellaro is a writer and editor who lives in Brooklyn, New York with her husband and their almost-two-year-old daughter. You can visit her website at: www.pregnancystories.net

Some Other New Harbinger Self-Help Titles

Family Guide to Emotional Wellness, $24.95
Undefended Love, $13.95
The Great Big Book of Hope, $15.95
Don't Leave it to Chance, $13.95
Emotional Claustrophobia, $12.95
The Relaxation & Stress Reduction Workbook, Fifth Edition, $19.95
The Loneliness Workbook, $14.95
Thriving with Your Autoimmune Disorder, $16.95
Illness and the Art of Creative Self-Expression, $13.95
The Interstitial Cystitis Survival Guide, $14.95
Outbreak Alert, $15.95
Don't Let Your Mind Stunt Your Growth, $10.95
Energy Tapping, $14.95
Under Her Wing, $13.95
Self-Esteem, Third Edition, $15.95
Women's Sexualitites, $15.95
Knee Pain, $14.95
Helping Your Anxious Child, $12.95
Breaking the Bonds of Irritable Bowel Syndrome, $14.95
Multiple Chemical Sensitivity: A Survival Guide, $16.95
Dancing Naked, $14.95
Why Are We Still Fighting, $15.95
From Sabotage to Success, $14.95
Parkinson's Disease and the Art of Moving, $15.95
A Survivor's Guide to Breast Cancer, $13.95
Men, Women, and Prostate Cancer, $15.95
Make Every Session Count: Getting the Most Out of Your Brief Therapy, $10.95
Virtual Addiction, $12.95
After the Breakup, $13.95
Why Can't I Be the Parent I Want to Be?, $12.95
The Secret Message of Shame, $13.95
The OCD Workbook, $18.95
Tapping Your Inner Strength, $13.95
Binge No More, $14.95
When to Forgive, $12.95
Practical Dreaming, $12.95
Healthy Baby, Toxic World, $15.95
Making Hope Happen, $14.95
I'll Take Care of You, $12.95
Survivor Guilt, $14.95
Children Changed by Trauma, $13.95
Understanding Your Child's Sexual Behavior, $12.95
The Self-Esteem Companion, $10.95
The Gay and Lesbian Self-Esteem Book, $13.95
Making the Big Move, $13.95
How to Survive and Thrive in an Empty Nest, $13.95
Living Well with a Hidden Disability, $15.95
Overcoming Repetitive Motion Injuries the Rossiter Way, $15.95
What to Tell the Kids About Your Divorce, $13.95
The Divorce Book, Second Edition, $15.95
Claiming Your Creative Self: True Stories from the Everyday Lives of Women, $15.95
Taking Control of TMJ, $13.95
Winning Against Relapse: A Workbook of Action Plans for Recurring Health and Emotional Problems, $14.95
Facing 30: Women Talk About Constructing a Real Life and Other Scary Rites of Passage, $12.95
The Worry Control Workbook, $15.95
Wanting What You Have: A Self-Discovery Workbook, $18.95
When Perfect Isn't Good Enough: Strategies for Coping with Perfectionism, $13.95
Earning Your Own Respect: A Handbook of Personal Responsibility, $12.95
High on Stress: A Woman's Guide to Optimizing the Stress in Her Life, $13.95
Infidelity: A Survival Guide, $13.95
Stop Walking on Eggshells, $14.95
Consumer's Guide to Psychiatric Drugs, $16.95
The Fibromyalgia Advocate: Getting the Support You Need to Cope with Fibromyalgia and Myofascial Pain, $18.95
Working Anger: Preventing and Resolving Conflict on the Job, $12.95
Healthy Living with Diabetes, $13.95
Better Boundries: Owning and Treasuring Your Life, $13.95
Goodbye Good Girl, $12.95
Fibromyalgia & Chronic Myofascial Pain Syndrome, $19.95
The Depression Workbook: Living With Depression and Manic Depression, $17.95

Call **toll free, 1-800-748-6273**, or log on to our online bookstore at **www.newharbinger.com** to order. Have your Visa or Mastercard number ready. Or send a check for the titles you want to New Harbinger Publications, Inc., 5674 Shattuck Ave., Oakland, CA 94609. Include $3.80 for the first book and 75¢ for each additional book, to cover shipping and handling. (California residents please include appropriate sales tax.) Allow two to five weeks for delivery.